PLATE I.

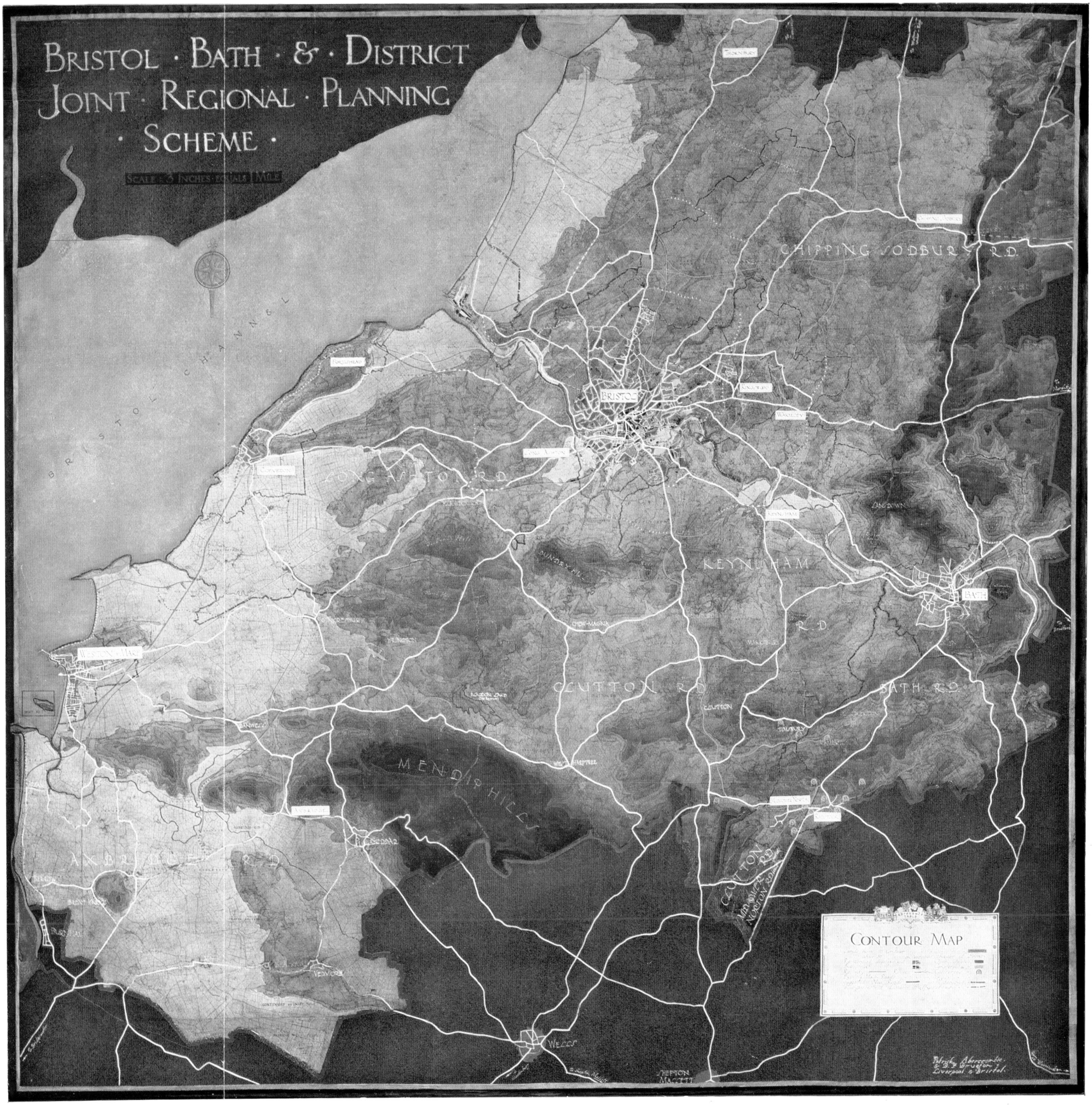
BRISTOL · BATH · & · DISTRICT
JOINT · REGIONAL · PLANNING
· SCHEME ·
BRISTOL CHANNEL
CHIPPING SODBURY RD.
BRISTOL
KEYNSHAM
BATH
BATH RD.
CLUTTON RD.
MENDIP HILLS
CONTOUR MAP
WELLS
SHEPTON MALLET

THE REGION, ITS CHIEF PHYSICAL AND ARTIFICIAL FEATURES.

BRISTOL AND BATH REGIONAL PLANNING SCHEME

Prepared for

THE BATH AND BRISTOL AND DISTRICT JOINT REGIONAL PLANNING COMMITTEE

By

PATRICK ABERCROMBIE

Department of Civic Design, University of Liverpool

and

BERTRAND F. BRUETON

Town Planning Officer to the Corporation of Bristol

The UNIVERSITY PRESS *of* LIVERPOOL

and

HODDER & STOUGHTON LTD., LONDON

1930

PRINTED BY
JOHN WRIGHT AND SONS LTD.,
BRISTOL
BINDING, PRINTING OF MAPS
AND ILLUSTRATIONS BY
PARTRIDGE AND LOVE LTD.,
BRISTOL

FOREWORD

THE formation of the Bath and Bristol and District Joint Regional Planning Committee is due to the initiative of the Bristol Town Planning Committee, who realised that no effective scheme could be produced for their area without considering the development of neighbouring areas, as physical features of nature take no account of administrative frontiers, and no authority can plan successfully in isolation. Although the Town Planning Act made it obligatory for urban authorities of 20,000 or more population to prepare plans, it was evident that the rural and smaller urban authorities were equally affected and their need to look ahead was as potent. Further, it was considered that the interests of the City, the neighbouring recreative and country towns and the intervening rural areas are closely interwoven and interdependent; in short that the whole tract of country lying west of the Cotswolds and north of the Mendips formed in reality one economic unit, or "Region."

Accordingly steps were taken on the advice of the Minister of Health to invite the Authorities in this area to attend a Conference to consider the preparation of a comprehensive outline plan. The Conference was held in the Council House, Bristol, on October 11th, 1923, Mr. G. L. Pepler, Chief Town Planning Adviser to the Minister of Health, in the chair, when it was resolved that it was desirable to set up a Joint Committee under the Town Planning Act

"To advise in the promotion and co-ordination of Town Planning Schemes, and if considered necessary to prepare in outline a Regional plan."

The Joint Committee was formed in due course, and it was decided to prepare a Survey of the Region and a Regional Scheme for the area extending from Thornbury in the north to the Mendip watershed in the south, and from the coast to the Wiltshire county boundary on the east. The work of preparing the Regional Survey and Scheme was placed in the hands of PROFESSOR PATRICK ABERCROMBIE, M.A., F.R.I.B.A., Past-President of the Town Planning Institute, and by consent of the Bristol Town Planning Committee, MR. B. F. BRUETON, A.R.I.B.A., M.T.P.I., has collaborated with Professor Abercrombie in its preparation.

The area of the Region has since been extended at the request of the Axbridge Rural District Council to include the whole of their district, although the portion of that district lying south of the Mendip plateau is not, economically speaking, within the Region. The Region is defined on Plate 15 : it comprises the whole areas of fifteen Authorities and a portion of another :—

Bristol City and County.	Axbridge Rural District.
Bath County Borough.	Bath Rural District.
Weston-super-Mare Urban District.	Chipping Sodbury Rural District.
Clevedon Urban District.	Clutton Rural District.
Portishead Urban District.	Keynsham Rural District.
Midsomer Norton Urban District.	Long Ashton Rural District.
Radstock Urban District.	Thornbury Rural District (part of).
Kingswood Urban District.	Warmley Rural District.*

All the Authorities except two (Clutton and Long Ashton Rural District Councils) have concurred in the establishing of the Regional Planning Committee, and have delegated to the

---

* Later subdivided into Mangotsfield U.D. and Warmley R.D.

**

FOREWORD

Committee such portion of their Town Planning powers as enable it to function in an advisory capacity. They have also contributed towards the expenses of the Joint Committee a sum representing the product of one-tenth of a penny rate over a period of three years.

The Joint Committee consists of two representatives from each City and one from each Urban and Rural District, together with the Clerk and Surveyor of each Council acting in an advisory capacity.

On the formation of the Committee, SIR JOHN SWAISH, K.B.E., J.P. (Bristol), was appointed Chairman; ALDERMAN C. H. LONG, J.P. (Bath), was appointed Vice-Chairman, and MR. E. J. TAYLOR, Town Clerk of Bristol, was appointed Honorary Secretary. In 1926 Sir John Swaish retired and was succeeded by ALDERMAN ALFRED DOWLING, J.P. (Bristol); in 1926 also Mr. E. J. Taylor retired and was succeeded by the present Town Clerk of Bristol, MR. JOSIAH GREEN.

The present membership (April, 1929) is :—

Authority.	Representatives.	Clerk.	Surveyor.
Bristol City & County	Ald. A. Dowling, J.P. *Chairman* Ald. A. Senington, J.P.	Mr. Josiah Green *Hon. Sec.*	Mr. L. S. McKenzie M.I.C.E.
Bath County Borough	Ald. C. H. Long, J.P. *Vice-Chairman* Ald. Wills, J.P.	Mr. J. Basil Ogden	Mr. F. P. Sissons
Clevedon U.D.	Mr. G. H. Gould	Mr. H. C. P. Day	Mr. I. J. Leach
Kingswood U.D.	Mr. A. G. Randall, J.P.	Mr. Percy Baldwin	Mr. H. G. Warne
Mangotsfield U.D.	Mr. H. F. Wren	Sir Seymour Williams	Capt. W. H. Knee
Midsomer Norton U.D.	Mr. F. A. Boulter	Mr. W. J. Landray	Mr. C. H. Sunderland
Portishead U.D.	Mr. Hedley Stevens	Mr. J. Chaffey Glyde	Mr. F. Smith
Radstock U.D.	Mr. W. J. Beard	Mr. C. H. Perry	Mr. E. Stockdale
Weston-s.-Mare U.D.	Mr. T. E. Macfarlane, J.P.	Mr. S. C. Smith	Mr. H. A. Brown
Axbridge R.D.	Mr. W. J. H. Porter, J.P.	Mr. F. R. Burdge	Mr. J. K. Dunster and Mr. J. Lovell, *Highways* Mr. H. R. Day, *Sanitary*
Bath R.D.	Mrs. Hignett	Mr. R. H. Whittington	Mr. F. Tiddy, *Highways* Mr. F. W. Kelway, *Sanitary*
Clutton R.D.	No representatives		
Chipping Sodbury R.D.	Capt. J. L. Brown, J.P.	Mr. R. Wilson	Capt. C. K. Henderson, *Highways* Mr. H. S. Hale and Mr. W. H. Williams, *Sanitary*
Long Ashton R.D.	No representatives		
Keynsham R.D.	Mr. W. A. Salmon	Mr. F. G. Whittuck	Mr. J. Johnson, *Highways* Mr. H. W. Argile, *Sanitary*
Thornbury R.D.	Mr. H. G. Bush	Mr. J. G. Wicks	Mr. F. A. Steer, *Highways* Mr. F. W. Davies, *Sanitary*
Warmley R.D.	Mr. A. Lear	Sir Seymour Williams	Capt. W. H. Knee

The Joint Committee has throughout sought the assistance of the County Councils of Gloucestershire and Somerset, and although a County Council is not a " Town Planning Authority " within the meaning of the Town Planning Act, the County Councils have willingly co-operated and have given valuable assistance to the Joint Committee.*

The representatives appointed from the County Councils are :—

GLOUCESTERSHIRE : Major F. W. B. Cripps, D.S.O., *Chairman County Highways Committee* ; Col. E. S. Sinnott, C.M.G., M.I.C.E., *County Surveyor* ; Mr. E. T. Gardom, O.B.E., *Clerk to the County Council.*

SOMERSET : Sir Frank Beauchamp, Bart., C.B.E., *Chairman County Works Committee* ; Lieut.-Col. E. H. Stead, M.I.C.E., *County Surveyor* ; Mr. Harold King, *Clerk to the County Council.*

The following, also, have kindly accepted invitations to attend the meetings and advise the Joint Committee on matters connected with the Scheme :—

Sir George H. Oatley, F.R.I.B.A., representing the Bristol Society of Architects.
Mrs. Falk, representing the Garden Cities and Town Planning Association.
Mr. J. J. Simpson, representing the Bristol Kyrle Society.
Mr. C. F. W. Dening, F.R.I.B.A. (Bristol).
Mr. Mowbray A. Green, F.R.I.B.A. (Bath).
Col. P. Burges, O.B.E. (Chipping Sodbury).
Mr. H. R. Griffiths, Divisional Superintendent, G.W.R.

The Regional Report and plans prepared by Professor Abercrombie and Mr. B. F. Brueton were submitted to a Meeting of the Joint Regional Planning Committee on June 6th, 1929, and on the motion of Alderman C. H. Long, seconded by Sir Frank Beauchamp, it was unanimously resolved that the Regional Survey and Report be generally approved and ordered to be published.

---

* By the Local Government Act, 1929, County Councils will be enabled to exercise Town Planning powers from April 30th, 1930.

The Council House,
   Bristol,
      June, 1929.

JOSIAH GREEN,
   Hon. Secretary.

AUTHORS' NOTE

THE Authors wish to take this opportunity of thanking those who have given them help in the production of this Report and its accompanying plans. In the first place thanks are due to Mr. Lessel S. Mackenzie, M.I.C.E., City Engineer of Bristol, whose advice has been continuous, and to the Surveyors and other officers of the other Local Authorities comprised in the scheme: without their co-operation the Survey could not have been compiled.

Mr. G. L. Pepler (Town Planning Adviser to the Minister of Health) has added his invaluable and constructive criticism. The Authors have also received much useful information about special aspects of the scheme from: Mr. A. H. Bennett, on Coal-mining; Professor Reynolds and Dr. Bolton, on Geology; Mr. Walter Bryant, on Quarrying; Mr. E. K. Tratman, on Archæology; Mr. Inglis (City Forester), on Afforestation.

These gentlemen are not to be held responsible for the use which has been made of their information, but the authors realise that without it the Report would have been less comprehensive in character. Mr. T. F. Thomson, A.M.T.P.I., has taken a great interest in the collection of information for the Survey and the drawing of the diagrams; also the Authors are indebted to Mr. N. L. Webber, P.A.S.I., for care and trouble taken in obtaining photographs.

The Authors, in conclusion, would like to draw the attention of the Committee to the need for immediate action: at this moment buildings are being erected in the Region, of design and materials that are unworthy of their situation and without due regard to their position, advertisements are erected in the line of vision of famous views, petrol stations present their disorderly fronts to the main roads and destroy the charm of village streets. These are obvious defects, but equally important deviations from just forms of development are going on where there is no town-planning scheme in operation: town planning should be applied without delay to the whole Region if an economic and orderly future is to be secured to this piece of singularly beautiful country and these attractive towns and villages.

CONTENTS

CONTENTS

PART THE THIRD. THE EFFECT OF THE REGIONAL PLAN

PART THE FOURTH. THE REALISATION OF THE REGIONAL PLAN

LIST OF ILLUSTRATIONS.

LIST OF ILLUSTRATIONS

MAP.

Folding Map in Envelope : 3-inch Scale ; showing general proposals for the Region.

PART THE FIRST

SURVEY OF THE REGION

PLATE 2.

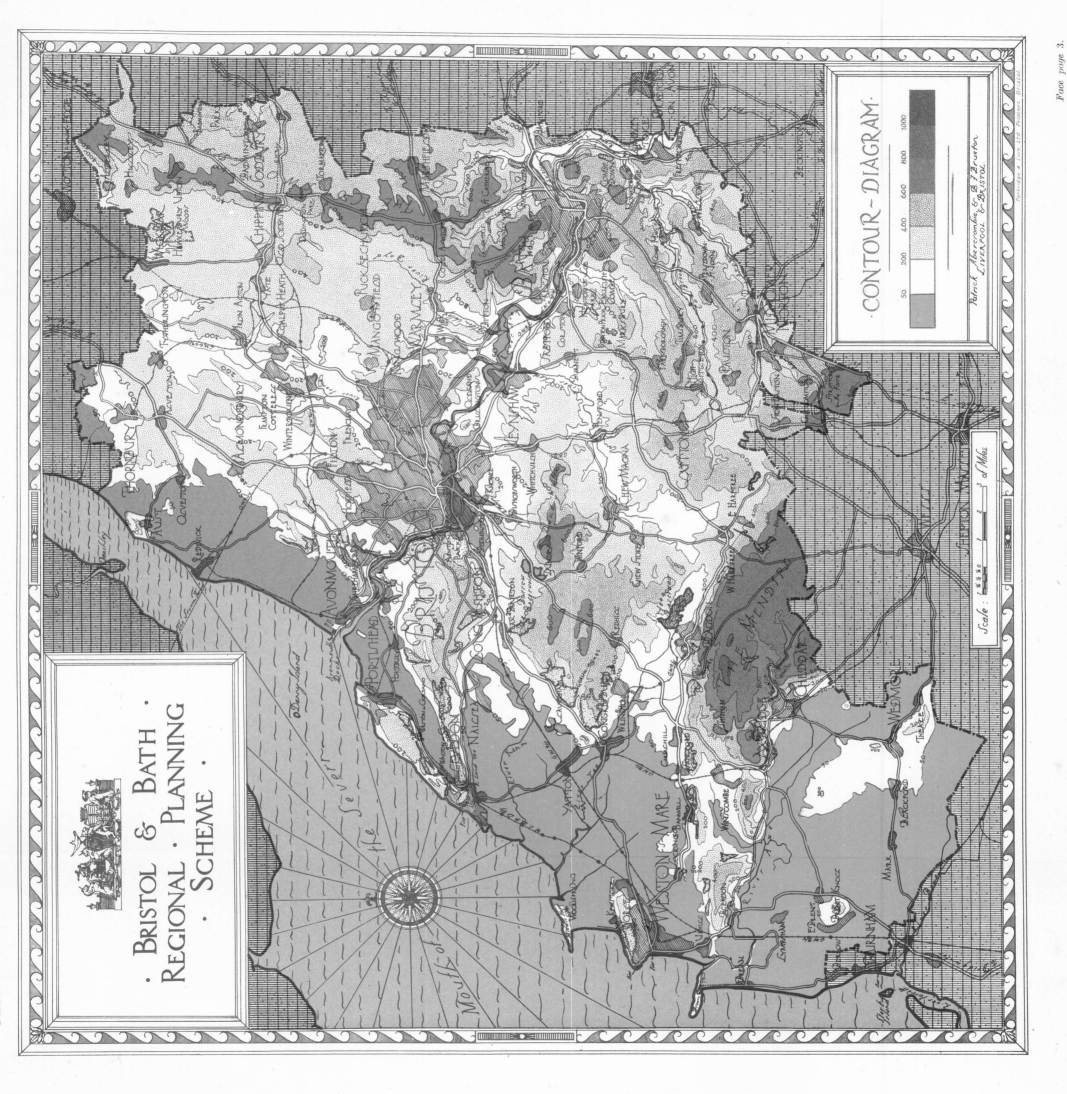

· BRISTOL · & · BATH ·
REGIONAL · PLANNING
· SCHEME ·

CONTOUR ~ DIAGRAM.

50   200   400   600   800   1000

Patrick Abercrombie, & B. F. Brueton.
LIVERPOOL & BRISTOL.

Scale : 1 : ⅛ inch to 1 mile

0   1   2   3   of Miles.

PART THE FIRST. SURVEY OF THE REGION

CHAPTER I.   PHYSICAL SURVEY

SECTION 1.   CONTOURS

THE contours of the Region are very much bound up with the geological formation. There is a flat alluvial coastal plain, unbroken, north of Avon, impinged upon in the south by several of the limestone ridges, or remains of former loftier folds. North of Avon, however, the wide terrace between the alluvial flats and the Cotswold escarpment does not indicate the varied geological formation. It is a slightly undulating plain, rising to 450 feet south of Chipping Sodbury and falling towards the Avon, intersected by a number of river valleys of which the Frome, Boyd, and Trym are the most marked. Geological formation is indicated at the Cotswold escarpment where there is a sudden rise, steepest from the Avon to Lansdown, of 700 feet: further north at Old Sodbury the ground rises to 500 feet. A typical ascent from the middle Terrace to the upper is made by the London road at Tog Hill (717 feet): the high ground is maintained to Marshfield (600 feet), beyond which there is a fall towards Chippenham.

Bath is situated in the main breach made in this plateau by the Avon, from which several lesser valleys radiate, all cut through to about the same level. The tops of the hills or downs surrounding Bath are almost flat and are above 600 feet. To the east of Bath the deep valley of the Avon takes a sudden bend to the south, when the Limpley Stoke Valley is joined by those of the Cam and Wellow (or Somer) Brook. These contours round Bath are extremely restless: there is no repose except on the tops of the Downs.

South of Bristol the coastal marsh lands are brought to a full stop in the narrowing " Gordano " valley, enclosed within ridges over 400 feet on the south and over 300 feet on the north. The latter forms the largest extent of elevated coastline in the Region. The next section of the Marsh or Moor extends more deeply inland, namely to Flax Bourton on the north and beyond Congresbury on the south: it just manages between Uphill and the sea to establish continuity with the Bridgwater Plain. This great expanse of low-lying and comparatively recently reclaimed alluvium extends far outside the Region to Bridgwater, the Polden Hills, Glastonbury and Pennard Hill, and closes in towards the Mendips. In this region it is broken in three places only: the two small hills of Brent Knoll (457 feet) and Nyland Hill (253 feet) and the larger Isle of Wedmore which rises a little over 200 feet. The area of these low-lying lands administered by the Commissioners of Sewers in Gloucestershire and Somerset is shown on the folding map.

The low ground penetrates along the Avon Valley inland beyond Bristol: there is land below the 50-foot contour almost touching the Bath boundary at the New Bridge. These Avon flats are not controlled by the Commissioners of Sewers.

The elevated lands south of the Avon may be taken in three groups: first the Clevedon–Portishead and Clevedon–Clifton ridges; second the Dundry–Barrow–Wrington group; thirdly, the Mendips and their outliers. A characteristic of all three groups is the abrupt descent into the coastal plain by which the most is made scenically of comparatively modest elevations and at the same time main lines of communications have been daunted from ascending them directly. This has been the fortunate means of their preservation.

The Clevedon–Clifton ridge, which widens out as it approaches the Avon, affects, beyond the river, the north-western portion of Bristol and Clifton : the varied levels which add so much interest and also tax the engineer's skill to avoid steep road gradients are the offshoots of this important feature. The Leigh Woods facing Clifton and Durdham Downs, Ashton Park, Kings Weston Hill, and Blaise Castle are the most obvious beauties.

Backwell Hill and Dundry (disparate geologically) combine to place a barrier to the southward march of Bristol : this high ground is breached at one point between Dundry and Backwell Hill by the Bridgwater Road, which, however, has to rise to 475 feet for the purpose. The other main road, to Weston-super-Mare, skirts round the wooded slope of the Backwell and Wrington Warren massif. At one place only, the Roddy Hill, does it cut through the higher ground near Cadbury Camp. Between the Backwell and Dundry group and the Mendips there is a piece of lower ground formed by the valleys of two rivers : the Yeo on the west and the Chew on the east.

Mendip is the most imposing mass in the Region. It is compared unfavourably with the Quantock Hills for variety—but the very simplicity of its shape adds to its impressiveness. The highest point, Blackdown, 1024 feet, by no means indicates the sense of elevation and remoteness of the whole tableland, a large part of which is over 850 feet high. This simplicity of form breaks up at the western end and there is, enclosed by hill fragments, the Winscombe Valley into which runs an arm of the marsh land on either side of the Lox Yeo River. Bleadon Hill, Brean Down and Steep Holm (three miles out in the Bristol Channel) complete the Mendip ridge westwards. Two other coastal fragments of inland ridges must be mentioned : Worlebury Hill north of Weston, and Middle Hope north of Sand Bay.

There remains the most difficult piece of country to describe from the point of view of its levels : namely that which lies S.E. of the Valley of the Chew. With the exception of the valleys of the Cam and Wellow which link it to the Bath country, there seem to be no main lines or dominating features. The caprice of geological denudation will largely explain this.

SECTION 2. GEOLOGY

A. Formation

§ i. *The Drama of Formation*

It is not easy for anyone other than an expert to understand the geological formation of this Region : the surface geology map is extraordinarily complicated owing to its patchiness and the juxtaposition of rocks of widely different periods. Compare it for example with that of Yorkshire and Lincolnshire where strata succeed strata, gently dropping eastwards, forming gigantic bands running north and south from carboniferous limestone to chalk. The Bristol map is of course supplemented by cross-sections, but these must be taken in many directions and at many points. But for a thorough grasp it is necessary to follow in a general way the history of the formations, which will alone explain an apparent jumble of strata. No apology is needed for an attempt to describe and illustrate in a simplified form the Geology of the Region, seeing that it forms the underlying basis of many of the practical features of the scheme : for industry, in its relation to coalmining and quarrying ; for residential use, showing suitable building land and places to avoid ; for scenic preservation ; for water supply.

Professor Lloyd Morgan in his admirable introduction to Dr. Reynolds' Excursion

Handbook* has adopted the dramatic method and has grouped the Earth Drama of the Bristol Region into four Acts, as preliminary to the fifth in which man steps on the scene.

§ ii. *The First Act*

The First Act discovers the Carboniferous series of rocks, resting upon beds of Old Red Sandstone (the oldest rocks exposed in the Region) and comprising the Carboniferous Limestone, Millstone Grit and the Coal Measures. These rocks were laid down in successive layers under apparently undisturbed conditions, save for one active volcano during the Limestone period, evidences of whose eruptions are visible in several places.† The thickness of these rocks is enormous—at least eleven thousand feet, i.e., 2 miles—and it is probable that they were formed in water which was never one thousand feet deep : it was a period therefore of continual gradual depression, but at unequal pace, the deposits sometimes being more rapid and thus shallowing the water.

§ iii. *The Second Act*

The Second Act is in violent contrast with this calm period of deposit : the strata are now " caught in the strong embrace of straining earth pressures " and thrust up to ridges and domes, with troughs and basins in between. Generally speaking, these colossal folds are uniform throughout this group of rocks, which for all the world appear like layers of blankets, black, grey, blue‡ and dull red, rumpled but following each other's convolutions. Occasion-

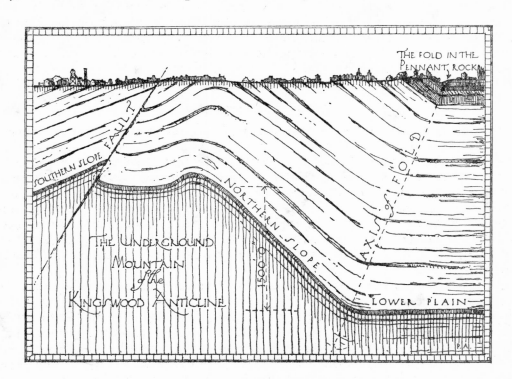

ally the folding slipped, causing faults, of which the one at Clifton is visible in the gorge. What was the scope within which these folds were bent—the height of the top of the highest

---

* And in his Geological History of the Neighbourhood of Bristol : *British Association Handbook*, 1898.
† At Middle Hope and Worle near Weston-super-Mare and on Wrington Warren.
‡ The colour for Limestone.

coal fold to the bottom of the lowest Old Red Sandstone? It is impossible to say: one might hazard the guess that the top dome of the Mendips would be at least 12,000 feet (over 2 miles) above sea level; but it is a harder matter to determine to what depth descends the lowest layer of the Sandstone where it plunges nearly vertically downwards south of Sandford Hill.

The second scene in this Act was of a quieter nature: while in other parts of this country thick deposits of Permian Limestone and New Red Sandstone (Triassic rocks) were being formed, in North, East and West Bristol the rolls and hollows were left bare and were subject to denudation. Our credulity is put to a severe test to believe what denudation—prolonged over ages of time—can effect; what we here see resembles more the work of a joiner's plane. The great sweeping curves of the folds have hardly affected the shaving process; whatever the different hardness of the strata, Coal Measures, Limestone and Sandstone are equally levelled off. In some places the folds have left stunted ridges such as the Mendip Hills: in other places the even contour gives no indication of the varied strata, as where Coal, Millstone and Limestone succeed each other going north from Rangeworthy, nor does it suggest the subterranean agitation of the Kingswood anticline. No more vivid impression of the underground mountain which persists under this planed level surface can be gained than from a visit to the Speedwell Pit, situated near the top of the anticline, with its workings carried down the sloping strata, northwards. A few figures will perhaps indicate the scale of these occurrences: the straight drop down to the coal seam is about 1200 feet, the gallery then cuts through the underground mountain somewhat below its apex for about ¼ mile, before the escarpment of its northern side is reached; the descent then begins at an angle of approximately 45 degrees: the vertical drop on this slope is about 1500 feet until suddenly the strata turn northward into a horizontal direction. There is also a similar slope on the southern side: this underground mountain is therefore half as high again as the Mendips. Not a sign of it appears on the surface.

§ iv. *The Third Act*

The Third Act opens with the Triassic age, now nearing its close, but at length reaching Bristol in the Keuper period: a salt lake submerged the level upturned edges of the carboniferous rocks, from which the Mendips emerged and other smaller islands. As the waters crept up the slopes of these islands, masses of loose stones of various sorts were cemented together into a composite rock called the Dolomitic conglomerate—it is found all over the Region and always indicates hollows or creeks in the earlier rocks, thus filled up and further effacing the original folds. Next in regular succession the normal Triassic Red Sandstone and Marl, followed by the Lias clays and Limestone, and lastly after a separating layer of Midford sands, the Oolites. It is not clear whether there was ever the Chalk on top, as is found in Wiltshire, further east.

There are several incidental scenes in this otherwise continuous peaceful Act: one, and a tragic one, can be reconstructed between the Triassic and Liassic periods: at this time the Rhætic deposits, some 2000 feet thick, were being laid down in the Eastern Alps. An expedition of the creatures which flourished during this period must have reached our area only to perish in millions owing to the over-saltiness of the water: these Rhætic or Penarth beds are thin, but clearly recognizable; they cap, for example, the New Red Sandstone at Beach Hill, north of Blagdon, and can be seen in section at Aust Cliff. It would seem also that during this period the older rocks sank, as in some cases the later Lias and Oolites rest directly on them, without the interposition of the New Red Sandstone.

In looking at this Third Act two salient features appear: (i) the thinness of the beds compared with the massive nature of the carboniferous series: the thickness from the bottom of the New Red Sandstone to the top of the Great Oolite is in many places not more than 1000 feet; (ii) the regularity and evenness of the deposits: these have a slightly eastern dip,

PLATE 3.

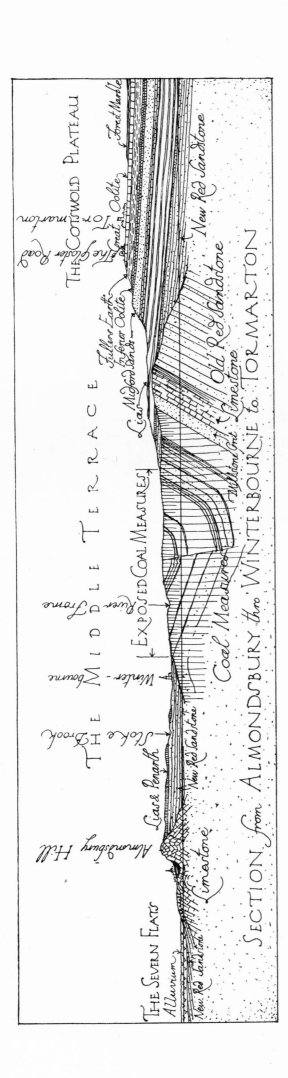

THE COTSWOLD PLATEAU

Tormarton

THE MIDDLE TERRACE

THE SEVERN FLATS

Forest Marble
Great Oolite
Fullers Earth
The Roman Road
Midford Sands
Inferior Oolite
Lias & Penarth

Coal Measures

EXPOSED COAL MEASURES

Water - Bourne

Ruin Stone

Stoke Brook

Almondsbury Hill

New Red Sandstone

Lias & Penarth

Alluvium

New Red Sandstone

Limestone

Coal Measures

Millstone Grit

Limestone

Old Red Sandstone

New Red Sandstone

SECTION from ALMONDSBURY thro WINTERBOURNE to TORMARTON

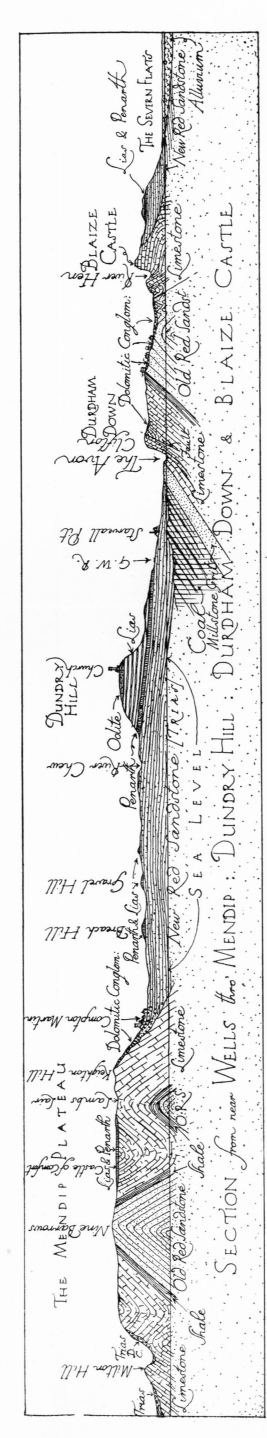

THE MENDIP PLATEAU

Milton Hill

Thrias Pit

Nine Barrows

Castle of Comfort

Lias & Penarth

O.R.S.

Lambs

Rookham Hill

Dundry
Church

DUNDRY HILL

Compton Martin

Dolomitic Conglom:

Penarth & Lias

Penarth & Lias

Breach Hill

Grant Hill

River Chew

Penarth

Oolite

Lias

G.W.R.

Stowell Pk

The Avon

Clifton

DURDHAM
DOWN

Dolomitic Conglom:

River Hen

BLAIZE
CASTLE

Lias & Penarth

THE SEVERN FLATS

New Red Sandstone

Alluvium

Old Red Sandstone

Limestone

Limestone

Shale

Old Red Sandstone

New Red Sandstone (Trias)

SEA LEVEL

Coal

Millstone Grit

Limestone

Shale

Limestone

SECTION from near WELLS thro' MENDIP : DUNDRY HILL : DURDHAM DOWN. & BLAIZE CASTLE

The vertical scale is approximately six
times the horizontal.

Sketch sections showing the geological
formations within the Region.

The sharpness of the fold
is exaggerated

Shute-shelve Hill

Axbridge

Sandford Hill

Slicoet

Churchill

Alluvium

New Red Sandstone

Dolomitic Conglom:

Dolomitic Conglom:
New Red Sandstone
Alluvium

Limestone
Shale
Old Red Sandstone
Limestone
Shale

SEA LEVEL

Old Red Sandstone

Limestone

New Red Sandstone

SECTION thro' MENDIP from AXBRIDGE to SANDFORD

but for miles their level courses can be traced, on the sections, across the country. They lie quietly, but in geological phrase unconformably, on the contorted strata of the older rocks.

§ v. *The Fourth Act*

The Fourth Act begins with the district re-elevated to form dry land and a second period of denudation sets in. The first scene might consist of marine denudation: as the land gradually rose, covered with a continuous coating of clay (or chalk), the waves would eat away the soft new deposits. The Cotswold escarpment has the air of sea coast cliffs which have been washed by waves: it was probably this gradual upheaval that dipped the level strata eastwards.

And now set in the real shaping of the landscape under those twin agents, wind and water. If any place could vindicate the Chinese theory of Feng-shui or Wind-Water as the principal producer of landscape effect, it is this Bristol Region. Undisturbed geological deposits tend to give an unbroken level surface capped by the latest strata ; Wind and Water carve it into fantastic shapes. The country round Bath—some of the most "mouvementé" in England— is carved out of these level strata, which assert themselves occasionally on the billiard-table tops of the downs, such as Lansdown and Charmy. The sandpaper action of the wind, the file-cutting action of the streams set to work, the latter not only cutting their channels continually deeper, but carrying vast quantities of silt to create the alluvial flats along the Bristol Channel.

And here a feature of river denudation must be mentioned : when a watercourse has once established its direction, it generally tends to stick to it. A slight depression would cause the first flow of the Avon : gradually as it wore through these late deposits it reached the Lime-stone ridge of Durdham Down, which was but thinly covered : the stream is not diverted, but in place of the wide shallow valley at Keynsham where the soft later deposits are largely denuded, it cuts the Clifton Gorge, directly across the strata. The Trym, and in the north the Little Avon, cut similar defiles through the limestone, which was hidden when they began to flow. The Boyd, again, suddenly for a brief passage becomes a romantic stream as it pierces an emergent knob of limestone.

It is interesting to speculate as to how much this later denudation affected the older rocks, when they were laid bare of their later coverings. The top of the Mendips was probably never covered, but other areas such as the Clevedon and Portishead ridges were only revealed by denudation. It seems fairly certain that the surfaces so revealed were not much remodelled by later forces of erosion, but their hollows and crannies, filled in, were left, with the later rocks, forming continuous surfaces, as may be seen north and south of Coombe Hill and Blaise Castle. Denudation in these has removed all the softer layers, except those which form continuous surfaces with the exposed early rocks : but possibly the finishing touches to the smoothness of both period rocks were put during the later stages of erosion.

Such is the Geological drama of the district : its scenes " stir our imagination with a display of activity more swift and forceful than is to be seen in the quiet life of to-day's sleepy hollows in Gloucester and Somerset." After this dynamic survey of the formation, it is time to examine the static conditions of the ground to-day.

B.   Static Geology

§ i. *North of Avon*

The actual position in the Region of the main geological masses can be gathered from the map, qualified as it must be by a study of the cross-sections ; the most important qualification is that of the small area of visible coal measures as compared with their real extent, covered with a thin veneer of later deposits (see Plate 4).

In every way the region north of the Avon is simpler than the south. The central area is occupied by the largest expanse of uncovered coal measures, these being in the form of a shallow saucer of Pennant rock holding the Upper Measures and succeeded by the deeper Lower Measures, which in the south (at Kingswood) are violently faulted so as to appear more suddenly at the surface than one could expect. There are clear indications of an enclosing ring of Carboniferous Limestone, which effectively encircles the northern end of the coalfield : on the west the sides are visible at Almondsbury, Westbury and Clifton, and on the east continuously to Chipping Sodbury and momentarily at Wick. On both sides of this limestone ridge (which in many places is rather a level band than a ridge) lies the New Red Sandstone (Keuper Marl and Rock) capped by the Lias clays : the Keuper only appears therefore on the surface in three narrow strips, the easternmost one, which passes through Yate, Wick and Bitton, being remarkable for Celestine and ochre and raddle deposits.

The Lias and Rhætic beds are much wider and give a characteristic appearance to areas on which are situated Filton on the west and Pucklechurch and Doynton on the east. The Rhætic beds are found as an extremely regular fimbriation or edging to the Lias wherever the latter rests on the New Red Sandstone.

If the Lias formations are not scenically remarkable, the Oolite group sufficiently compensates : it forms that remarkable line, running nearly due north and south from Wotton-under-Edge to Radstock and Frome. But north of the Avon its descent to the Lias plain is much more abrupt and straight than it is in the south. West of this line, this group is not found except as capping Dundry Hill, whose conspicuousness is therefore geologically justified.

The Oolites are separated generally from the Lias by beds of Midford Sands (so called from the village near Bath) : then follow in succession the Inferior Oolite, Fuller's Earth, Great or Bath Oolite (which forms the level tops of Lansdown, Charmy Down, Banner Down and most of the high ground round Bath) and finally Forest Marble which is chiefly found in this Region at Badminton and Hinton Charterhouse. There is something very satisfactory (after the fragmentary, patchy, spasmodic and misleading appearance of the older rocks) in the logical sequence in which this Oolite group appears, following the face of the great escarpment of the Cotswolds and winding round the valleys, the geological map forming practically a counterpart of the contour plan. For simplicity of colouring these five layers have been grouped into three : but the full range of colours on the large scale Geological Ordnance Survey map is more vivid and expressive.

The Avon indeed forms a bad division of the Geological Map, for the Old Red Sandstone and Limestone Ridge of Clifton runs continuously (in spite of the gorge) to Clevedon. The Coalfield, of course, is continuous from north (at Cromhall) to south (at Radstock) : but its central feature, the great Kingswood anticline (earlier described as an " underground mountain ") is on the north of the Avon.

§ ii. *South of Avon*

The principal cause of complication of the southern part of the Region is an apparent change in the axis of the main folds of the primary rocks. The main axis of folding near the Avon appears clearly to be north and south, as may be seen in the cross-section through Winterbourne. It is true that the cup-shaped form of the coal measures indicates two axes of folding and the great Kingswood anticline is along an east to west axis. When we come to the great hog's back of the Mendip there is no longer any doubt about the east and west axis, with vertebræ and tail pieces complete. Worle Hill and Middle Hope indicate remains of other parallel ridges.

The denudation, too, in this southern area has been much more capricious : Dundry, an outlier of the Cotswolds, has been already mentioned : elsewhere (e.g., Backwell Hill), the Lias is found direct on the Limestone without any intervening Trias or Rhætic beds ; and

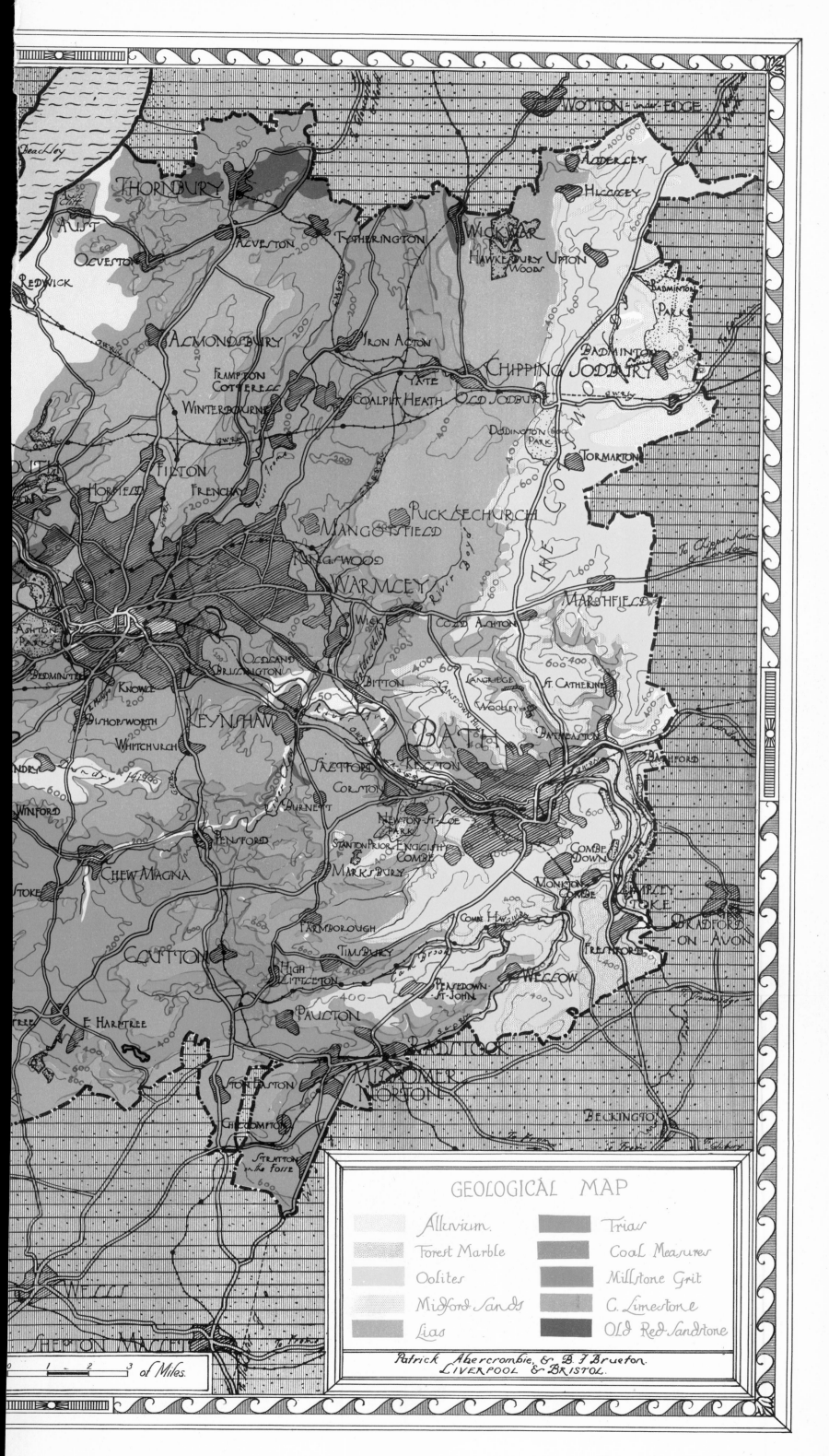

GEOLOGICAL MAP

Alluvium.
Forest Marble
Oolites
Midford Sands
Lias

Trias
Coal Measures
Millstone Grit
C. Limestone
Old Red Sandstone

Patrick Abercrombie. & B. F. Brueton.
LIVERPOOL & BRISTOL.

Face page 9.

PLATE 4.

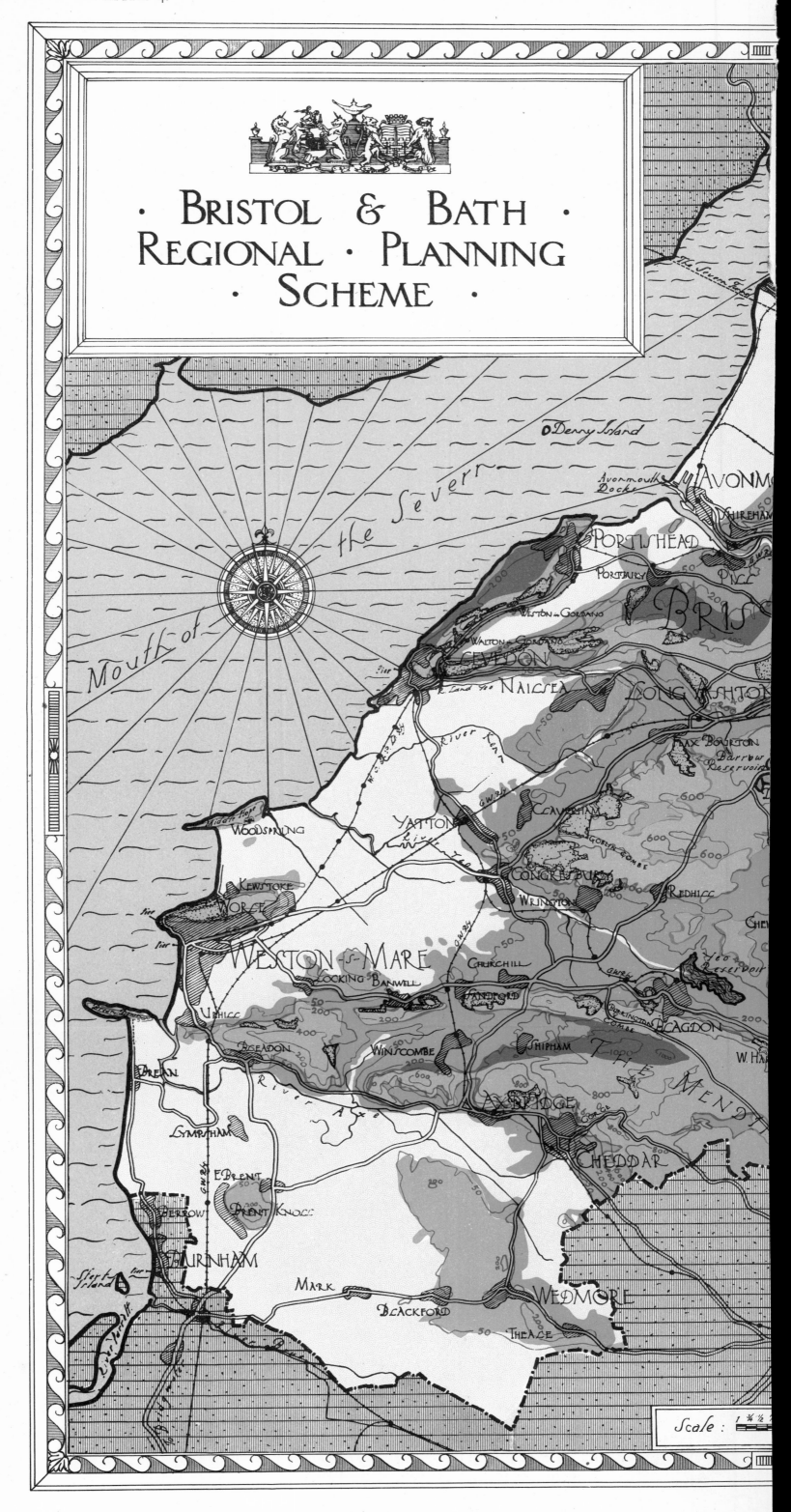

· BRISTOL & BATH ·
REGIONAL · PLANNING
· SCHEME ·

Scale :

there are numerous isolated patches of Lias on the New Red Sandstone.   Brent Knoll emerges as an abrupt island of Lias in the alluvial sea : the Isle of Wedmore is a flatter mound ; showing the Triassic base to the Penarth and Lias beds : Nyland Hill has a top of Carboniferous Limestone.

It is interesting also to trace, often side by side, features remaining from the earlier or Second Act, and those caused by the denudation of the Fourth Act.   Allusion has already been made to the Avon gorge, a work of the Fourth Act : the moderate hollow between Clifton and Durdham Downs, at right angles to the gorge, represents a landscape feature in the unbroken Limestone of Act 2 : this is proved by the partial filling in of the hollow by Dolomitic Conglomerate during the early part of the Third Act.   More remarkable still is the juxtaposition on Backwell Hill of several Second Act creeks up which tongues of Conglomerate run into the Limestone uplands, side by side with Brockley Combe (cut by a torrent through the Limestone during the Fourth Act).   Here the orientation of early and late features is much the same.

The Nailsea Coalfield is also a disturbing incident : separated from the other coalfield by a fold of the limestone and lying in a hollow between two folds (even as the main Coalfield does at Cromhall) it appears to extend seawards, between the two Limestone ridges of Clevedon and Middle Hope.   Its actual extent westward has not been determined.

One of the minor freaks of this geological map is the almost total absence of the Millstone Grit from the surface.   This is the chance result of its being covered by the later rocks : Millstone Grit, which is sometimes called " Farewell Rock " as it underlies the Coal Measures and shows the end of their productiveness, is not indeed thick here, but it should have made bands of noticeable width between the Coal Measures and the Mountain Limestone, as it does just south of Wickwar.   The only other considerable outcrop of Millstone Grit is in the form of a series of detached spots on the southern edge of the Limestone from Long Ashton to Brandon Hill in Bristol.

§ iii.   *Succession of Rocks*

The following is a list of the rocks in succession beginning with the oldest found in the Region, the Old Red Sandstone, and ending with the Alluvium :—

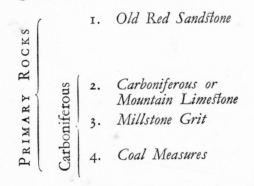

1. *Old Red Sandstone*	Forming Blackdown, the "Dome" of the Mendips : and long strips from Clevedon to Portishead, and from Charlton House, through Failand across the Avon to Stoke Bishop.
2. *Carboniferous or Mountain Limestone*	Found in four main masses from extreme north to extreme south of the Region.
3. *Millstone Grit*	Only sparsely outcropping, but carrying the coal measures throughout.
4. *Coal Measures*	The Upper and Lower, divided by continuous band of the Pennant Grit.

The above are folded "conformably," with well-marked faults, especially in the Coal Measures.

* * * * *

There is in this Region a gap betweeen the Primary and Secondary Rocks ; Permian, at the end of the Primary, and Bunter, at the beginning of the Secondary, are missing.

* * * * *

9

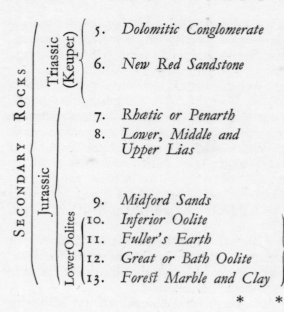

SECONDARY ROCKS	*Triassic (Keuper)*	5.	*Dolomitic Conglomerate*	Made up out of fragments of the older rocks, cemented together.
		6.	*New Red Sandstone*	Red soft stones and Marls: very large areas of this are found, lying unconformably on the Carboniferous rocks, the beds being often quite thin.
	Jurassic	7.	*Rhætic or Penarth*	Shallow beds separating the Trias from the Lias.
		8.	*Lower, Middle and Upper Lias*	Largely clay but also containing a grey slightly crystalline limestone. Found in large and small patches generally on the New Red Sandstone, but occasionally direct on the Mountain Limestone.
		9.	*Midford Sands*	Parting Beds between the Lias and the Oolites.
	Lower Oolites	10.	*Inferior Oolite*	These beds follow in regular succession and are continuous on the eastern side of the Region, the rivers having cut through them, revealing their terraced slopes.
		11.	*Fuller's Earth*	
		12.	*Great or Bath Oolite*	
		13.	*Forest Marble and Clay*	

*   *   *   *   *

Oxford Clay to Chalk are missing.

*   *   *   *   *

POST TERTIARY ROCKS	14.	*River Gravel*
	15.	*Old Alluvium* (Brick earth)
	16.	*New Alluvium*
	17.	*Blown Sand*

SECTION 3.   RIVERS, MOORS, COAST AND TIDES

A. The Rivers

§ i. *The Avon*

The River System of the Region is dominated by the Avon and its tributaries, which drain about two-thirds of the whole area. Entering the Region at the eastern boundary near Bradford at the point where it is joined by the Wiltshire Frome (which in itself drains a very large area outside the Region), it is next joined by the combined Cam and Wellow (which has absorbed the Somer). After passing through the lovely Limpley Stoke and Claverton Valley it is joined by the By-Brook from Box, and then several small streams (such as the St. Catherine's brook) until the Boyd enters it from the Golden Valley at Bitton. Next comes the Chew at Keynsham, serving a wide area to the foot of the Mendips, the Warmley brook, and then the Gloucestershire Frome which joins it in the city of Bristol and which drains the largest area of any tributary in the Region. The Trym is the last tributary of any importance.

An interesting watershed occurs south of Dodington Park where the Gloucestershire Frome rises in the escarpment of the Cotswolds: about a mile north of it the Little Avon rises, and though there is nothing in the contours to oppose its joining the Frome and there is even the geological formation to cut through, it insists on flowing northwards through Wickwar and empties itself independently into the Severn. Finally there is a third stream which takes its rise on the top of the escarpment and starts flowing due east, exactly opposite to the Frome; nevertheless after fetching a wide compass it eventually becomes the Avon, flowing through Malmesbury and Chippenham, Bath and Bristol.

§ ii. *The Northern Flats*

These, north of the Avon, are drained direct into the Bristol Channel by an insignificant series of streams which are little more than Dykes.

§ iii. *The Southern Flats*

South of Avon the Flats are wider and are drained by a series of sluggish rivers mostly flowing parallel with each other and several bearing the name Yeo. The Gordano Marsh has a nameless brook; below the ridge of Tickenham Hill flows the Land-Yeo, emptying at Clevedon: next the Ken, having its rise somewhere near Brockley. Then comes the Yeo, a more important stream, being the exit from the Blagdon Reservoir, and serving an area as far inland as West Harptree. Next follows the Banwell, a short stream, having its rise near Banwell Hill and its mouth at the eastern end of Middle Hope.

The River Axe is a more important river than any of the foregoing: it drains a large area of the Mendip Hills (though these produce few streams as most of the rainwater is absorbed) and also a wide area of marsh: it has two tributaries, one which flows out of the Cheddar Gorge and the Lox Yeo from the Winscombe Valley. The estuary of the Axe is a fine curved cut between Uphill and the landward end of Brean Down.

The Brue (its mouth at Highbridge) is almost wholly outside the Region; it serves the marshlands south of the Axe watershed.

B.   The Moors

The low-lying lands, or as they are here called "Moors," are generally speaking below the 50-foot contour line, though there are places, as near Mark, where the level rises above this figure. A large part of these Moors has been reclaimed from the sea within historical times and is actually below the level of the adjoining sea; in fact when the sea wall burst near Burnham many miles of land were submerged to a depth of 10 or 12 feet. There is an elaborate system of ditches and dykes which drain into larger drainage channels (locally called Rhines); these latter drain into the rivers or direct into the sea at certain states of the tide. The fall is of course very slight and embanking is resorted to.

C.   The Coast

The coast of the Region can best be studied in relation to Geological formation and Contours. Where the flats border on the Severn, there is little of interest, a monotonous and muddy shore; but there are several points worth noting. Starting from the north: there is the promontory and cliff of Rhætic formation at Aust, which faces Beachley at the mouth of the Wye; this is the narrowest place for crossing the river for many miles above or below. Just below the headland is Old Passage, where was the ferry across the Severn.

There is a slight promontory, but of no elevation, at Redwick, near where the Severn Tunnel plunges under the River. There is then a straight piece of coast starting with Severn Beach, down to the mouth of the Avon which enters the Severn tamely between alluvial flats after the elevated grandeur of the Gorge.

At Portishead, beginning with Battery Point, a fine stretch of elevated coast line extends to Clevedon, for the greater part dipping into deep water and ending with the picturesque

11

headland of Wain's Hill. Then follows a piece of dull flat coast until after the estuary of the Banwell River, the Limestone promontory of Middle Hope thrusts its delicate nose into the Channel; the whole of whose north side descends direct into deep water—the longest extent of deep water frontage in the Region.

Sand Bay is the first well-marked bay to be encountered: it appears to be formed by nature for a seaside resort: it is divided from Weston Bay by Worlebury Hill, larger and loftier than Middle Hope and wooded on its seaward end; but at no point does it reach out to deep water.

Weston Bay, with the estuary of the Axe at its southern end and the almost-island of Brean Down, has the effect of a deeper bay than Sand Bay.

Brean Down disputes with Middle Hope the title to the most beautiful feature on the coast of the Region: its southern side is more precipitous than the northern face and it dominates the last piece of coast, from Brean to Berrow. This stretch, nearly straight for four miles and then slightly receding towards Burnham, has a continuous fringe of sandhill, cutting off the marsh from the sea.

D.   The Tides

The Tides of the Severn Estuary are remarkable as having the biggest variation between high and low water in the world except perhaps the Bay of Fundy, Newfoundland. This gives a very special character to the coast and especially to the river estuaries which at low tide have the appearance of deep gorges, lined with mud. The average variation between high and low spring tides is 41 feet at Avonmouth (King Road), and single tides reach the figure of 49 feet variation.

SECTION 4.   RAINFALL

The annual Rainfall incidence of the Region varies from about 28 inches in the Avon Valley between Bristol and Bath, and south-west of Brent Knoll, to over 45 inches on the Mendip plateau.

Plate 5, which shows graphically the relative intensity of the average rainfall over a period of 35 years (1881–1915), has been prepared from information supplied by the Meteorological Department of the Air Ministry. It is interesting to compare this with the contour map and to note that the isohyetes (lines of equal rainfall) follow to a marked degree the contour lines of the country, and that the areas of greater rainfall are, generally speaking, confined to the hilly portions of the Region.

The Mendips, Cotswolds, and the Dundry-cum-Brockley uplands, areas of great rainfall, form valuable gathering grounds generally free from pollution owing to absence of population.

The average annual rainfall of the entire Region is about 30 inches, which is only very slightly higher than the average (about 27 inches) for the country as a whole.

PLATE 5.

RAINFALL

showing the Average Rainfall in inches for 35 years (1881 — 1915)

27½	30	32½	35	37½	40	42½	45	47½

Patrick Abercrombie & B. F. Brueton.
LIVERPOOL & BRISTOL.

Partridge & Love Ltd. Printers, Bristol.

Scale: 1 63360

Scale of Miles 1 2 3

· BRISTOL · & · BATH ·
REGIONAL · PLANNING ·
· SCHEME ·

CHAPTER II.   HISTORY

SECTION 1.   GENERAL

§ i. *Archæological*

THE Region abounds in archæological remains representative of all periods of human activity, and it is especially rich in remains of the various prehistoric periods. Only a comparatively small portion of the prehistoric remains within the Region have yet been systematically investigated, but enough has been done to indicate its importance in those far-off times. It has been ascertained, for example, that the Mendip plateau was as thickly populated in prehistoric times as were the downlands of Wiltshire.

The sites known as " Aveline's Hole " at the foot of Burrington Combe and Gough's Cavern, Cheddar, are two of the most important in Britain for remains of the Upper Palæolithic (i.e., Old Stone) age. Rowberrow Cavern and other caves in the Mendip area have yielded remains definitely referable to both this and the succeeding Neolithic (i.e., New Stone) age. The closing portion of the Neolithic period and the beginning of the Bronze-using age are marked by the erection of large stone (megalithic) monuments and long-shaped burial mounds ; examples of the former are found in the Stone Circles at Stanton Drew and the dolmens at Wrington, Wick and Bristol (Druid Stoke), also single stones remain at Winscombe and Armoury Square (Bristol).

Mr. E. K. Tratman, of Bristol, states that

> " A number of the Mendip caves have yielded remains of the Bronze Age, but as yet " no open living sites of the period have been discovered and explored. It is evident, " however, that the population was large, from the great number of round burial mounds " or tumuli that are to be found scattered all over the Region, for it has been proved by " excavation that the majority of these mounds do date from this period, though a few " have been found to belong to the succeeding Early (or Prehistoric) Iron Age.
>
> " Of the sites occupied during the Early Iron Age, that have been fully explored, " perhaps the most important are Read's Cavern near Burrington Combe and Wookey " Hole (just outside the Region) ; other cave and open sites are known to have been " used during this period, but they have not yet been fully investigated. Of the open " living sites perhaps the best known are Dolebury and Worlebury Camps."

On referring to Plate 6, it will be noted that there is an absence of prehistoric remains in the low-lying portions of the Region, and this tends to suggest that in prehistoric times they were uninhabited, either by reason of inundation as a shallow sea, or as a waterlogged morass. In support of this theory may be cited the result of excavations near Clevedon, which are thus described by Mr. Tratman :—

> " The gravel deposits abutting on the old cliff face near Walton Castle have been " excavated of late years, revealing the old cliff face, that existed when the sea was approxi- " mately 50 feet above its present level. Here also is the site of the Clevedon bone cave ; " the gravels and the old sea cave which they filled have yielded many remains of animals " belonging to the latter part of the Old Stone Age."

In addition to caves and camps, the Region contains a number of prehistoric roads or tracks some of which are delineated on the diagram. Their characteristic features are that they take sinuous courses and generally follow the hill tops—apparently to avoid dangers lurking in the forests and swamps of the lowlands. In more modern times it became unnecessary for travellers to seek safety by confining themselves to the hills and open stretches of country, and more direct routes were opened up, the old tracks in many cases falling into disuse as traffic routes. It is interesting, however, to note that some are still in use.

§ ii. *Roman*

The prehistoric period may be considered as ended with the coming of the Romans, and as they mixed with the native population the latter acquired some culture; thus for the next few centuries we have a period best described as Romano-British. All the " lived-in " caves of Mendip (except Aveline's Hole and Read's Cavern) show remains dating from this period, as also do the great camps such as Dolebury, Worlebury and Bury Hill, to cite but three of the great number that exist. Sodbury Camp is the only camp in the Region that is apparently of purely Roman origin.

With the coming of the Romans a fundamental change in the process of development took place; they made use of defence works which they found in existence, but they incorporated them into a system of defence of their own devising, which was based upon a scheme of new roads, the characteristic features of which are :—

(i) A preference for the higher levels;
(ii) Progress by straight lines; and
(iii) Deviations in direction effected by angles instead of curves, the angles occurring generally on high land, less frequently at rivers and stations.

The Roman Roads in the Region (see Plate 10) which now remain are :—

Via Julia.—This formed part of the road from Londinium (London) through Calleva (Silchester) to Aquæ Sulis (Bath) and thence to the mouth of the River Avon at Abone (Sea Mills), which was the point of embarkation for Caerleon and Wales.

Fosseway.—The road from Isca (Exeter) through Aquæ Sulis (Bath) to Lindum (Lincoln).

Road over the Mendip Plateau, which is thought to have terminated at or near the mouth of the River Axe with a camp and settlement of which all trace is lost.

Mr. E. J. Burrows, in his book on the Earthworks of Gloucestershire, advances the theory that the camps lying to the north of the River Avon formed a system of defence against invasion from the west; but this is not supported by any evidence of a Roman road-system in that neighbourhood, and these camps, if used in that way, must have been of the nature of outposts only.

It is evident that under Roman occupation the Region enjoyed a large measure of peace and security, since we find their great centre Aquæ Sulis (Bath) to be a Spa situated in the midst of hills and totally unsuited for defence. Confirmation may also be found in the remains of Roman villas scattered about in positions remote from fortified bases. Except for the Roman settlement at Sea Mills and the villa at Bedminster Down there are no known traces of Roman civilisation on the site now occupied by Bristol.

Another incident in the Roman occupation was mining for lead on the Mendip plateau. These mines are thought to have been started in pre-Roman days, but the Romans developed an extensive industry there and the works, though now abandoned, are not yet worked out.

§ iii. *Post-Roman*

Of the dark days following the withdrawal of the Romans little is definitely known, but from the fact that villages which were established about this period are generally found to be

PLATE 6.

. BRISTOL & BATH .
REGIONAL · PLANNING ·
· SCHEME ·

ARCHÆOLOGICAL · SURVEY

PRE-ROMAN   ROMAN

Patrick Abercrombie & B.F.Brueton.
LIVERPOOL & BRISTOL.

Scale : 1:253440
0   1   2   3
Scale of Miles

just off the line of the Roman roads,* it has been deduced that brigandage was rife and that the villages were deliberately placed within the shelter of the bush or forest as a measure of safety to prevent surprise from sudden descent of marauding bands who doubtless made good use of the Roman highways in their raids.

The principal monument of this period is the Wansdyke. This great earthwork extended from the coast near Clevedon across Somerset into Wiltshire and is thought to have been erected by the victorious Scandinavian invaders, to protect their newly acquired territories, after they had driven the British inhabitants into the western corner of the country.

SECTION 2.   BRISTOL

§ i. *Early Days*

It is probable that the site now occupied by Bristol attracted the Scandinavian and other invaders of post-Roman times as a favourable situation for a town, as it was protected by Wansdyke, served by the old Roman road (Via Julia), accessible from the sea, and sheltered by the natural ramparts of the Avon Gorge. There are, however, no records of these early days in the city's history, but it is known that the Scandinavian settlers in Ireland had a mint in Bristol, and there are in existence two Saxon coins (about A.D. 1000) struck at Bristol.

§ ii. *Mediæval*

The development of the Manorial system in Saxon times would see the development of communities into Boroughs at strategic points like Bristol, and the military system inaugurated after the Norman Conquest led to the turning of these communities into military strongholds, e.g., the building of Bristol Castle.

The growth of Christianity in the country also received an impetus from the Norman Conquest by the linking up with continental religious foundations, and the Region became honeycombed with religious institutions, Bristol being one of the chief religious centres. All this was closely associated with commercial activity, encouraged by Royal grants and local enterprise. It would appear that Scandinavian settlement, Saxon borough, port for Irish trade, military station and religious centre, commercial town, County and City, is the order of Bristol's development. The earliest known Charter is dated 1155 ; in the twelfth century

---

* *Note*.—Saxon village name terminations are -TON and -HAM, and examples within the Region are illustrated in the following sketch :—

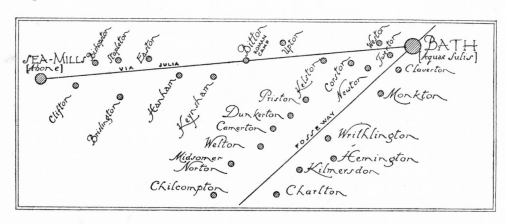

a large trade with Ireland was associated with St. James' Fair and Bristol Castle was built; in 1373 Edward III (in return for services rendered in ships and men at the siege of Calais) granted a Charter making Bristol an independent County; later came the great merchants and Bristol commerce extended into all known seas; in 1497 John and Sebastian Cabot, sailing from Bristol, discovered North America; on the suppression of the monasteries, Henry VIII created the town a City and Bishopric; Bristol was the centre of western campaigns during the Civil War, the line Bristol–Bath–Chester protecting Wales, a Royalist stronghold.

Bristol, however, retained its mediæval character to the end of the seventeenth century; in 1671 no fewer than sixteen city gateways were in existence*; the streets of the old city were narrow, tortuous and gloomy to a degree. Only scattered fragments remain of these old streets; to envisage such a thoroughfare one should visit St. Mary-le-Port Street and recall the days when the old houses with their overhanging upper stories occupied both sides of the street, excluding both light and air.

§ iii. *Eighteenth Century*

The eighteenth century saw the development of the City as a centre of culture and recreation; no better indication of the great reconstruction that took place in this century can be obtained than by consulting some of the many excellent maps produced towards the end of the seventeenth and the beginning of the nineteenth centuries. To the stagnation of building in the seventeenth century succeeded a period of great activity; town planning became dominant and the results are seen in the numerous squares and new streets which were laid out and developed both within and without the City. It may have been the last legacy of importance bequeathed by the seventeenth century—Colston's Almshouses on St. Michael's Hill—which inspired the development of the " Marsh," but it is significant that a Council Minute in 1699 records that the City Surveyor be asked to report upon the development of the Marsh—now Queen Square—for the *uniform building of houses*. By 1717 most of the houses in this—the finest and most important—square, covering nearly seven acres, had been completed and 240 trees planted by special order of the Council. Within the century over a dozen other open spaces or squares came into being.

The interesting Hall of the Society of Merchant Venturers is of this period: it bears the date 1701.

In addition to many isolated buildings of a public and private character, many new streets were set out in a formal and architectural manner and a good deal of remodelling took place within the old city walls. The most notable contribution of this century is John Wood's Exchange with its attendant buildings and the markets; of this period also is Redland Green Chapel by John Strachan.

§ iv. *Nineteenth Century*

With the dawn of the nineteenth century the rise of Clifton as a health resort resulted in various building schemes, some of them of gigantic proportions. For example, Royal York Crescent, on the hill top, with its notable sweeping line, dominates the skyline for miles. It is at Clifton that the majority of buildings displaying Greek motifs are to be found; Worcester House and Clifton Park House are individual examples; whilst Worcester Terrace and Vyvyan Terrace are examples in the grand manner.

Some notable city buildings are the Council House, by Sir Robert Smirke; the Bank of England by Professor Cockerell, who also designed Holy Trinity, Hotwells, and the Philosophical Institute, Park Street, the latter being one of his earliest public works.

---

* Reduced to four by 1789; to-day only one, St. John's, remains.

PLATE 7.

The Avon Gorge at Bristol.

In the early part of this century Bristol became noted as a Spa, and the Hotwells was a fashionable resort.   Bristol's interests were, however, concerned more with commerce than with development as a health resort, and when the great industrial revolution came, the clash of interests prevented wholehearted competition with the industrial development in the North. Bath concentrated on being a pleasure resort, but Bristol suffered for a considerable period from the conflicting interests; the City has now, however, rebuilt its fortunes as a port and trading centre.

SECTION 3.   BATH

§ i.   *Threefold Fortune of Bath*

It is not possible in a Regional Report to deal adequately with the City of Bath—its history, its architecture and its planning. Volumes have been written upon it and will continue to be; but a few notes must be included, however brief and devoid of original research.

Perhaps the first thing that strikes one in Bath is the irregularity of the greater part of its site.   The Roman town situated on the flat tongue at the turn of the Avon and the late eighteenth century suburb, the Pulteney Estate on the north-east, practically exhaust the level ground. For the rest, the most perverse levels oppose the regulating hand of the Renaissance town-planner, who was intent upon the most ambitious and formal of all shapes, the circus and the crescent.   The level hilltops which would have suited the formal plan were avoided as being too exposed; the top of Charmy Down would have accommodated the whole of eighteenth-century Bath.

The origin of Bath of course accounted for this singular choice of site—singular both as to its remarkable irregular beauty and as to its obstinacy towards human artifice.   This was no place for a fortified post like Chester from which to dominate the countryside : no road-junction like Cirencester : but a site pointed out by nature as a Spa—whether to Briton or Roman in the first instance ; so the town that followed must accommodate itself to whatever site was available—hence the present-day difficulty of improving the road system.

That wonderful Thermal Spring, which has been flowing at the rate of half a million gallons a day since the dawn of history, has determined the site of Bath.   Another stroke of fortune gave it one of the most beautiful of building materials in the world—Bath stone ; a third, found at the moment of its greatest period of prosperity since Roman times, a succession of first-rate architects, who designed the city we admire to-day.

§ ii.   *Roman and Mediæval*

The Roman City was a rough pentagon, one side being practically on the river, its angle opposite Bridge Street.   The intersection of Westgate and Cheap Streets and Union and Stall Streets represents about the centre point.   The Roman Baths are situated immediately to the east of Stall Street ; the Temple of Minerva to the north.

Mediæval Bath grew little beyond these limits : the great Abbey Church was apparently sited without any knowledge of the Roman remains—but it is approximately axial with them and falls into the plan comfortably.   The High Street now opening in front of the north transept was formerly divided by houses and contained the isolated Guildhall.

The map drawn by Joseph Gilmore, " teacher of the Mathematics in the City of Bristol," in 1694 and illustrated in the margin with the principal buildings shows a completely stone-mullioned, Elizabethan or Jacobean city, with straggling growth along Southgate Street towards the river and the old bridge, and northwards in two directions, forking along Broad Street towards Lansdown and along Walcot Street to London.

§ iii. *The Eighteenth Century*

Bath may be said to have begun its modern period of thermal prosperity with the patronage of Charles II, and more especially the first visit of Queen Anne in 1702. For the first quarter of this century the annual rush of visitors was accommodated in the old town-within-walls or in the neighbouring villages. In spite of much rebuilding that was taking place everywhere it was overcrowded, and night disgraced by brawls which occurred with painful frequency after the balls between the Sedan chairmen and the gentlemen with their poles and swords : the city authorities, it is true, attempted to improve the paving and lighting of the streets, but otherwise Bath was unprepared for the rôle of chief Spa and fashionable amusement centre of England.

But again Bath was fortunate : at the right moment appeared the three men who were capable of creating one of the most beautiful cities in Europe. To Nash must be given first credit as the social organiser, recognised by the Corporation and appointed Master of Ceremonies. He was a gamester by profession, but this is not surprising when it is remembered that gambling was recommended as part of the Cure by the Medical Profession. Nash set to work upon a code of rules for the Visitors, a tariff for Lodging-house Keepers, and " induced the Corporation to apply to Parliament for special powers to oblige the inhabitants to keep the streets and public ways clean and to maintain a Watch for the protection of the community." He raised sums of money for the repair of roads in the neighbourhood and dealt with the unruly Sedan chairmen by the ingenious device of having them all enrolled as special constables. Duelling among nobility and gentry he prohibited, and forbade the wearing of swords.

The second man to enter the scene was Ralph Allen, the philanthropist and business man. He quickly realised the possibilities of Bath and especially its unrivalled building material, Bath stone. His great mansion, Prior Park, was erected chiefly to show the monumental capabilities of the stone. But his genius was behind the scheme for the expansion of the City, and he gave his first job, the building of a Town House in Lilliput Alley (now North Parade Passage), to the third maker of Bath.

This was John Wood, the architect, who came to Bath at the age of 23, and who soon realised that the old town was too small—both in size and scale—for the spacious life which was already attempting to expatiate there. Wood was that type of architect, not always wholly approved by his profession to-day, who combined real estate enterprise and speculative building with architecture and town planning. But his great merit was that all four aspects of town expansion were carried through with triumphant success.

It would appear to have been the fortunate chance of a lack of encouragement from the Corporation within walls that set Wood to work on the free ground without. He began at the north-west corner of the walls in 1728. Between that date and about 1770 was completed the sequence of Queen Square, The Circus and the Royal Crescent, the latter being carried out by his son. The new Bath is here to be seen on a scale of monumental magnificence which yet continues to be comfortable and habitable. There is not space to describe this famous piece of domestic town planning in detail ; but suffice it to say that there is continuity with variety ; the Square, the Circus (with its three openings only, so that from wherever you enter you face the noble sweep of the opposite segment), the Crescent (facing its expanse of open parkland), are thus not only different in shape and setting but in architectural treatment ; the enriched three tiers of pilasters of the Circus give way to the simple sweep of the great columns of the Crescent. The natural levels are made full use of : the rising ground of Gay Street approaching the Circus and the Crescent parallel with the contour and facing the drop in the ground. At the opposite corner of the old city he planned and built the Grand (now North) Parade, facing the lower-level triangular open space, now the Institution Gardens. This with the South Parade and other streets was to be the fashionable promenade near the Baths and Nash's Assembly Rooms (where the Royal Institution now stands).

It is unfortunate that this boldness of planning was not carried out as a comprehensive

PLATE 8.

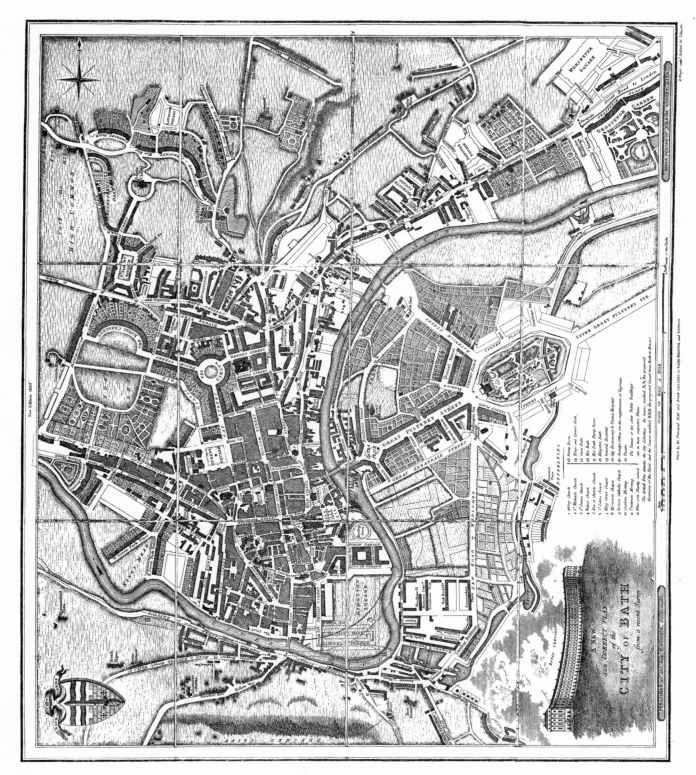

Bath at the end of the Eighteenth Century, from an old engraving.

scheme—but as before suggested, it was perhaps the difficult site that daunted the planners, combined, it is to be feared, by a lack of central control. The rest of Bath, beautiful as it is, consists chiefly of semi-isolated pieces: thus the Assembly Rooms designed by John Wood, jun., have no proper relation to the Circus; St. James' Square (by John Palmer) has no connection with the Crescent or even with Marlborough Buildings. Farther out, the charming Norfolk Crescent is isolated by the river, but on a level site; whereas Lansdown and Camden Crescents illustrate the way in which the formal planning was breaking down on the steep hillsides. Lansdown Crescent (by Palmer) with its east and west wings and Somerset Place makes a gallant attempt to conform by lines of contraflexure to the wavering contours. Camden Crescent, mounting uphill, carries a curving and rising cornice (a sort of gigantic spiral) and ends abruptly as though the author had not known how to extricate himself from the difficulty of completion.

Nearer the centre more articulated work was being done. Milsom Street (probably laid out by Baldwin) works in with Wood's squared planning and is well closed in at the top. Thomas Baldwin was also responsible for the chief remodelling of the central area carried out in a more delicate manner than that of the elder Wood. He built in 1795 the open colonnade north of the Pump Room and its closed fellow on the south which forms the terminal feature to Bath Street which he laid out at right angles to Stall Street. There is some uncertainty whether the western end of Bath Street was to expand into a circus round the Hot Bath (exquisitely designed by the younger Wood); but the manipulation of the levels in the colonnade of Bath Street is extremely skilful.

There remains to be described the Bathwick Estate, the largest piece of level ground available for eighteenth-century town planning. Unfortunately, like Withenshawe from Manchester, it

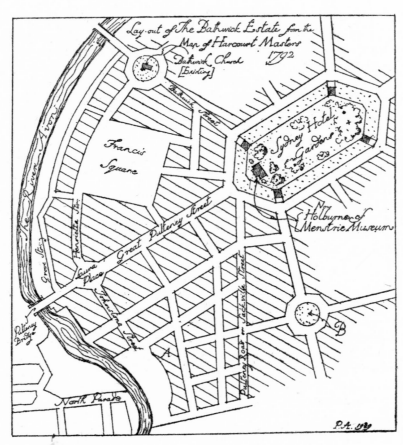

was cut off for lack of a bridge which was not authorised until 1768, when the Trustees of Sir William Pulteney obtained permission to erect it and proceeded to develop the estate. There is some uncertainty as to the authorship of the design of this Bathwick estate: it is generally ascribed to Adam, who actually built the Pulteney Bridge and is supposed to have laid down the lines of Pulteney Street. The plan of the estate has several different versions, that shown by Harcourt Masters being not without traces of gaucherie, as for example the road that forestalls the present continuation of North Parade from the Place at B (see diagram): this should never have ended up at the back of the great crescent A (a design for which by Adam is in the Soane Museum). Anyhow, neither of the flanking pieces of the plan has been carried out: the irregular Henrietta Park occupies what should have been formal Francis Square, and the Bath and County Recreation Ground the site of the Crescent and several rather uninteresting blocks. But by great good fortune the centrepiece of the Plan was completed and under architects so sympathetic to the notion of the original designer as Baldwin, John Eveleigh and Harcourt Masters. It thus happens that the Pulteney Bridge, Argyle Street, Laura Place, Great Pulteney Street and the Sydney Hotel and Gardens are a complete piece of unified design. In its delicate way this sequence is as fine as Wood's robuster group across the water: which means that these two town features will stand comparison with anything in Europe. The Bridge, beautiful in mutilation; Laura Place, a square on the diagonal which does not interrupt the forward movement; Great Pulteney Street, of justest proportion—100 feet wide and 1100 feet long, with a modestly emphatic central feature; the Sydney Hotel (now the Holburne of Menstrie Museum, restored with care by Sir Reginald Blomfield) closing the vista with perfect restraint, while the road sweeps round and up to Claverton. No better example of the achievement of the later eighteenth century art of Civic design could be found in this country.

§ iv. *The Material*

The influence of good material in producing fine architecture is well known. We do not know exactly the standard of its Roman design, but from the numerous remains of the Baths and Temple of Minerva it is clear that Bath was one of the most monumental cities in Latin Britain. Of its mediæval buildings, the Abbey remains almost alone, a noble piece of conscious design. It is one of the latest Gothic churches and possesses one of the finest interiors. There is little of the stone-mullioned period of Elizabeth and the seventeenth century, so that there is a clean jump to the eighteenth century which appears to continue the Roman tradition of design, the Abbey alone witnessing the intervening 1200 years.

This eighteenth-century outburst of prosperity and consequent building was coincident with the use of Bath stone, which before then had chiefly been used for peddled ornaments. Under Ralph Allen's business ability and Wood's architectural guidance the new city was soon faced entirely with its own material. It is probably only faintly realised how much of the charm of Bath depends upon the beauty of its plain stone walling. It is only necessary to compare the cold austerity of Edinburgh New Town with the mellow warmth of Bath to realise the importance of colour and texture of material in building.

§ v. *Prior Park*

Prior Park, Ralph Allen's great house, has been mentioned; but no report on the Region would be complete which did not mention the view of the city from the portico. It is unsurpassed in this country as an urban landscape: the valley foreground with the Palladian Bridge in the middle distance spanning the fishponds of the monks of Bath Abbey with the silver-grey city in the background. If Oxford from Boar's Hill shows more towers, domes and spires than Bath, there is no such foreground as this combe nor such portico and steps from which to view the scene.

PLATE 9.

The Centre of Bath.

Photos: Aerofilms Ltd

The Circus and Royal Crescent.

AIR VIEWS OF BATH.

CHAPTER III.　COMMUNICATIONS

SECTION 1.　ROADS

§ i.　*History of the Road System*

(A) PRE-ROMAN.

THE origin of some of the roads in the Region is lost in the prehistoric past; there is evidence that the country south of the Avon contains a number of roads and tracks which are believed to have been in use by the native Britons in pre-Roman days.

The ancient tracks appear to have been centred on Keynsham and Bath, and their general direction was west or south-west from these points.　The district north of the Avon has not been so fully explored, but it may be inferred that the choice of Keynsham and Bath was deliberate and that there were fords at these spots, communicating with roads into Gloucestershire whose general direction would probably be the line of the Cotswold escarpment, avoiding the flat country watered by the Frome, which is thought to have been at that time very densely wooded.

The routes taken by these prehistoric tracks appear to be based on no system, except that they show a preference for the higher levels.　Several of these are still in use including (see Plate 10). :—

(*a*) The upper Clevedon Road through Failand (B3128).

(*b*) The east to west road on Dundry Hill.

(*c*) The road from Keynsham through Publow and Stanton Drew, obliterated in the vicinity of Bishop Sutton, but shortly after re-appearing, passing on the west of West Harptree village, and over the Mendips to Cheddar and Axbridge.

(*d*) The Banwell–Worle–Kewstoke Road.

(*e*) Part of the Lower Bristol Road from Bath (A36) continuing as A368 through Corston, Stantonbury, Marksbury and Hallatrow, proceeding thence as A37 through Farrington Gurney and Ston Easton to the Regional boundary at Old Down.

(B) ROMAN.

The Romans made some notable additions to the roads in the Region, viz. (Plate 10) :—

(*f*) *The Fosseway :* entering the Region east of Marshfield (from the direction of Cirencester) the road ran southward for about three miles along the ridge of Banner Down, and, descending into the Avon valley, it there made junction with the road from London via Silchester; it was here deflected to the south-west and passed through Bath; leaving Bath on the south it ascended to Odd Down and proceeded still in a south-westerly direction to the southern boundary of the Region near Nettlebridge (*en route* for Ilchester), after crossing the valley of the Somer between the sites of the twin towns of Radstock and Midsomer Norton.

(*g*) *The western exit from Bath :* this was on the north of the River Avon, it ran along the shoulder of Lansdown Hill through Bitton (Roman Camp) across the site of northern Bristol and Durdham Down, to a settlement and point of embarkation on the River Avon at Sea Mills (Abone).

(*h*) *The Road along the Mendips :* this was the western portion of a route from Winchester via Old Sarum to the lead mines on Mendip. It ran in a westerly direction near Priddy and through Charterhouse (Settlement) to Blackdown, where there was a small Station. Thence it probably continued westward to the mouth of the River Axe via Banwell and Bleadon (Roman Camps).

(*j*) *The northward road from Abone :* this is believed to have run from the River Trym at Sea Mills, over the Kings-Weston ridge to Henbury : from thence along " Cribbs Causeway " to Almondsbury ; continuing along the line of the modern road towards Gloucester.

The greater part of (*f*), (*g*) and (*j*) are still in full use to-day, but (*h*) has for the most part degenerated into a bye-lane or field track.

(C) Post-Roman.

During post-Roman and mediæval times many new routes came into existence, but there is little evidence of any policy or scheme of construction as in Roman times. Some of them probably originated as Church paths, and the fact that in the middle ages Bristol was declared a " Staple Port " would account for the appearance of most of the routes converging on that town. Mediæval routes were evolved first as bridle or pack-horse ways, and developed during the 16th and 17th centuries as rough vehicular tracks ; some of them were widened and improved into " turnpike " roads during the coaching era, others remain as byeways to this day. The turnpike roads shown on Plate No. 10 are taken from an old map dated 1820, and it is interesting to note that the British Tracks (*a*), (*b*), (*d*), and the Roman road (*h*) do not appear on this map ; and that whilst the road (*e*) and parts of road (*c*) were the only surviving British tracks shown, three of the four Roman roads were then still in use. In addition there appears a network of new routes radiating from Bristol ; of these, the following have proved their worth and are now ranked as " First-class " main roads :—

      Bristol–Gloucester (via Filton) (A38).
      Bristol–Chipping Sodbury (A432).
      Bristol–Kingswood–Chippenham (A430).
      Bristol–Keynsham–Bath (A36).
      Bristol–Whitchurch–Shepton Mallet (A37).
      Bristol–Bridgwater (A38).

Others which are now ranked as Second-class roads include :—

      Bristol–Winterbourne–Wotton-under-Edge (B4058).
      Chipping Sodbury–Wickwar (B4060).
      Bristol–Henbury–New Passage (B4055).
      Chew Stoke–Harptree (B3117).
      Old Sodbury–Acton Turville (B4040).
      Fosseway (Odd Down)–Woolverton (B3110).

Others which have not been since promoted to " Classification " and for the most part still remain as narrow tortuous lanes, are :—

      Aust (Old Passage)–Ridgeway–Iron Acton.
      New Passage–Old Passage.
      Wotton-under-Edge–Hawkesbury Upton.
      Westbury–Brentry–Cribbs Causeway.
      Hambrook–Earthcott Green.
      Downend–Codrington–Tormarton–Acton Turville.
      Mangotsfield–Pucklechurch–Hinton.
      Bitton–Siston.

PLATE II.

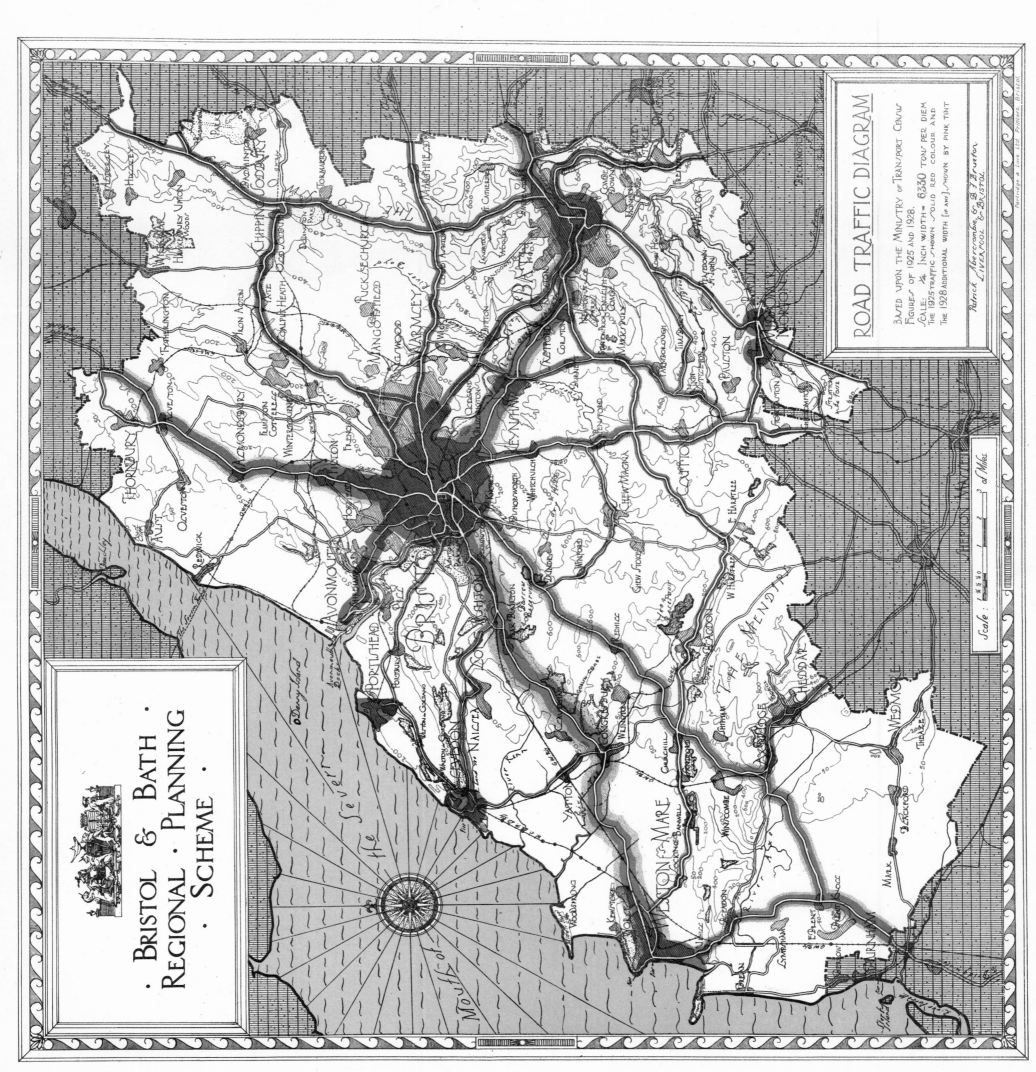

ROAD TRAFFIC DIAGRAM

BASED UPON THE MINISTRY OF TRANSPORT CENSUS
FIGURES OF 1925 AND 1928.
SCALE: ¼ INCH WIDTH = 6,330 TONS PER DIEM
THE 1925 TRAFFIC SHOWN SOLID RED COLOUR AND
THE 1928 ADDITIONAL WIDTH [IF ANY] SHOWN BY PINK TINT

Patrick Abercrombie & B.F. Brueton
LIVERPOOL & BRISTOL.

· BRISTOL & BATH ·
· REGIONAL · PLANNING ·
· SCHEME ·

Partridge & Love Ltd. Printers, Bristol.

PLATE 10.

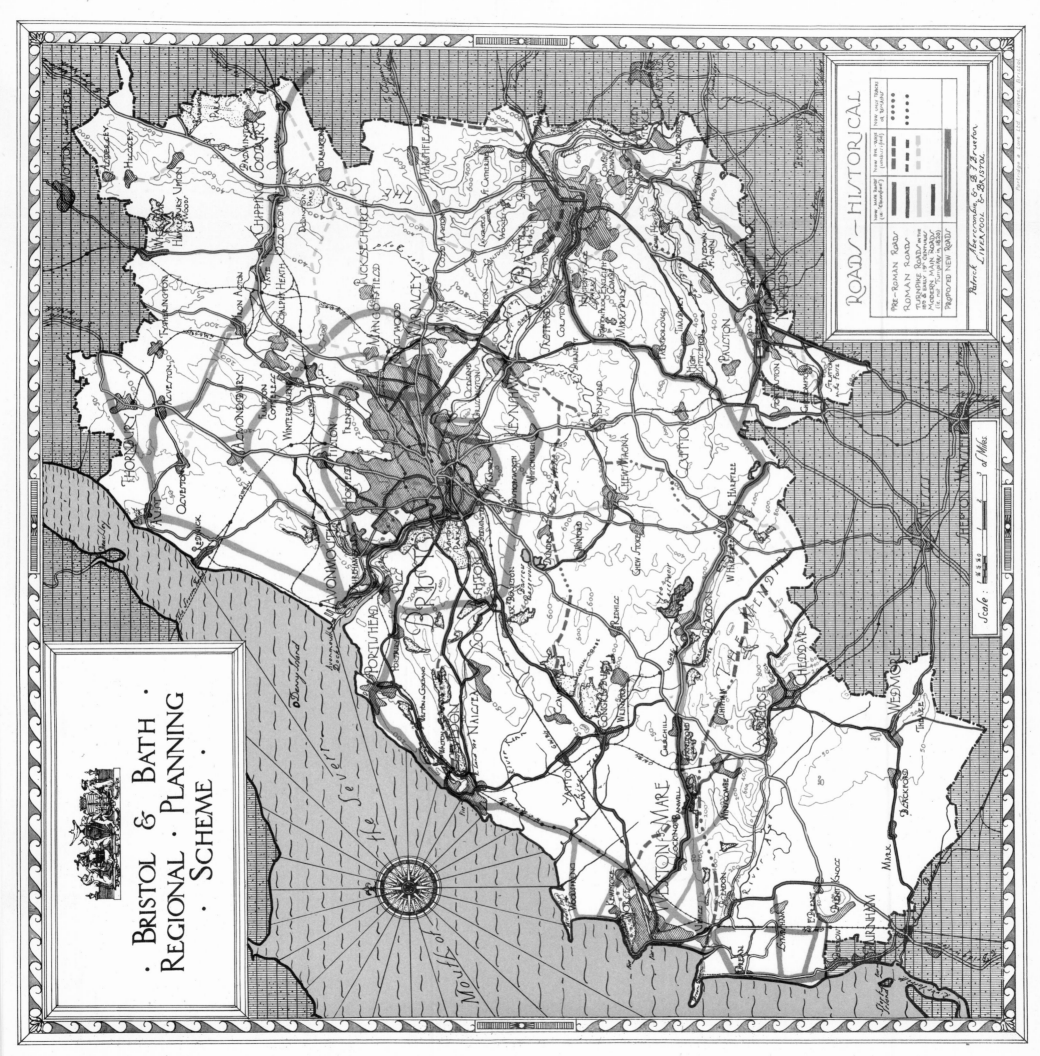

. BRISTOL & BATH .
REGIONAL · PLANNING
· SCHEME ·

ROADS — HISTORICAL

Patrick Abercrombie & B. F. Brueton
LIVERPOOL & BRISTOL

Scale: of Miles

Partridge & Love Ltd. Printers, Bristol.

Wick–Bath.
Corston–Twerton–Odd Down.
Bedminster–Bishopsworth–Dundry Hill–Chew Stoke.
Harptree–Castle Comfort (2 routes).

§ ii.   *The Existing Road System*

Perhaps the best way to approach the Road System of this Region is by means of the Map of Classified Roads issued by the Ministry of Transport.*

From this map it may be seen that of all the first-class roads in the Region, four stand out as being of National as well as Regional importance, viz. :—

The North to South route through Bristol (A38), which commences at Derby and runs through Birmingham, Gloucester, Bristol and Exeter to Plymouth.

The North to South route through Bath (A46 and A367), commencing at Cheltenham and proceeding via Bath to Shepton Mallet where it joins A37 (to Weymouth).

The West to East route through Bristol and Bath (A36): this commences at Avonmouth and terminates at Southampton.

The London Road (A4) having its Western terminus in Bath, where it makes junction with A36.

The map also shows that within the Region there are two main foci—Bath and Bristol—with a double connecting link north and south of the Avon, and that, as may be expected, the " national " routes run through one or other of the foci.   Further, there is a marked tendency for the main routes (with the exception of the double link referred to above and the London road via Marshfield) to run North and South rather than East and West.   Even the old coaching road that ran through Chipping Sodbury to Aust, having now lost its western objective, turns south after Yate, attracted by the Bristol magnet.   It will be convenient, therefore, in studying the roads within the Region, to take those that radiate from the two foci, and afterwards to deal with those few main roads that have no connection with them.

There are seven Class A roads radiating from Bath ; four of them, two on the west (A36 and A431, to Bristol) and two on the east (A4 to London, and A36 to Southampton), cling to the Avon valley ; the London road branches north to Gloucester (A46), and south (at Bathford) to Trowbridge, via Bradford (A363), thus making six radials ; the seventh is the southern exit from Bath, A367, it follows very nearly the Roman fosseway and leads via Radstock and Shepton Mallet to Wells.   A46, the northern road, is that noble old coaching road from Stroud which follows the escarpment of the Cotswolds, it joins the London road at the eastern end of Bath.   The roads to Bristol, the northern by Kelston and Bitton, the southern by Saltford and Keynsham, are united by a short length of switch road (second class, B4044).   The eastern exits (A4, A36, A363) are entirely dominated in their direction by the contours ; they both start in a north-easterly direction, though both Southampton and Bradford-on-Avon are on the south-east of Bath.

The second focal point, Bristol, is the meeting place of no fewer than ten radial roads, six north of the Avon and four on the south of the River.   These amalgamate within the City and concentrate most of their traffic on Bristol Bridge and the central part of the old city. North of the Avon are the Northern road (A38) to Gloucester, the North-eastern (A432) to Chipping Sodbury, the Eastern, which branches at St. George, one arm (A430) leading due east through Kingswood to Chippenham and London, the other (A431) leading south-east

---

* On this map main roads are numbered and classed as first or second class ; a clue to the relative importance of the roads may be obtained from their numbering: the through routes of national importance are called " A " routes and are given single or double numbers, local first-class roads receive three-digit numbers, and second-class roads have four digits and the prefix " B."

to Bath, and two other roads (A36 and A4018), which connect the City with its port at the mouth of the River (Avonmouth).

South of the Avon, the four radials (taken from West to East) are the Weston-super-Mare Road (A370), the Bridgwater Road (A38), the Wells and Shepton Mallet Road (A37), and the Bath Road (A36).

The First-class Roads which have no direct connection with either of the two foci consist of cross-country links and connections. They include the following :—

A368 Weston to Bath, branching from the Wells–Weston Road at Banwell, and proceeding via Banwell, Blagdon, West Harptree, Marksbury and Corston, where it joins the Bath–Bristol Road.

A370 Weston to Brent, joining the Bristol–Exeter Road at East Brent.

A371 Weston to Wells, branching from the Bristol-Weston Road and proceeding via Locking, Banwell, Winscombe and Cheddar.

A369 Marksbury to Hallatrow, and Rush Hill to Wells.

A362 Farrington Gurney, via Midsomer Norton and Radstock, to Frome.

The First-class Roads are supplemented by a number of others which are graded as " Second-class " : these consist for the most part of local roads and subsidiary connections. The most important of them perhaps are B3124, 3128, 3130/1/3, roads connecting the coastal towns of Clevedon and Portishead with Bristol and the trunk road A38 ; B3117, the Chew Valley Road ; and B3139, the Highbridge–Wedmore–Wells Road.

Within the Region are many other roads, not classified by the Minister of Transport ; some of them have possibility of becoming of importance in the evolution of a Regional Road System, and among these may be mentioned :—

> Aust to Alveston.
> Ridgeway to Iron Acton.
> Downend (Bristol) through Westerleigh to Acton Turville.
> Bleadon to Axbridge.
> Uphill to Banwell.
> Portishead to Walton.
> Westbury to Pilning.
> Bitton, via Oldland to Siston.

§ iii. *The Main Roads, and Traffic Statistics*

The function of each main road in the Region has been described in § ii of this chapter. Thanks to grants from the Road Fund their condition generally leaves little to be desired, and many widenings and minor diversions have been carried out in recent years. Generally speaking also their width between hedges appears to be adequate in many of the undeveloped areas, but in some of the villages houses actually abut on the road in such positions as to make widening an expensive matter ; in such cases one remedy is " bye-passing," and this is dealt with in a later section. The use to which the existing main roads are put varies greatly on different routes ; all the " First-class " roads are by no means of the same importance ; this is clearly shown graphically in Plate 11, which indicates by red bands of different widths the volume of traffic in the summer of 1925 according to the Traffic Census taken by the Ministry of Transport. The diagram also shows (by pink colouring) the relative increase in traffic at the 1928 Census. Bristol, as may be expected, is the principal focus of all traffic in the Region, and some of the improvements in the road system which are suggested in a later section of this Report are aimed to relieve the congestion which the concentration of this enormous volume of traffic causes in that City. In 1925 the heaviest traffic occurred on the Bristol–Keynsham portion of the Bristol–Bath Road ; next came the Bristol–Gloucester Road,

PLATE 12.

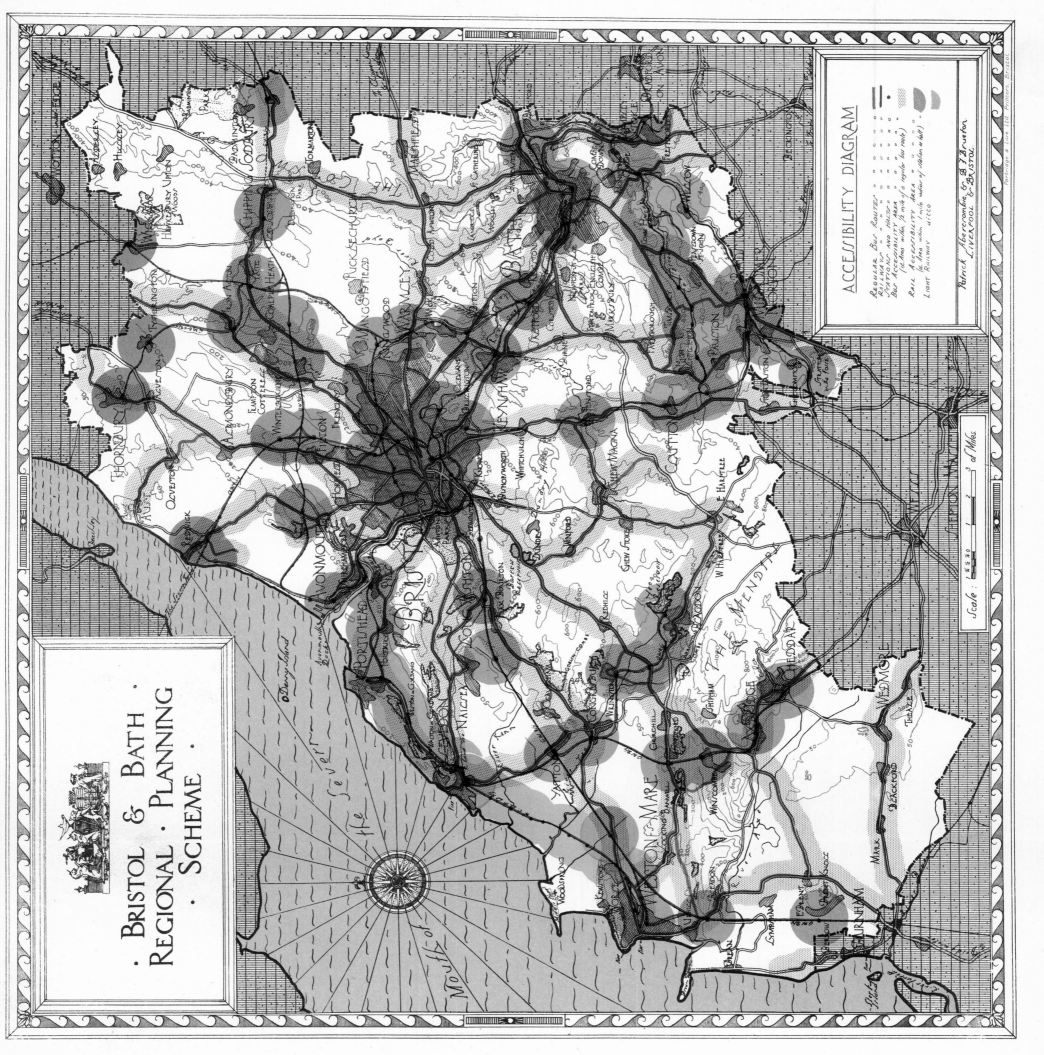

ACCESSIBILITY DIAGRAM

Patrick Abercrombie & B. F. Brueton. Liverpool & Bristol.

· BRISTOL · & · BATH · REGIONAL · PLANNING · SCHEME ·

and this was followed closely by the Bath–London Road and the Bristol–Weston Road. In 1928 the Bristol–Weston Road has forged ahead to first place ; the Bristol–Bath–London Road comes second, and the Bristol-Bridgwater Road third.

A table is given in Appendix A showing the traffic census figures for 1922, 1925 and 1928, so far as they are available ; and also a table, compiled from these figures, showing the percentage of increase in the six-year period.

In view of the growing popularity of road transport it were idle to assume that road traffic in the Region is nearing its maximum, and the question arises as to whether saturation point has been reached, or is imminent, on any of the main routes. Apparently in Bristol itself this point has been reached, if not exceeded, and this makes it all the more imperative that some at least of the proposals outlined in this Report for the relief of Bristol should be put in hand with the least possible delay.

§ iv. *Accessibility, Bus Routes, etc.*

On Plate 12 are shown the areas rendered accessible by rail and motor-bus services. The growth of road transport by motor-bus has been so great in recent years that there is hardly a village or hamlet in the Region that has not been made accessible by this means ; it follows that from the point of view of accessibility the existing road system leaves little to be desired, but not all of the roads are of sufficient width for motor-bus use, and much remains to be done in the way of widenings and minor diversions.

§ v. *Defects of the Road System*

A modern road system has to provide for three kinds of traffic : through, inter-regional, and local. Defects in a system may be grouped under two headings—inadequacy of existing routes and absence of routes. Under the first head may be placed anything which acts as a check to the smooth flow of traffic and causes congestion at any given point ; such checks may be expected to occur where the route is narrow, at points where traffic routes converge, where there are local obstructions (e.g., tram standards) and where local traffic attains to such dimensions that the influx of any through traffic puts a strain on the capacity of the route.

Absence of route not only retards development and hinders intercommunication but forces traffic to use other routes, or portions of them, and tends to add to the congestion of the traffic using those routes legitimately.

The particular defects of the road system in this Region may be broadly cited as :—

(*a*) The absence of ring roads round the foci.
(*b*) The absence of adequate coastal connections.
(*c*) The inadequacy of the routes north and south of Mendip.
(*d*) The inadequate approach to Avonmouth except through Bristol.
(*e*) The absence of an eastern outlet from Radstock and Midsomer Norton.

To these may be added (in view of the projected road crossing of the Severn) a sixth, viz. :—

(*f*) The absence of adequate roads to the site of the proposed crossing.

SECTION 2.   RAILWAYS

The G.W.R. main line from London to Penzance runs through the Region, via Bath and Bristol ; also the G.W.R. main line from London to South Wales, via Badminton and the Severn Tunnel ; the latter effects a fly-over crossing at Stoke Gifford where two branches originate, one to Bristol and the other to Avonmouth.

The L.M.S.R. route from the Midlands terminates at Bristol, and a branch runs from Mangotsfield junction to Bath.

Other lines of local importance are :—

      Bristol–Radstock–Frome (G.W.R.).
      Cam Valley (G.W.R.).
      Bath–Radstock–Shepton Mallet (S. & D.J.R.).
      Bath–Limpley Stoke–Bradford-on-Avon (G.W.R.).
      Bristol–Portishead (G.W.R.).
      The Clevedon Branch (G.W.R.).
      The Blagdon Branch (G.W.R.).
      The Cheddar–Wells Branch (G.W.R.).
      The Thornbury Branch (L.M.S.).

There is also a light railway working between Portishead, Clevedon and Weston-super-Mare.

THE AVON GORGE

CHAPTER IV.   THE ACTIVITIES OF THE REGION

SECTION 1.   REGIONAL RELATIVITY

§ i.   *A Local Entity*

EVERY Region, if properly demarcated so as to form a geographic unit (either a county or two inter-county areas as happens in this case, and in many others where a navigable river forms the boundary), may be regarded as a little world, or microcosm : here may be traced the interrelated activities of town and country, of work-place and play-place, of producing spot, marketing centre and consuming area.   This Region is singularly complete— almost, one might suggest, self-sufficing—in this respect, as will be explained shortly.   But it is equally remarkable in its external relationships : for every one of the aspects of human existence which are so completely furnished for local use are equally connected with and essential to the outer world.

First let us consider the Region as a local entity.   There is the centre of industry, the Bristol Group : to be considered a manufacturing area, but of even greater importance as a business centre for marketing for the whole Region, and as a port.   As compared with the scattering of several big towns found on other navigable rivers, it is satisfactory to have one centre, not indeed too large, but a focus of commercial activity.   In this century no commercial or industrial centre can be considered as adequately placed without a convenient source of power. Accordingly we find a regional coalfield, in full operation at Radstock and Midsomer Norton and in course of development near Bristol.   As the power is available locally, so the coalfield has its market at its door.   Next, it is usually found that a business district develops its residential areas somewhat apart from the evidences of work : either close by, as at Clifton, or in an independent town, as at Bath.   But the people also, wherever they live, need active relaxation—pleasure towns—so there are Weston-super-Mare, Clevedon and Portishead ; or for those who like the greater contrast there is the country, and of *every* variety : simple pastoral scenes, dense woodlands, open downs and deserted hilltops, river valleys, and limestone headlands thrust out bare into the channel ; while for those who require to gape at the marvellous, there are stalactite caverns and goblin combes.   The Region has also its ancillary services to hand ; for water supply it is not necessary to parcel out distant mountains for whose partition there is a scramble between contending urban communities : the local hill countries within the Region are amply sufficient.   For building materials there is clay for bricks and tiles, building stones of various kinds, lime for mortar, and road metalling.

Side by side with what might be called the townsman's view of the Region, there is the countryman's.   The agricultural world goes on in spite of depression, with its crops varied according to the nature of the soil, which follows the geological structure, and the countryside is parcelled out into farms and hamlets, villages and country towns, forming a complete system of life wherein are carried on agricultural occupations of first importance to the urban population.   So much for the self-contained aspect of this Region.

§ ii.   *External Relations*

Its external connections are equally complete.   Bristol is, of course, more famous as a world port than as the capital of this Region.   In the middle ages Bristol was second only to London : to-day, the port at the river mouth shows that a town originally chosen for mediæval security behind a bend of the Avon (after passing through a wild and forbidding gorge) can be adapted to meet modern requirements by the creation of docks readily accessible to deep water.

Bath has been a national possession since the days when its hot springs healed the father of King Lear; it is the richest town in England in Roman remains and eighteenth-century architecture, and disputes with Oxford and Edinburgh the position of the most beautiful town to-day.

Weston-super-Mare is much more than the seaside resort of Bristol. It has a reputation now in open competition with Scarborough, Southport, Torquay and Bournemouth.

The marvels of the Cheddar Gorge and Caves attract from all parts of the country and, finally, the Cheddar Cheese has become an international possession.

The completeness of the Region, therefore, has nothing parochial about it, seeing that its components, in addition to their local functions, have their important places in the outer world.

SECTION 2. DEVELOPED AREAS

§ i. *The Bristol-Kingswood-Mangotsfield-Warmley Conurbation.*

Professor Geddes has coined this somewhat ugly but expressive word to indicate a constellation of urban communities. It rarely happens that a commercial town exists separately and Bristol is no exception. Regarded quite apart from boundaries of local authorities, the main urban area consists of an almost circular mass surrounded by satellites and several tentacles stretching out from the body. This central block is about three miles in diameter, more than two-thirds being on the north of the Avon; it lies in a shallow hollow, the well-marked limestone ridge up which Clifton climbs, and which still preserves its open tableland, cutting it off from any view of the open sea. It would be interesting to know what the mediæval, seventeenth or even eighteenth century voyager by water to Bristol thought of this approach to a mighty city, through a wild limestone gorge, of whose imminence the tame estuary of the Severn gave no indication.

The existing satellites consist of Avonmouth, the modern port and industrial area on the northern bank; Shirehampton, a village rapidly being transformed into a housing area for the port; Pill, on the south side of the River. Portishead, containing as it does part of the Bristol Docks, might also be included as a coastal satellite. Of more or less completeness of detachment is a group of suburban satellites on the north-west—Henbury, Lawrence Weston, Westbury-on-Trym, and Sea Mills. All these are affected by the broken country of King's Weston Hill, Blaise Castle, and the valleys of the Trym and Hen. Clifton is in direct contact with Bristol: indeed it is one of the most solid attractions of the city that, a short half-mile from the traffic centre, Docks, Cathedral and College Green, up Park Street, past the noble University and Brandon Hill with its civic campanile, one enters the suburb whose beauty is best described by saying that she is the true daughter of Bath. On the south-west, Bristol and Clifton are brought up sharp against the Avon gorge with Leigh Woods on its opposite bank and the great expanse of Ashton park. There are only two suburban* satellites on this side—Abbots Leigh and, at a mile's distance, the straggling ribbon of Long Ashton. Bristol furnishes a dramatic surprise at the point where the Avon turns sharply to the east and the new course of the river branches from the old, which now becomes a floating harbour; here the town suddenly ends—Ashton park and green fields approach the commercial docks; the urban landscape is punctuated by vast isolated tobacco warehouses and backed by the formality of Clifton's crescents; a disused colliery adds its industrial note and reminds one that we are here on still unexhausted coal measures. From this spot it is possible to walk out into the unspoilt, almost deserted country behind Ashton park or to climb to the top of Dundry Hill. It is rare that the full blast of urban existence is found cheek by jowl with country life.

---

*It would be quite reasonable to describe Nailsea, Flax Bourton, Yatton and Congresbury as satellites of Bristol—but they are dealt with as growing villages of the Region.

PLATE 13.

DAILY MIRROR.

Air View of Bristol showing the docked Avon and Queen Square.

On the South, the urban area has kept within three-quarters of a mile of the new cut of the Avon, except for a satellite Housing Scheme on Bedminster Down at the fork of the roads to Bridgwater and Dundry. Bishopsworth on the latter road is another suburban satellite, showing signs of growth. The high ground of Totterdown near the Avon has been built on, and the two remaining masses south of the river follow the Wells and Bath roads, spreading between rather than straggling along them. Knowle, on the former, is completed by a large Corporation Housing scheme, built up to the city boundary: Brislington on the Bath road spills over it.

On the North there is marked ribbon development along the Gloucester road, extending for four miles from the centre of the city to Filton.

So far, i.e., on the West, North and South, the growth of Bristol has been compact, with satellite offshoots and considerable space between, caused frequently by irregular ground or large private ownerships. Towards Filton alone, a narrow, almost continuous ribbon is apparent.

The eastern portion of the Bristol conurbation presents a very different and, it must be confessed, less attractive method of growth. It coincides to a large extent with the coalfield and succeeds the mediæval Forest of Kingswood. Here most of the roads follow the original forest tracks and the fringing houses are the descendants of squatters' cabins. An unobservant person motoring along the London road from St. George's Park to Warmley, some 3½ miles, might be under the impression that he was passing through the same sort of built-up area that he had already passed through from the centre of the city, two miles back. But a closer inspection would show him that it is a thin edging of ribbon building, and that the crossroads are equally thinly edged. The difference between this ribbon and the Filton sample is not only one of length, but of age: the Filton ribbon is modern; the Kingswood ribbon is of greater age. The whole of this eastern end of Bristol in the triangle between the Avon and the two branches of the Midland line, containing about 9 square miles, is an example of low average density: but this is not sufficient for urban satisfaction when unaccompanied by logical road planning. The Bristol housing schemes at Fishponds and Speedwell show how these interior vacancies can be filled on more satisfying lines. Mangotsfield, Warmley and Oldland form the boundary of this semi-developed area.

A special feature of this eastern fringe is the large number of Commons: Rodway Hill, Siston Common, Goose Green, Webb's Heath, Lyde Green, Bridgeyate Common, Vinney Green, etc.

North of the Midland Railway, the principal natural feature is the valley of the Frome, which separates parallel roads both of which lead to an industrial satellite growth at Winterbourne, Frampton Cotterell and Coalpit Heath: growth which at the moment appears arrested and consequently somewhat forlorn.

The southern part of this east end of the Bristol conurbation is less fully developed; the Bath road links up the satellite villages of Hanham, Longwell Green, Willsbridge and Bitton, the latter being regarded as the extreme eastern limit of the conurbation.

The Avon is industrialised on the north bank almost up to Conham, after which it is free until the Keynsham Hams are reached, except for an outburst of squatters' cabins in the gorge at Hanham Abbots.

Keynsham and Saltford are, indeed, on debatable ground between Bristol and Bath, but the recently built works of Messrs. Fry indicate an industrial satellite of Bristol.

§ ii. *Bath*

Like Bristol, Bath has its satellites and its ribbon extensions. Down stream there is Twerton: up stream Batheaston (joined by ribbon) and Bathford on the north bank, Bathampton on the south. The three northern valleys contain Weston, straggling along the Roman Via Julia; Swainswick isolated beside the Gloucester road; and a ribbon up St. Catherine's valley. Nor has the jutting promontory of Lansdown prevented the town from creeping up, and now it threatens to invade the wind-swept plateau. On the southern side there is the extension of Twerton : the scattered building along the Fosseway at Odd Down : Combe Down at the back of Prior Park, and choicest of all, the village of Claverton. The other villages round Bath have fortunately so far remained isolated and have not been swept into her system of growth.

§ iii. *Weston-super-Mare*

Weston-super-Mare occupies the northern end of a bay enclosed by two lofty headlands, Worlebury Hill on the north and Brean Down on the south : communication with the latter is cut off by the estuary of the Axe. The greater part of the town is on low flat land, but it climbs the slopes of Worlebury Hill, and has an extension inland, with a suburb at Worle on the Bristol Road. There is also scattered building round the northern and eastern end of the hill to Kewstoke. At the southern end of the bay, on higher ground forming the first step of Mendip, lies Uphill, once a separate village.

A good deal of outlying growth which may be attributed to Weston occurs in the neighbourhood, e.g., on the western slopes of Bleadon Hill, and at places along the northern escarpment of the Mendip range, as at Hutton and Banwell.

North and south of Weston there are bays, as yet undeveloped, but showing signs of seaside growth. Sand Bay to the north, smaller than Weston Bay, is enclosed by the narrow and graceful limestone promontory of Middle Hope, on whose southern slope is Woodspring Priory, the most remarkable beautiful group of mediæval monastic buildings in the Region. The Banwell estuary forms a natural northern boundary to this area. South of Brean Down there is a four-mile stretch of sandhills to Burnham : scattered bungalow building is already taking place here, which demands immediate organisation and control.

§ iv. *Clevedon and Portishead*

Clevedon and Portishead are situated at either end of the ridge of Old Red Sandstone and Limestone. They are both residential towns and seaside resorts, on irregular and picturesque sites. On the south, Clevedon quickly descends into the marsh lands, and beyond the picturesque Wains Hill with its isolated church* the coast becomes flat and dull. Between the two towns, the noble sweep of steep rocky coast has already been partly ruined by a disorderly rash of shacks and bungalows.

Portishead contains one of Bristol's Docks and has been chosen as the site for a super power station. The low-lying land between the dock and the Avon is at present inaccessible : it will probably become an industrial area, corresponding to that on the northern side of the estuary.

§ v. *Radstock, Midsomer Norton and the Cam Valley*

Towards the south-east corner of the Region there are two areas partially urbanised for industrial purposes : the twin communities of Radstock and Midsomer Norton, and the group of villages found on either side of the Cam Valley, from Dunkerton westwards. Nowhere are the Coal Measures exposed, but they are only hidden by a thin veneer of secondary rocks.

Radstock and Midsomer Norton occupy the valleys of the River Wellow and its tributary the Somer : but they also straggle up and down the steep hills in the wake of different collieries. The area is not very densely developed, and a large extent of ground is covered with pitheads and colliery tips, with attached groups of houses.

Building in the Cam Valley is considerably more scattered : it contains the following villages, beginning in the east : Dunkerton, near where the Fosseway crosses the Cam ; Peasedown St. John, on the Fosseway ; Camerton, an old village by the Park, a modern one on the river ; Radford on the river ; Timsbury, north of it ; Paulton, the largest of these quasi-industrial villages ; Hallatrow ; High Littleton ; Farmborough ; and Clutton, the capital of the district, which connects this area to the Wells road. In several of these villages

---

* Here Tennyson wrote " In Memoriam."

the industrial element is not very pronounced, but nevertheless they form a well-marked group, situated in extremely broken country and all presenting problems as to future growth which require careful study.   Though coal-mining has been the cause of a change from purely rural communities, there are already other industries in the neighbourhood.

SECTION 3.   THE COALFIELD

§ i.   *A Single Field*

The Regional Coalfield, though it has been commercially known as two (or even three) separate areas, the Bristol, the Radstock and the Nailsea, is in reality a single one, with two small outliers.   The main field extends from Cromhall, just beyond the northern boundary of the Region, to somewhere near the villages of Vobster and Mells, a couple of miles from Frome : the two outliers are the Nailsea field and a fragmentary strip overlooking the Gordano marsh.   The actual extent from north to south is about 26 miles : from east to west (along the line from Bristol to Bath) about 12 miles.   The area is approximately 238 square miles : about one-fifth of the whole is visible on the surface.

A large portion of the Bristol coalfield is exposed as may be seen on Plate 4. The Radstock coalfield is entirely covered with later rocks, though of no great thickness ; but the Measures are visible in four patches south of the Avon : (i) in the valley of the Chew where the later rocks appear to have been eroded by that river or by its predecessor in early times ; (ii) at Clutton, where they stretch across the valley of the Cam nearly to Farrington Gurney ; (iii) covering a small triangle between Corston, Newton St. Loe and the Avon ; (iv) outside the region at Coleford.

The Nailsea area is also to a considerable extent exposed, the growing residential area of Nailsea being situated actually upon the Coal Measures.   A small strip near Clapton-in-Gordano is also exposed.

But though it is virtually a single coalfield, an important distinction must be made between the Upper and Lower Coal Measures, separated by a band of Pennant rock.   This latter is a Coal Measure Sandstone for the most part barren of coal* and varying in thickness from 1500 to 3000 feet ; it is also heavily watered.   Where, therefore, it is necessary to penetrate through it to the Lower Measures it presents one of the economic problems of the Field, and it is of importance to show the areas (i) where the Upper Measures are accessible, and (ii) where the Lower are attainable without passing through the whole thickness of the Pennant rock.   This occurs as the result of anticlinal folds and faults which cut across the field in several directions.

The Kingswood anticline, which has already been mentioned in the description of under-ground geology, is the cause of the main division of the coalfield along these lines.   The effect of the anticline or fold is to bring the Lower Measures up to the surface, denuded of their covering of Pennant rock.   It will be seen therefore from Plate 14 that the Upper Measures occur in two oval areas, a small one in the north and a large one in the south, fringed by the Lower Measures which also cut across the waist on the line of the Kingswood anticline.

The total thickness of the strata varies, but in the Somerset basin, from the top of the Coal Measures (or the underside of the Trias) to the Millstone Grit, may be taken to be about 7000 feet divided as follows :—

Upper Division .	.	.	.	2200
Pennant Rock .	.	.	.	2000
Lower Division .	.	.	.	2800
				7000 feet.

---

* There are a few thin seams giving a total thickness of 5 feet of coal: one of them, the "Graces Coal," has been worked at Nailsea.

§ ii. *Economic Coalfield*

An attempt has been made on Plate 14 to show the economic extent of the general Coalfield, divided into Upper and Lower Measures. For this practical purpose, there are certain gaps within the area included on the geological map in which it is not considered likely that coal will be commercially worked. The area of the upper coalfield in which mining developments are at present taking place or will be likely to take place in the future is shown single-hatched. The reputed areas of the Lower Coal Measures in which access to these Measures has already taken or is now taking place or may be expected in the future is shown cross-hatched. It must not, however, be taken that throughout the single-hatched or cross-hatched areas coal would be as intensively worked as it is, say, in the neighbourhood of Radstock : but it is intended to show that, if coal-mining remains a normal and profitable commercial undertaking, these are the areas where it may be anticipated that pits may be sunk. If it is desirable anywhere to prevent mining operations for reasons possibly of the preservation of amenities (e.g., in the immediate neighbourhood of Bath) this map indicates the need for action at an early date, before commercial exploitation has been begun.

Of great advantage to this coalfield is the absence of firedamp, which has never been met with in the Upper Division and in the Lower is confined to the deeper seams, and there is not found to any great extent.

As mentioned above, the water-bearing strata of the Pennant rocks are a difficulty in sinking to the Lower Measures, where these rocks have not been eroded. The Lower Division, however, is generally considered to be the most productive, so that the presence of the Pennant (which is three times as thick as in the Forest of Dean and South Wales) is a real obstacle to rapid development.

The Upper Division on the Somerset side contains seams varying from 10 to 12 in number in different localities and having an aggregate thickness of about 24 feet of coal.   In the northern basin of the Upper Division there are only 4 seams and an aggregate thickness of 10 feet of coal.

The basin of the Lower Division is of course far more extensive than that of the Upper (see Plate 14), and it cannot be said that the amount of coal has been everywhere tested.   But from actual borings and pits sunk there are from 20 to 25 seams with an aggregate thickness of over 60 feet of coal ; several of the seams are of 4 to 7 feet in thickness.

The Royal Commission on Coal Supplies estimated the quantities of coal reserves in this Region as follows :—

Total tons down to 4,000 feet	.	.	.	4,587,635,708
Less abstracted since computation	.	.	.	25,000,000
				4,562,635,708 tons.
Total at all depths .	.	.	.	.	6,993,897,568
Less abstracted since computation	.	.	.	25,000,000
				6,968,897,568 tons.

§ iii. *The Bristol Coalfield*

The term Bristol Coalfield may be taken to include all the Coal Measures on the Gloucestershire side of the Avon, both the small patch of the Upper Division and the larger encircling Lower Measures. The most intensive development has occurred along the line of the Kingswood anticline extending as far as Warmley, comprising the collieries of Ashton Vale, Malago Vale, Bedminster, Easton, Hanham, Kingswood, Speedwell, Soundwell and California, etc. The Lower Coal Measures, as already stated, at this point are freed from the incubus of the Pennant, which has made sinking comparatively easy and the rich series of the Lower

Division accessible direct. But hitherto there has been, owing to insufficient geological information, a serious deterrent to the fullest development of these Lower Measures on the northern slope of the anticline in the direction of Winterbourne, where (see Plate 14) it will be seen that they are of widest extent. It has been the belief that the steep northern slope of the anticline was continued until unworkable depths were reached. In the neighbourhood therefore of Mangotsfield and Coalpit Heath, only the comparatively unprofitable Upper Division was available (some 10 feet of coal). The Bristol Coalfield, profitable as it has been in the past, has thus been freely described as a moribund area : the coal (Lower Division) was known to be there, but was for the greater part supposed to be at unworkable depths and buried beneath the formidable water-bearing Pennant rocks (which supervene as soon as the anticline dips sufficiently).

It has been discovered, however, that the coal seams of the anticline, after steeply descending for some 2000 feet, suddenly become horizontal. So far as can be ascertained this lower level with minor undulations is continued for long distances in all directions. At present this seam is being worked from the old shaft at the top of the anticline, but when coal-mining is again in the ascendant, new shafts could profitably be sunk to the horizontal seams. The supposed drawback to the Bristol Coalfield—a progressively deepening series of seams—is thus seen to be eliminated.

It is interesting to note that projections from this underground angle (between the slope and the horizontal lower level) to the ground-level revealed an exactly corresponding bend in the Pennant rocks actually visible on the surface, and that to the north of this the Pennant at the surface is horizontal. This significant fold had escaped the eye of the Geological Survey and hence the current misapprehension as to the coal seams.

The workings in these seams have been in the past under the grave disadvantage of being at a high inclination : they are now being conveniently worked on the flat.

This Lower Series comprise House, Steam, Manufacturing and Coking coals. From several seams the coal is very low in sulphur content and high in agglutinating power. It makes a good metallurgical coke and has a high yield of bye-products, as the following test will show :—

The yield of Coke	79·62%

The Volatile Products :—

Tar	2·68%
* Ammonia liquor . . .	5·04%
Carbon dioxide	·99%
Sulphuretted hydrogen . . .	·23%
Benzol	·79%
	————
	9·73%
† Gas, by difference . . .	10·65%
	————
	20·38%
	————
	100·00%

<table>
<tr><td>* Ammonia .. ..</td><td>3·107%</td><td>† The yield of gas :—</td><td></td></tr>
<tr><td>Volatile ammonia as sulphate</td><td>1·113%</td><td>@ 760 mm. pressure, 0° C., dry ..</td><td>9,683 c.ft.</td></tr>
<tr><td>Fixed ammonia as sulphate</td><td>·093%</td><td>@ 760 mm. pressure, 15° C., moist</td><td>10,389 c.ft.</td></tr>
<tr><td>Total sulphate .. ..</td><td>1·206%</td><td>Total yield of gas, including carbon dioxide, sulphuretted hydrogen, benzol .. ..</td><td>10,696 c.ft.</td></tr>
<tr><td>Residue .. ..</td><td>·727%</td><td></td><td></td></tr>
<tr><td></td><td>————
5·040%</td><td></td><td></td></tr>
</table>

It may be anticipated, therefore, that the Coalfield on the north-east of Bristol in the direction of Winterbourne, Frampton Cotterell and Coalpit Heath will develop in the future, utilising the Lower Series of Coal Measures, as a mining and manufacturing area.

Further to the north-east of the anticlinal workings in the Lower Series lies the patch of the Upper Series of the Coal Measures. At the southern end of this area is the Parkfield Colliery: this is working several seams in the Upper Series, varying in thickness from 2 feet to a joint vein of 5 to 6 feet, which is worked as one. The Fuel Research Board have recently carried out an exhaustive test* upon coal drawn from these veins known as "Parkfield Large Gas Coal." As a gas producer this coal proves to be very similar to the Mitchel Main coal at Derby; indeed it gives a somewhat higher yield.

It does not appear likely that these Upper Series will be exploited much further: the future of the Bristol Coalfield would seem to lie in the horizontal seams north of the anticline and possibly south of it in the direction of Brislington and Whitchurch.

§ iv. *The Radstock Coalfield*

This is geologically the southern end of the Bristol Coalfield; here the Upper Measures have been extensively worked over a long period. The workings have been in the past confined mostly to the topmost layer of the Upper Series of Coal Measures (the "Radstock" seams); this layer—the smallest in extent by reason of the saucer-like shape of the Coalfield—is not entirely exhausted, but seven of the principal pits (the Radstock, Camerton, Braysdown, Norton Hill, Kilmersdon, Writhlington and Old Mills pits), having exploited the layer to the full extent of the area available to them, have within the past fifteen to twenty years deepened their shafts and tapped the Second or "Farringdon" Series of the Upper Measures. These latter seams are more extensive than the "Radstock" seams and the coal is found in workable thicknesses on a fairly level floor.

Below again lies the Lower Series of Measures, after an intervening band of Pennant rock estimated at from 1500 to 1800 feet thick; these Lower Measures are as yet unworked within the Region. Their depth in the vicinity of Radstock itself is thought to be too great for economic working, but towards the "rim of the saucer," where the Measures approach more nearly to the surface, extensive developments are expected to occur; this will be to the south-east of Radstock, beyond the Regional boundary.

The coal now being obtained (from the Upper Series) is particularly suitable for the extraction of gas, it is used at Bath Gas Works (said to be the cheapest gas in the Country) and the Bristol, Weston, Clevedon, Aldershot, and other Gas Undertakings; in fact it is the main source of gas coal in the West of England. It is also a good house coal; for steam-raising, however, South Wales coals compete with the products of this area.

§ v. *The Nailsea Coalfield*

In the isolated Nailsea Basin the Upper and Lower Series are present, separated by the Pennant rock. Hitherto the workings have been somewhat superficial and have been flooded out owing to insufficient machinery. But there does not appear to be any reason why a revival of coal-mining should not occur in the area, under modern methods of pit sinking, and pumping.

The extent of the field seawards is uncertain, which makes an estimate of the amount of coal doubtful, but it has been put at 20,000,000 tons. If so it could be exploited by two pits raising between them half a million tons annually, which would give a life of forty years to the coalfield.

Though the residential area of Nailsea proper is actually on the exposed Coal Measures, it is probable that it would not be necessary or desirable to sink a pit here seeing that a certain

---

* *Bristol and Somerset Coalfield: Carbonisation of Parkfield Gas Coal.* H.M. Stationery Office, 1928. 1s. 6d.

amount of coal has already been extracted; this higher ground, therefore, would form a suitable area for housing the colliers. If each pit employed 2000 men (including surface workers) and one miner is taken to form a unit of a general population of four persons, there would be a population of some 16,000 to be housed in the immediate neighbourhood for that period. Being situated on the G.W. main line it is probable that a certain amount of industrial development would follow the coal working.

§ vi. *Subsidence*

It is always difficult to estimate the amount of subsidence that is likely to take place. Luckily only in the Nailsea basin is any very low lying land involved, and flooding here should not effect the housing as higher ground is available all round.

It has been stated that Pennant rock, expensive to bore through, barren of coal and pregnant with water, has yet this virtue—that its thickness and stiffness will prevent subsidence being experienced on the surface by the working of the Lower Series.

§ vii. *Revision of Geological Maps and Sections*

It appears that the Bristol, Somerset and Nailsea Coalfields have been somewhat neglected from the point of view of research. The Geological maps have not been revised: in many directions they are incomplete and in certain particulars they are inaccurate. The western limit of the Nailsea basin has not yet been discovered: the Severn Tunnel proved the existence of Coal Measures quite distinct from and far to the west of the Gloucestershire Basin. The sudden bend to the horizontal in the Lower Series north of the Kingswood anticline has been fully explained: but how far the seams remain horizontal is still unknown. Private research is being actively undertaken, but it requires the authoritative guidance of the Geological Survey to establish the new material on a scientific foundation.

SECTION 4. ECONOMIC GEOLOGY OTHER THAN COAL

§ i. *Introductory*

In a Region of such varied geological formation, it is to be expected that there would be a wealth of minerals of commercial value. These have been grouped according to their strata, though as a result of this method it may be found that neighbouring quarries working different rocks appear in widely separated groups. Plate 14 shows the position of the principal quarries and brickfields and a comparison with the geological map will indicate the nature of the material worked.

§ ii. *The Old Red Sandstone*

There does not appear to be much use made of either the Upper or Lower beds of the Old Red Sandstone. Much of the ground consists of barren tracts of conglomerate and hard sandstone. Where the softer sandstones and marls occur, the ground forms rich areas suitable for orchards.

§ iii. *The Carboniferous Limestone Series*

Mountain Limestone and the Upper and Lower Limestone Shales represent this Series in the Region. In some districts they are used on a limited scale for walling stone and other building purposes, but the demand is not great as the cost exceeds that of other building materials. The Mountain Limestone is hard and bluish-grey in colour, the Upper Limestone Shale has bands of grit connecting it with the Millstone Grit; much of the Limestone is stained pink with iron ore; it is extensively quarried for road stone and for chippings. Large quarries, well equipped with machinery, exist in the Avon Gorge, at North Weston, Portishead, Clevedon, Backwell, Weston-super-Mare, Sandford, Tytherington, Chipping Sodbury, Wickwar, and Failand. Most of these quarries possess plant for drying and the manufacture of tar-macadam.

Limestone in its various forms is mostly used for local purposes, and the industry is expected to continue to supply the needs of the Region.

Mountain Limestone is also burnt for lime at Shipham, Weston-super-Mare, Failand and other places.

§ iv. *Millstone Grit*

This consists of a hard pale quartzite and is not quarried commercially, probably because there are not many places where it is visible on the surface. The soil upon it is for the most part poor. Brandon Hill in the City of Bristol has the typical black and starved look of the Millstone Grit.

§ v. *The Coal Measures*

As usual the Coal Measures are rich in many materials besides coal. The Pennant Grit which divides the Upper from the Lower Series is exposed over much of the Northern portion of the coalfield; it is a grey and reddish hard sandstone, extensively used for building and engineering purposes (e.g., in steps and landings), also as street kerb and channel. It is also broken by machinery and screened for concrete work. The quarrying and dressing of Pennant stone is an important industry within the Region; the supply is inexhaustible and it can be marketed economically and on a successful competitive basis. Some of the principal quarries are within the City of Bristol, at Fishponds and Stapleton; it is also found and worked around Winterbourne, Frenchay and Hallatrow; also at Conygar near Clevedon, where there is a Pennant quarry on the small coal-measure outcrop. Pennant stone is also found on the River Avon at Hanham, at Mangotsfield, at Nailsea and other places where quarries have been worked in the past but are no longer active.

Fireclay is quarried as a bye-product of the Collieries; the supply exceeds the demand. A certain amount of brick earth also occurs in the Coal Measures.

§ vi. *The Triassic (Keuper) Series*

The Keuper is divided into the Dolomitic conglomerate, Red Sandstone and Marl: the Sandstone is too soft for building, but the Marl is used for brickmaking near Bristol.

Celestine (Sulphate of Strontium) is quarried in the narrow band of marl that occurs between the coal measures and Oolites near Wickwar and Yate. It has also been quarried at Milbury Heath and on the Mendips, but in that locality the supply is nearly exhausted. The demand is not as great as formerly, but supplies appear to be still available.

Ochre is worked at Wick and Winford; the industry is alive and likely to improve, but it is not expected to extend to other places.

Alabaster and Gypsum in small quantities have been quarried at Aust cliff.

§ vii. *The Lias*

The Lower Lias is quarried for building purposes around North Bristol and near Bitton, Doynton and Pucklechurch; the demand is local and is limited, being in competition with bricks. A certain amount of inferior road-making material is quarried in the Lower Lias.

Brick Earth, Shales and Clays occur in the Middle Lias and are quarried in the Bristol area, at Patchway and Stoke Gifford on the G.W. Railway.

Ironstone occurs in the Middle Lias and has been quarried at Upton Cheney and near Winford, but the industry is now defunct as the beds were not sufficiently rich to repay the cost of working.

The Upper Lias consists for the most part of clay and shale; it has been used for brick-making. Blue Lias is quarried at Bishopsworth.

PLATE 14.

· BRISTOL & BATH ·
REGIONAL · PLANNING
· SCHEME ·

INDUSTRIAL SURVEY

THE COAL INDUSTRY

Patrick Abercrombie & B. F. Brueton.
LIVERPOOL & BRISTOL.

Scale: 1:63360

of Miles

§ viii.   *Midford Sands*

These are used for mortar-making and also for polishing: they occur almost invariably fringing the inferior Oolite, and following the extraordinarily complicated lines which watercourses and denudation have made.

§ ix.   *Inferior Oolite*

This consists of an oolitic and shelly limestone with occasional sand and clay: the largest deposits are found at Dundry Hill and north of Radstock.   These strata contain the principal building stones of the Cotswold Hills, the famous Larne Freestone, but lack of rail facilities in the portion of the Cotswolds lying within the Region has hindered the development of this material in the Region itself.

§ x.   *Fuller's Earth*

These strata extend throughout the Cotswold escarpment, but they actually contain only small quantities of true Fuller's Earth; it used to be worked near Bath and at Wellow and Midford, but it is not now obtained commercially.   Otherwise the strata consist of grey calcarean clays, which are occasionally used for marling.

§ xi.   *Great (or Bath) Oolite*

Though a large amount of this occurs within the Region forming the characteristic capping to the hills round Bath, the actual quarrying of this, perhaps the most famous (with Portland stone) of all English building stones, is carried on further east over the border of Wiltshire.

§ xii.   *Forest Marble*

This is also called Bradford Clay from a thick bed found near Bradford-on-Avon.   There is no economic deposit within the Region, but the upper layers, containing irregular bedded Oolitic Limestone, are quarried for building and road metal in the neighbourhood of Frome and Cirencester.

SECTION 5.   OTHER INDUSTRIAL ACTIVITY

Outside Bristol and the coalfields of the Region this is not an industrial area.   A sufficient indication of the location of the factories is given on the Industrial Survey (Plate 14).   The industries of Bristol are remarkable for their variety, and it would be difficult to find an industry not represented.   One effect of this is that the city is spared the extremes of high pressure and depression experienced in centres depending upon one or two staple industries. Chief among the industries of Bristol are the manufacture of chocolate, tobacco, soap, leather, boots and shoes, ship-building and repairing, aeroplanes, chemicals, spelter, seed, oil, lead, galvanised iron, artificial silk, the wine and spirit trade, tar and resin works, and paper and printing.   The Imperial Tobacco Company has its headquarters and chief factories in Bristol, as also have Messrs. J. S. Fry & Sons.   Other works of national and world-wide repute are the Bristol Aeroplane Company, the Bristol Potteries, Douglas Motor Cycle Works, the Bristol Tramway and Carriage Company's Motor Works, Lysaght's Galvanized Iron Works, and Hills' ship-building yard, where the *Great Western* steamship was constructed.

The trade and industries of Bristol are of course largely connected with the docks of the Port, which is one of the chief centres of maritime trade of the United Kingdom.   The port not only serves the city but a large area, including the western and south-western counties, Birmingham and the Midlands.   Bristol takes over 10 per cent of the grain imported into the United Kingdom, more than half the bananas (it is the premier port of Europe for this traffic) and 26 per cent of the tobacco. Extensive installations have been established by the leading oil companies, the quantity of oil imported exceeds half a million tons a year. Other large trades of the port are flour-milling, provisions, fruit, timber, oil seeds, metals, and wines and spirits. There is a large area of land adjacent to the docks most suitable for the erection of

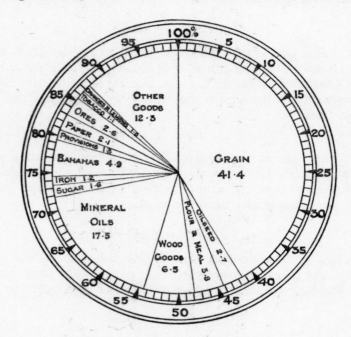

BRISTOL DOCK EXPORTS DIAGRAM

works and factories. In the City of Bath there are a lead works and the engineering works of Messrs. Stothert & Pitt, who manufacture cranes, lifting, crushing, screening and washing plant for the home, colonial and foreign market. At Keynsham, Messrs. J. S. Fry & Sons have recently established a new factory for the manufacture of chocolate and cocoa; this is a natural extension of Bristol's Industrial Area. Mention should also be made of the large electric generating station now being erected by the Bristol Corporation at Portishead, upon a site specially selected for the facilities for cooling water and the supply of coal, both seaborne and railborne. This Power Station is destined to be of more than local interest in the future. Other industries in the Region are for the most part purely local, such as gas-works, etc.

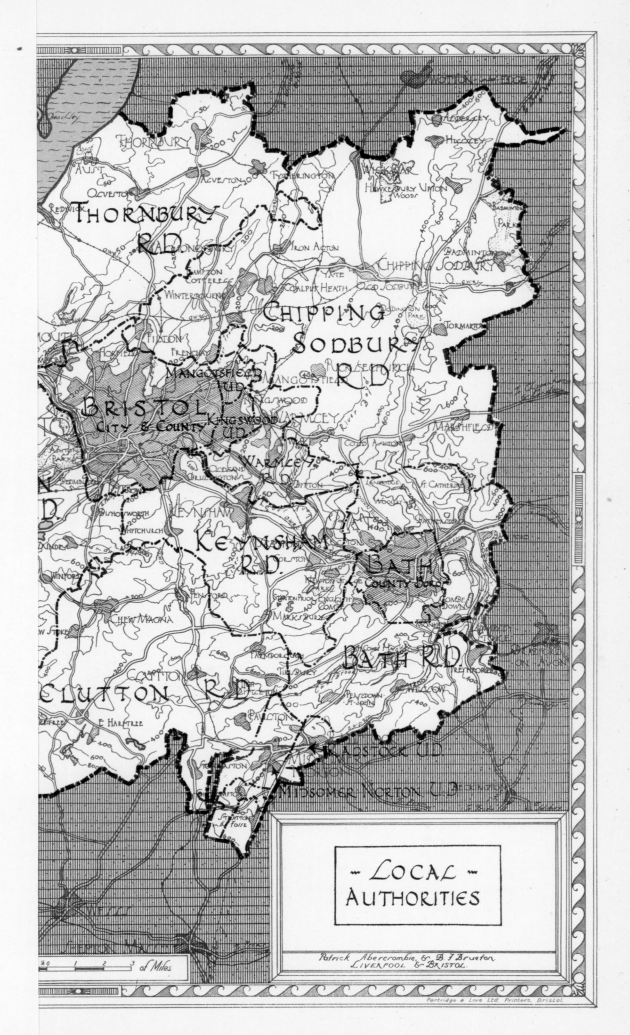

THORNBURY R.D.

CHIPPING SODBURY R.D.

BRISTOL
City & County

KEYNSHAM
R.D.

BATH
County Boro.

CLUTTON R.D.

BATH R.D.

MIDSOMER NORTON U.D.

- LOCAL -
AUTHORITIES

Patrick Abercrombie, & B.F. Brueton.
LIVERPOOL & BRISTOL.

of Miles

CHAPTER V.   ADMINISTRATION

§ i. *Local Government*

County Authorities.   The Region includes portions of the Counties of Gloucestershire and Somerset, together with the City and County of Bristol.

Local Authorities.   The Local Authorities concerned, with their areas and rateable values, are :—

Name.	Area : Acres	Rateable Value, March, 1929.
Bristol City and County . (excluding River Severn and Foreshore)	18,686	£2,843,713
Gloucestershire—		
Kingswood U.D. . .	1,530	£46,900
Mangotsfield U.D. . .	1,153	£35,549
Chipping Sodbury R.D. .	69,736	£120,157
Thornbury R.D. . . (the parishes of Almondsbury, Aust, Alveston, Elberton, Henbury, Littleton, Northwick, Rangeworthy, Redwick, Tytherington only)	33,872	£66,684
Warmley R.D. . .	8,936	£33,699
Somerset—		
Bath County Borough .	5,152	£588,083
Clevedon U.D . . .	3,017	£46,203
Midsomer Norton U.D. .	3,970	£30,040
Portishead U.D. . .	1,029	£28,869
Radstock U.D. . . .	1,014	£16,840
Weston-super-Mare U.D. .	2,412	£229,629
Axbridge R.D. . . .	93,062	£308,151
Bath R.D. . . .	27,360	£90,109
* Clutton R.D. . . .	41,133	£80,528
Keynsham R.D. . .	21,405	£98,120
* Long Ashton R.D. . .	47,852	£157,437
Total . .	381,319	£4,820,711

* Although within the Regional Area, these Authorities have not yet (June, 1929) adhered to the Regional Committee.

§ ii. *Drainage Commissions*

Certain portions of the Region are subject to special control in the matter of land drainage ; this control is independent of the administration by the County Councils and the local District Councils, but may be said to be supplemental thereto. The lands concerned are those low-lying areas which are below the level of the highest spring tide and certain other neighbouring lands which drain into these ; the boundaries of the areas under this special control are indicated by dotted lines on the folding map.

North of the Avon the drainage area is controlled by the Commissioners of Sewers for the lower level of the County of Gloucester ; south of the Avon, from Pill to Uphill, by the Somerset Commissioners of Sewers (Northern Division) ; south of Uphill by the Somerset Drainage Board. The two Commissions are of ancient formation : they were first appointed under an Act of Henry VIII ; the last-named body is set up under the Somerset Drainage Act 1877.

In both Counties the Commissioners are local gentlemen appointed for life or as long as they shall continue to qualify by holding property in the area of the yearly value of £100 or by acting as agent for an estate of not less than £300 yearly value.

The Somerset Commissioners appoint *Dyke Reeves*, local farmers, who hold office for a period of five years ; the Dyke Reeves receive no salary ; they appoint from among themselves a *Foreman*, who receives a nominal salary, and the foreman reports on their behalf to the Commissioners twice yearly. The Gloucestershire Commissioners work under a different system ; they appoint local *Surveyors*, who act independently and report twice yearly direct to the Commissioners. The principal duties of the Dyke Reeves and Surveyors are to inspect and report to the Commissioners upon the condition of the main drainage channels and banks, and to see that the principal ditches (known as " commissioned " ditches) are kept clear by the owners or tenants of the adjoining lands. Defaulters are reported to the Commissioners, who have power to levy fines. The Commissioners are also empowered to levy special rates, which are applied to the general maintenance of the drainage system.

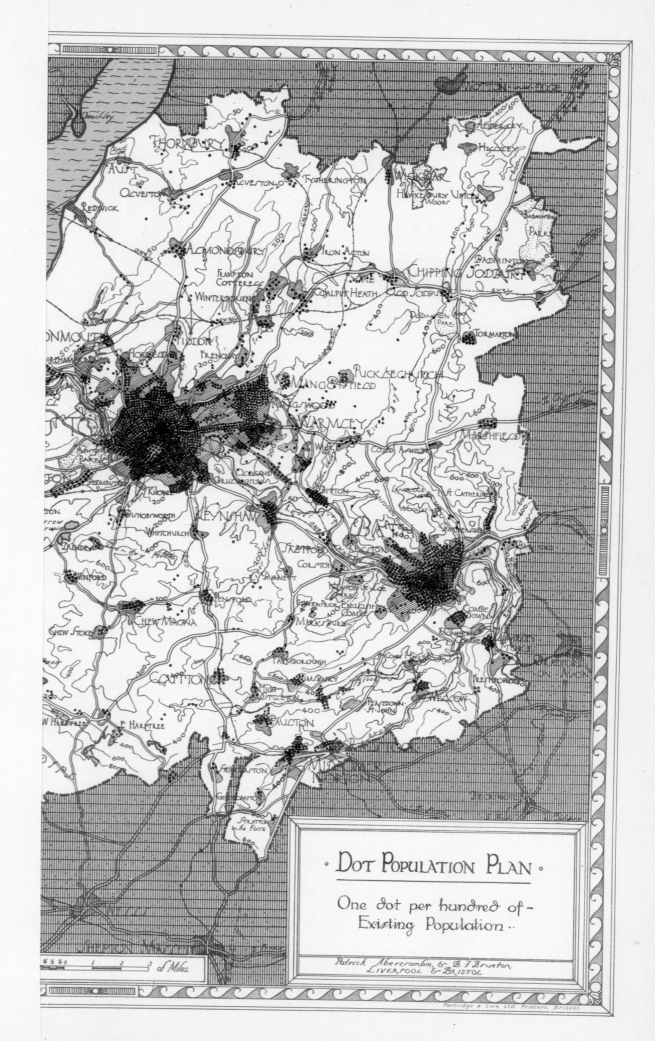

· DOT POPULATION PLAN ·

One dot per hundred of
Existing Population

Patrick Abercrombie & B.F. Brueton
LIVERPOOL & BRISTOL

of Miles.

Partridge & Love Ltd. Printers, Bristol

CHAPTER VI.   POPULATION

§ i.   *Census Figures*

THE Population figures, taken from the Census Tables, and the average rate of increase, or decrease, computed therefrom are as follows :—

Local Authority.	Population.			Rate of Increase or Decrease (per cent).		Estimated average rate of increase or decrease in ten years (per cent).
	1901.	1911.	1921.	1901–1911.	1911–1921.	
Bristol City . .	339,042	357,114	376,975	+ 5	+ 6	+ 5·5
Bath City . .	65,956	69,173	68,669	+ 4	— 1	+ 1·5
Weston U.D. . .	19,845	23,235	31,643	+ 17	+ 36	+ 26·5
Clevedon U.D. .	5,900	6,111	6,724	+ 3	+ 10	+ 6·5
Portishead U.D. .	2,544	3,329	3,815	+ 30	+ 15	+ 22·5
Midsomer Norton U.D.	5,809	7,299	7,780	+ 25	+ 6	+ 15·5
Radstock U.D. .	3,355	3,690	3,661	+ 10	— 1	+ 4·5
Kingswood U.D. .	11,961	12,700	12,958	+ 14	+ 2	+ 8
Axbridge R.D.. .	22,947	22,655	23,293	— 2	+ 3	+ ·5
Bath R.D. . .	11,648	14,794	14,571	+ 27	— 2	+ 12·5
Chipping Sodbury R.D.	22,104	20,955	21,105	— 6	+ 1	— 2·5
Clutton R.D. . .	16,599	16,074	15,794	— 3	— 2	— 2·5
Keynsham R.D. .	8,269	10,141	10,575	+ 23	+ 4	+ 13·5
Long Ashton R.D. .	15,694	16,181	17,619	+ 3	+ 9	+ 6
Thornbury R.D. . (part of)	10,297	10,669	10,758	+ 3	+ 1	+ 2
Warmley R.D. .	15,945	17,188	18,476	+ 7	+ 7	+ 7
	577,915	611,308	644,416	+ 5·7	+ 6·9	+ 6·3

Plate 16 shows the distribution of population, each dot represents 100 persons.

§ ii.   *Occupational Analysis*

From the 1921 Census Tables the figures for " males over 12 " have been extracted; they are given in the Tables under 32 group occupations; these have been condensed to eleven groups, and the resulting figures reduced to a percentage basis for ease in comparison. The numbers and percentages are shown in the table overleaf, and the figures are illustrated graphically on Plate 17.

Population (1921 Census)

The male population over twelve years of age—Ordinary figures.
The equivalent percentage of the population of the town or rural district—Italic figures.

	Agricultural workers	Mining and quarrying	Metal workers	Workers in skins, leather, and textiles	Building trade and workers in wood	Makers of food, drink, and tobacco	Professional, clerical, and commercial	Transport, public services, administration and defence	Personal service, entertainment and sport	Other occupations	Unoccupied and retired	
	1	2	3	4	5	6	7	8	9	10	11	
Bristol	1,526	1,726	12,795	5,466	14,017	4,820	23,253	23,864	3,621	24,529	18,572	134,189
	1·1	*1·3*	*9·5*	*4·1*	*10·4*	*3·6*	*17·3*	*17·8*	*2·7*	*18·3*	*13·9*	*100*
Bath	948	305	2,058	749	2,974	529	4,300	3,288	1,117	3,024	4,167	23,459
	4·0	*1·3*	*8·8*	*3·2*	*12·7*	*2·2*	*18·4*	*14·0*	*4·7*	*12·9*	*17·8*	*100*
Weston-super-Mare	297	124	488	240	846	222	2,651	1,352	534	907	2,013	9,674
	3·1	*1·3*	*5·0*	*2·5*	*8·7*	*2·3*	*27·4*	*14·0*	*5·5*	*9·4*	*20·8*	*100*
Clevedon	234	34	94	92	223	45	390	263	67	193	403	2,038
	11·5	*1·7*	*4·7*	*4·5*	*10·9*	*2·2*	*19·1*	*12·9*	*3·3*	*9·4*	*19·8*	*100*
Portishead	90	11	86	25	99	24	216	225	28	150	451	1,405
	6·4	*1·0*	*6·2*	*1·8*	*7·0*	*1·7*	*15·4*	*16·0*	*2·0*	*10·6*	*31·9*	*100*
Kingswood	184	237	674	1,522	340	115	449	347	95	534	525	5,022
	3·7	*4·7*	*13·4*	*30·3*	*6·8*	*2·3*	*8·9*	*6·9*	*1·9*	*10·6*	*10·5*	*100*
Midsomer Norton	132	1,400	84	110	192	42	260	143	49	160	546	3,118
	4·2	*45·0*	*2·7*	*3·5*	*6·2*	*1·3*	*8·3*	*4·6*	*1·6*	*5·1*	*17·5*	*100*
Radstock	23	736	67	6	89	25	149	100	15	108	142	1,460
	1·6	*50·4*	*4·6*	*0·5*	*6·1*	*1·7*	*10·2*	*6·9*	*1·0*	*7·4*	*9·6*	*100*
Axbridge Rural	3,404	237	248	114	780	142	762	590	168	672	1,366	8,483
	40·2	*2·8*	*2·9*	*1·4*	*9·0*	*1·7*	*9·0*	*7·0*	*2·0*	*7·9*	*16·1*	*100*
Bath Rural	1,161	1,200	218	49	467	56	376	371	117	414	949	5,378
	21·6	*22·3*	*4·0*	*1·0*	*8·7*	*1·0*	*7·0*	*6·9*	*2·2*	*7·7*	*17·6*	*100*
Chip. Sod. Rural	2,153	1,205	294	139	766	141	550	652	170	738	1,279	8,087
	26·6	*14·9*	*3·6*	*1·7*	*9·4*	*1·7*	*6·8*	*8·0*	*2·1*	*9·4*	*15·8*	*100*
Clutton Rural	1,230	2,148	128	194	434	61	355	308	93	342	792	6,085
	20·2	*35·3*	*2·1*	*3·2*	*7·1*	*1·0*	*5·8*	*5·1*	*1·5*	*5·6*	*13·0*	*100*
Keynsham Rural	825	99	320	54	370	81	625	462	93	477	609	4,015
	20·5	*2·5*	*8·0*	*1·3*	*9·2*	*2·0*	*15·6*	*11·5*	*2·3*	*11·9*	*15·3*	*100*
Long Ashton Rural	1,752	252	212	103	617	148	662	791	162	713	947	6,359
	27·7	*4·0*	*3·3*	*1·6*	*9·7*	*2·3*	*10·4*	*12·4*	*2·5*	*11·2*	*14·9*	*100*
Thornbury Rural *	2,242	192	319	97	707	121	548	1,122	170	820	1,171	7,509
	29·9	*2·5*	*4·3*	*1·3*	*9·4*	*1·6*	*7·3*	*14·9*	*2·3*	*10·9*	*15·6*	*100*
Warmley Rural †	624	404	520	983	646	273	730	619	105	950	1,111	6,965
	8·9	*5·8*	*7·5*	*14·1*	*9·3*	*4·0*	*10·5*	*8·9*	*1·5*	*13·6*	*15·9*	*100*
Total Male Population over twelve years of age												233,246

* The whole Rural District.
† Prior to partition.

PLATE 17.

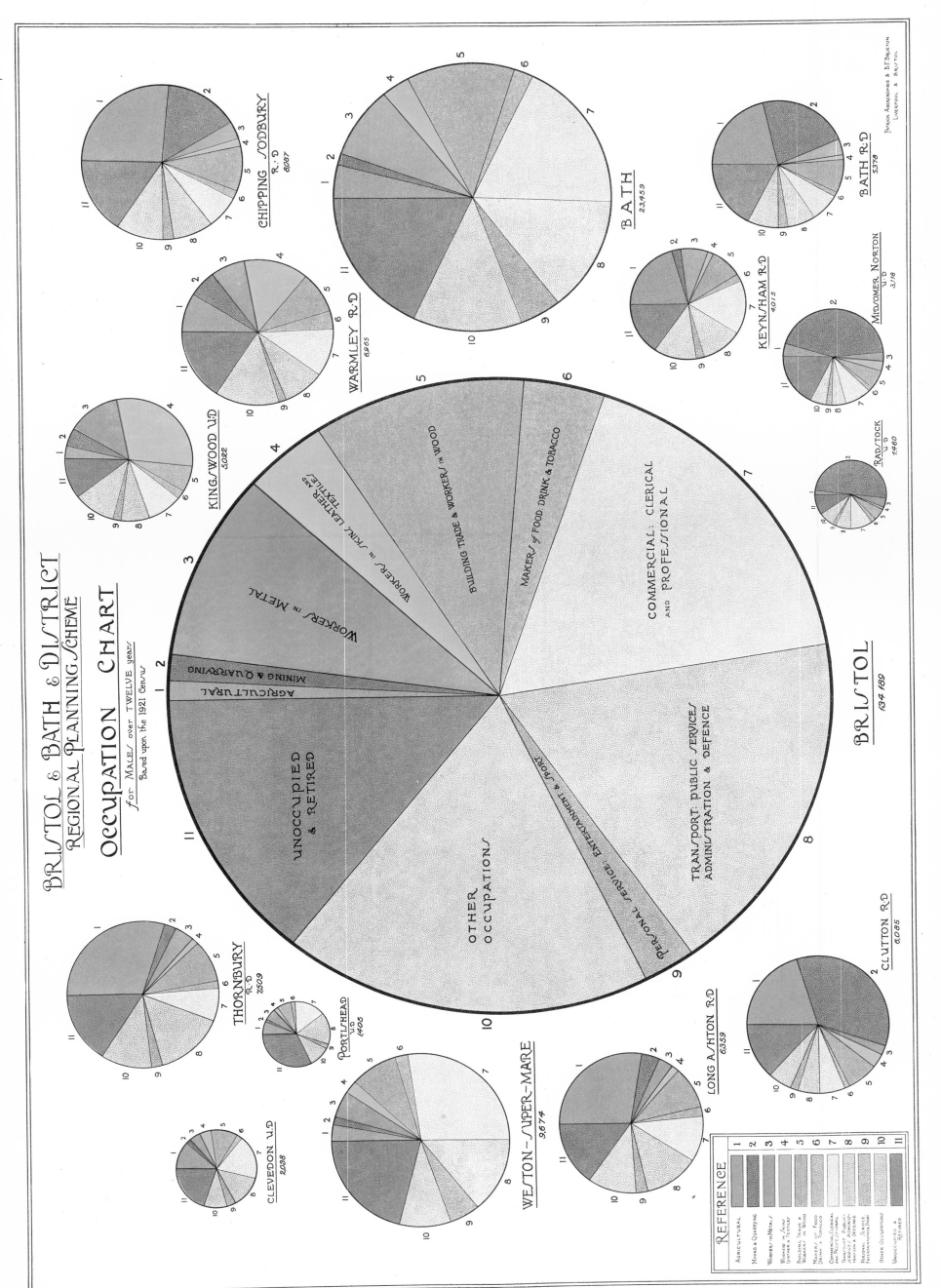

BRISTOL & BATH & DISTRICT
REGIONAL PLANNING SCHEME
OCCUPATION CHART
for Males over TWELVE years
Based upon the 1921 Census

CHIPPING SODBURY R.D
8,087

BATH
23,459

BATH R.D
5,378

KEYNSHAM R.D
4,015

MIDSOMER NORTON U.D
3,118

RADSTOCK U.D
1,960

WARMLEY R.D
6,965

KINGSWOOD U.D
5,022

BRISTOL
134,189

AGRICULTURAL
MINING & QUARRYING
WORKER IN METAL
WORKER IN SKIN, LEATHER AND TEXTILES
BUILDING TRADE & WORKERS IN WOOD
MAKERS of FOOD, DRINK & TOBACCO
COMMERCIAL: CLERICAL AND PROFESSIONAL
TRANSPORT PUBLIC SERVICES ADMINISTRATION & DEFENCE
PERSONAL SERVICE ENTERTAINMENT & SPORT
OTHER OCCUPATIONS
UNOCCUPIED & RETIRED

THORNBURY R.D
2,909

PORTISHEAD U.D
1,405

CLEVEDON U.D
2,038

WESTON-SUPER-MARE
9,674

LONG ASHTON R.D
6,359

CLUTTON R.D
5,085

REFERENCE
1 AGRICULTURAL
2 MINING & QUARRYING
3 WORKERS IN METAL
4 WORKERS IN SKIN, LEATHER & TEXTILE
5 BUILDING TRADE & WORKERS IN WOOD
6 MAKERS OF FOOD DRINK & TOBACCO
7 COMMERCIAL, CLERICAL AND PROFESSIONAL
8 TRANSPORT PUBLIC SERVICE ADMINISTRATION & DEFENCE
9 PERSONAL SERVICE ENTERTAINMENT & SPORT
10 OTHER OCCUPATIONS
11 UNOCCUPIED & RETIRED

Patrick Abercrombie & B.F Brueton
Liverpool & Bristol

§ iii. *Occupational Distribution*

The following should be read in conjunction with the foregoing table :—

(*a*) *Commercial, Clerical and Professional*. This, the largest group, contains 36,276 male workers (15·55 % of the total in the Region) ; of these Weston has the largest proportionate number, 27·4% of her population, which points to her use as a dormitory town. The percentage of population in the other towns is fairly constant at between 15 and 19%, except that Midsomer Norton, Radstock and Kingswood are down to between 8 and 10 % of their totals. The rural districts range between 5 and 10%, but one Rural District, Keynsham, has 15·6% in this Group, which is interesting and suggests that Keynsham is being used as a dormitory satellite to Bristol.

(*b*) The next largest group is *Transport, Public Services, Administration and Defence*, containing 34,497 (or 14·79 % of the whole), and Transport accounts for about 28,500 of these. Bristol predominates in transport ; it is a leading railway centre (4000) as well as a port ; there are also in Bristol 6700 engaged on Road Transport and 6000 on Water Transport (including 3400 dock labourers). Portishead, Bath, Weston, Clevedon, Thornbury, and Long Ashton have high percentages in this group ; Midsomer Norton and Clutton have very few in proportion to their population.

(*c*) The *Building Trade* group is the third largest in the Region with 23,567 (or 10·1% of the whole). It is fairly well distributed in proportion to population ; Bath has the highest percentage (12·7%) and Radstock the lowest (6·1%).

(*d*) *Agriculture* provides occupation for 16,825 male workers (or 7·21% of the total). The district having the greatest proportionate number of agricultural workers is Axbridge (40·2%) followed by Thornbury (29·9%), Long Ashton (27·7%) and Chipping Sodbury (26·6 %). The towns are, as would be expected, well below these percentages, but Clevedon Urban is remarkable for having 11·5 % of its population in this group.

(*e*) *Metal Workers* account for 18,605 (7·95%) of the male population ; they are located chiefly at Bristol (12,795) and Bath (2,058).

(*f*) *Mining and Quarrying* account for 10,310 males in the Region (4·42% of the whole). Half the male population of Midsomer Norton and Radstock are scheduled here ; Clutton has 35·3% in this group, and Bath Rural 22·3% ; the coalpits north of Bristol swell Chipping Sodbury's total to 1205 (15 %), but in the other districts the percentage is negligible.

(*g*) *Textiles, Skins, and Leather Trades* run Mining very closely ; this group amounts to 9943 (4·26% of the total). Most of the workers in the group are employed in the boot and leather trade and are located mainly in Bristol and Kingswood, no less than 30·3% of Kingswood's total being in this group ; 14·1% of Warmley are also scheduled here, but the percentage in other areas varies between 2 and 5.

(*h*) The *Food, Drink and Tobacco* group is just worth extracting ; it contains 6845 male workers (2·93% of the whole), 4820 of them being in Bristol.

(*i*) *Personal Service, Entertainment and Sport* : 6604 male workers (or 2·83%) are mostly located in Bristol (3621) and Bath (1117), but the highest proportionate number is at Weston, being 5·5 % of Weston's total. At Radstock there is only 1% so engaged.

(*j*) *Other Occupations*. Here are assembled 34,731 workers in miscellaneous trades, or 14·9% of the whole. Bristol with its complex structure absorbs 24,529 of these and Bath 3024. The remainder are fairly evenly distributed at about 10% of the male population in those areas.

(*k*) *Unoccupied and Retired*. These amount to 35,043, 15 % of the whole. Bristol has 18,572 of them, but this is only 13·9% of Bristol's male population. Other proportionate numbers in this group are :—

Portishead	.	.	. 31·9% (451)
Weston	.	.	. 20·8% (2013)
Clevedon	.	.	. 19·8% (403)
Bath City	.	.	. 17·8% (4167)
Bath Rural	.	.	. 17·6% (949)
Midsomer Norton	.	.	. 17·5% (546)

One would have expected Bath to head the list, but apparently other towns in the Region are popularly esteemed as places of retirement.

The lowest percentage is at Radstock with 9·6% (142 people).

§ iv. *Female Population*

It has not been thought necessary to analyse in detail the census figures for " females over 12," but it may be noted that whilst the women exceed the men by 44,065, 190,709 (or over 66%) of the former are returned as " unoccupied or retired " ; this includes, of course, women and girls at home.

The other principal female occupations are :—

(1) Persons employed in personal service, entertainment and
    sport . . . . 34,010 or 11·8%
(2) Commercial, clerical and professional . . . 24,394 or 8·5%
(3) Makers of textile goods and articles of dress . . 14,415 or 4·0%
(4) Makers of tobacco, food and drink . . . . 6985 or 2·4%
(5) Paper workers and printers . . . . . 5766 or 2·0%

COMPTON BISHOP CHURCH (UNDER WAVERING DOWN)

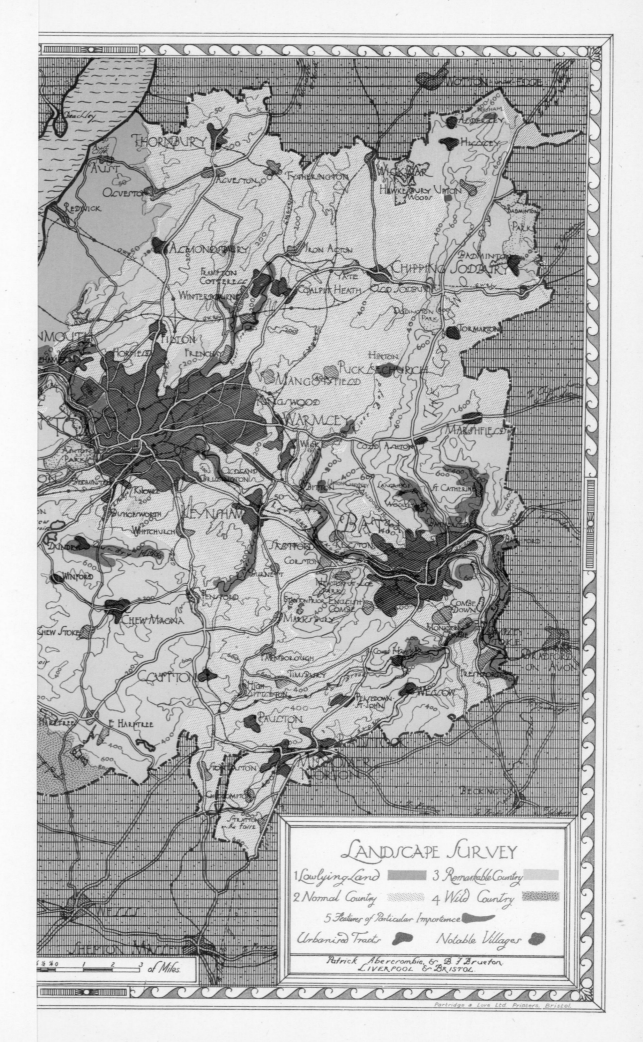

LANDSCAPE SURVEY

1 Lowlying Land   3 Remarkable Country

2 Normal Country   4 Wild Country

5 Features of Particular Importance

Urbanized Tracts   Notable Villages

Patrick Abercrombie & B. F. Brueton
LIVERPOOL & BRISTOL

CHAPTER VII.　LANDSCAPE SURVEY

SECTION 1.　THE COUNTRYSIDE GENERALLY

§ i.　*Introduction : Landscape Studies*

IN the present imperfect stage of Landscape Studies it is no easy matter to make a survey of the Landscape in so varied and complex a Region as this. There is the initial handicap of an imperfect means of notation or classification of Landscape effects. Dr. Vaughan Cornish, Past President of the Geographical Association, has announced that he hopes to put forward a system by which æsthetic Geography can be ascertained and mapped as scientifically as Political, Social, Vegetable, Orographical and Geological data. But pending this more precise instrument of study, a rough attempt has been made to divide up the Region into areas of different types of landscape and to analyse their components. By this means the predominant characteristics can be ascertained, the effect of future developments upon them gauged and existing discordances pointed out. Later in the report this Landscape Survey is correlated to the zoning plan, under which is shown the most suitable uses to which the land can be put with a view of developing economic resources and conserving natural amenities.

This section of the Report therefore is concerned with the Landscape Survey only ; and for this purpose the Region has been divided up into five types of area, within which types there are of course many sub-divisions : for these sub-divisions (owing to the early stage of the technique of landscape study) recourse will be had to the normal and unsatisfactory guide-book method of verbal description, supplemented by photographs. But if the result of this rough division and verbal description is enough to remind the inhabitants of the extraordinarily varied Landscape beauties which they possess and to make them better known to the world outside the Bristol and Bath Region, the Survey will have served its purpose. It will also, it is hoped, lead to the natural question, to be answered in Part the Second, how these beauties can be retained by a community which has to work for its living and to study true economy.

§ ii.　*Fivefold Division of the Countryside*

The following are the five main divisions into which the Countryside has been classified on Plate 18 ; they are discussed in Section 2 of this Chapter :—

(1) The *lowlying land*, chiefly along the coast and generally below the 50-foot contour and under the control of Commissioners of Sewers.

(2) The *normal agricultural land* which does not possess any striking landscape effects due either to varied contours or vegetation.

(3) The land, largely agricultural, which owing to contour, vegetation, water or other causes, is of *remarkable landscape value*.

(4) The *wilder areas* which owe much of their effect to remoteness, lofty elevation, or absence of human handiworks.

(5) Features of particular beauty or landscape importance ; these features are generally found embedded in areas 3 and 4, but occur also in certain cases in comparatively dull stretches of country (2). In selecting them we have been guided not only by personal preference, but

by the general consensus of opinion. It will usually be found that the general public has an unerring instinct for striking or astonishing Beauties (and this extreme popularity of appreciation is often their undoing), whereas the quieter charms of landscape pass unheeded (and are for the opposite reason liable to be defaced by lack of appreciation).

One of the inevitable drawbacks of this type of survey is that logically the Countryside must be presented in a series of disjointed divisions : thus the Cheddar Gorge is described in a different division from the Mendip Hills, and the reader must make his own synthesis with the help of the Map.

§ iii. *Town and River in the Landscape*

In this Landscape Survey continuous urban tracts, though as in the case of Bristol they may have originally possessed great landscape beauty, have of necessity been omitted ; but it must not be forgotten that these large towns are components in the Regional landscape and that an obligation rests upon them to be of seemly appearance from a distance. Their interior urban seemliness, no less desirable, belongs to another aspect of æsthetic geography.

The Villages and smaller Country Towns will be considered as an integral part of the countryside and a brief survey of them is included in another section.

It is not possible to include in its due relation to the landscape the Severn Estuary and the Bristol Channel : the spaciousness, the colour, the great range of its tide levels have their influence upon all coastal scenery and many inland prospects.

SECTION 2.   THE DIVISIONS OF THE COUNTRYSIDE

§ i. *The Lowlying Lands*

These alluvial flats border the Region on the coast in varying width, increasing from about a quarter of a mile wide in the north to over ten in the south. Except for the high ground between Portishead and Clevedon, they are only interrupted by isolated incidents, namely, the Sandstone headland at Aust and the three parallel Limestone promontories of Middle Hope, Worlebury Hill and Brean Down, the tip of the Mendip ridge. With these exceptions, therefore, the coast of the Region, bordered by the lowlands, is not interesting.

But it would be a mistake to dismiss this lowlying division of the Region as devoid of beauty. It possesses the very definite charm of all flat and fenny countries, great sky expanse and characteristic vegetation and warm-toned buildings. Also like all fens, it is easily defaced, being devoid of positive features ; but at the same time the defacements must be large enough to dominate its trees. A single small building which on an eminence in undulating country can shed a baleful influence for miles around, here could be hidden in the general flatness and free-growing willows. But desultory industrial buildings, a few tall chimneys pouring out smoke, can quickly convert the fen into a squalid bog : pleasant dykes, here called Rhines, rich in their special flora, can easily change into sluggish sewers, with slimy banks.

Where complete industrialisation is to take place, as for example north of Avonmouth, the fen landscape of course disappears. Generally speaking, however, it is anticipated that its nature will protect it from change ; except where, near the Bristol Channel, it forms a natural and suitable seaside building area.

The whole extent of lowlying land may be conveniently divided into four portions : (*a*) from Aust to Avonmouth ; (*b*) Gordano ; (*c*) from Clevedon Ridge to Mendip ; (*d*) South of Mendip.

(*a*) This area must inevitably become industrialised at the southern end : its landscape value is chiefly as a foreground to the splendid view from the Almondsbury terrace.

PLATE 19.

Photo: R. F. Warrilow.

Air View of Weston-super-Mare.

(*b*) The Gordano forms a beautiful valley running parallel with the coast between two ridges : it is so intimately connected with these two lovely limestone features, that its preservation is essential to their continuance.

(*c*) From Clevedon to Mendip the low land contains some of the most fully developed and some of the remotest portions. Weston-super-Mare occupies a large portion of the beautiful bay between Worlebury Hill (up which the town climbs) and Brean Down (from which man is excluded). Sand Bay, between Worlebury Hill and Middle Hope, is almost deserted, but awaits its development as a future seaside town. There are other large areas more inland, remote from change, and it is hoped that they will remain so. Many of the villages, like Kingston Seymour, and their surroundings, have a mellow quiet charm.

(*d*) South of Mendip the levels widen out rapidly and have all the air of a reclaimed country from which emerge islands, small and conical as Brent Knoll and Nyland Hill, and large and flat like that of Wedmore.

§ ii. *Normal Agricultural Land*

By this is meant country of the type which makes up the bulk of the English Landscape : of quiet charm, but not rising to any heights. It is not intended for a moment that, by relegating large tracts to this somewhat negative division, it is suggested that such countryside does not merit preservation : indeed the normal methods of rural conservation combined with reasonable development should apply to this type of area, otherwise England's rural beauty would only be preserved in chosen spots. But it so happens that this Bath and Bristol Region has so varied and rich a scenery that the normal countryside is not the preponderating type.

It would be idle to attempt to describe this usual English scenery : gently undulating ground, hedgerow trees, isolated trees in the fields, artificial copses, wooded parks, single farms and grouped villages dominated by Tower or Spire. Suffice it to give the four districts which fall in this division.

(*a*) The biggest stretch which has been scheduled in this division extends north of Bristol, Kingswood and Mangotsfield. A good deal of it has been marred by mining ; this stretch roughly forms the second of the three terraces, of which the lowest is the fenland already described, and the uppermost is the Cotswold plateau.

The edge of this middle terrace next the fen is formed by a narrow limestone outcrop— a sort of balustrade as it were which lifts this strip into a higher division of scenic beauty. For

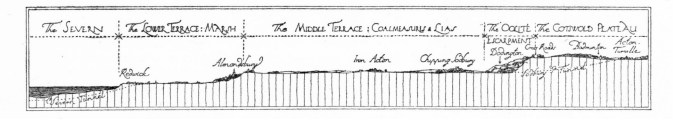

the rest the terrace is bordered by the Lias clays (and it is typical clay country) with the broad patch of the Coal Measures thrusting through in the centre, fringed by the New Red Sandstone. But this geological change is little remarked in the landscape. Incidents in this subdivision will be dealt with later.

(*b*) A small patch of country east of the Cotswold escarpment, in which Tormarton and Acton Turville are the villages, appears to belong to this division of country. It lies between the 550- and 400-foot contour ; the streams flow eastwards and just beyond the Region they cut for themselves deep valleys, making the highly picturesque Castle Combe landscape.

47

(*c*) The whole of the country south of the Avon (except the fen) is so complicated, both in its contours and surface geology, that one might easily assume that there could be no normal English country—all must be fantastic or at least remarkably picturesque. But a Region like this breeds fastidiousness, and an area selected originally on purely landscape grounds as not remarkable appears again to coincide with the area of Lias clay that forms a rough crescent north of Dundry extending from Bishopsworth through Whitchurch, Keynsham, Burnett, Marksbury and Farmborough to Timsbury. To the east of this crescent the Oolites, and to the west the New Red Sandstone, each in a different way produce more remarkable landscape effects. The small area of exposed Coal Measures is glorified by the valley of the Chew.

The Radstock area and upper Cam valley were designed by nature for a higher category than "normal landscape," but their beauty has been so daunted (though not destroyed) that they are conveniently attached to this sub-division.

(*d*) A small patch in the valley of the Yeo to the south of Wrington, the isle of Wedmore, and the neighbourhood of Nailsea, appear also to belong to this division.

§ iii.   *The Areas of remarkable Landscape Value*

A glance at Plate 18 will show that these areas are extensive, in some places forming large continuous tracts, in others isolated areas of limited extent but which in themselves could hardly enter the category of Specially Beautiful Features. It will also be seen that on the western spurs of Mendip this division and that of the Wild Country are closely interrelated.

Seven areas may be stated to belong to this division, and it will perhaps be clearest to begin at the northern extremity of the Region leading to the country round Bath, or what might be termed the landscape of the Oolites; next the parts immediately north and south of Bristol; then the area from Dundry to Mendip, and lastly the coast and neighbourhood of Bristol.

(*a*) In the extreme north-east of the Region is to be found a remarkable patch of country lying between Wickwar and the boundary which may be called the Hillesley area, from a village in its midst. It is in three parts : a portion of the central plain, a piece of Cotswold escarpment and the plateau above; a sense of remoteness pervades all three in spite of the great Road which traverses the plateau. The plain possesses several commons and large woodlands intersected by open drives and streams. The commons have that gypsy air, slightly untidy and reminiscent of the picturesqueness of eighteenth-century landscapes, such as Morland and Gainsborough painted. The Cotswold portion belongs, in conformation, to the Wotton-under-Edge and Dursley country, rather than to the long narrow escarpment which stretches southwards; that it is say it is violently cut up into a series of combes, locally called Bottoms, which run up into the plateau and thence double back again almost to the edge of the escarpment facing the plain. The combes have streams, they are wooded along the contours, and are of extraordinary beauty and quietness—the principal villages, Hillesley, Alderley, Hawkesbury, Tresham, are situated either at the openings to the plain or at the upper end upon the plateau. The latter has a grand air of solitude and austerity; it is traversed by the seven-mile-long plantation of beeches which encloses the western side of Badminton Park. Without great variety of contour, Badminton is one of the noblest English Parks, and there are still vestiges of the Avenues radiating from the house, which were the most ambitious attempt in England to dominate the country by formal Landscape design in the grand manner borrowed from France.

(*b*) South of the Hillesley area occurs one of the most impressive features of this Region, known generally as the Escarpment of the Cotswolds.* It runs from the village of Hawkesbury

---

* This escarpment is called the Cotswold (on some maps it arrogates exclusively that name), but really it is only a southern one-sided continuation southwards from Nailsworth or Wotton-under-Edge—one-sided because after the escarpment there succeeds a fairly level tableland which stretches for miles eastwards and is not typical Cotswold country at all.

PLATE 20.

Photos: N. L. Webber.

Cotswold Escarpment Country, Hawkesbury.

PLATE 21.

Photo: Exelby Reynolds

PHOTOGRAPH OF CONTOUR MODEL.

PLATE 22.

A Wooded Combe (Brockley)

Photos: N. L. Webber.

A Limestone Combe (Burrington)

TWO COMBES.

Parks, of which Ashton is the largest and most beautiful. The Avon Gorge also belongs to this sub-division.

(g) King's Weston Hill and Blaise Castle begin the terrace edge north of the Avon: the Limestone ridge disappears for a mile or two, although the edge still continues past Spaniorum Hill and Over Park, until at Almondsbury it emerges again whence there is a splendid prospect over the lowlying land and Bristol Channel. The main road then follows this narrow Limestone ridge, but where it widens out south of Thornbury, a less marked landscape character supervenes.

§ iv.   *The Wild Country*

Several areas of wild country have been taken with the preceding division, e.g., the hill tops round Bath and Wrington Warren; but there is one part of the Region in which the Wild predominates over the Remarkable, namely, the vast bulk of the Mendip Hills. It is unfortunate that "the Mendips" is not generally used in the singular—for though complex in structure, it is simple in shape except where it becomes somewhat disarticulated in its western extremities towards the sea. The great landscape merit of the Mendip consists in a steep escarpment on north and south with few breaches, leading up to a vast and slightly gloomy tableland, averaging 850 feet high, and only rising above the thousand feet at Blackdown and North Hill, where the oldest rocks, the Old Red Sandstone, thrust themselves above the Mountain Limestone. It is the unbroken shape of the greater part of the Mendip that gives it scale; compared with the grace and variety of the Quantocks, the Mendip is austere and bold, but it is always impressive.

This division in the Limestone caused by the Old Red Sandstone dome continues westwards in a series of narrow northern wooded knobs, Dolebury Warren, Sandford Hill, Banwell Camp, Banwell Hill, and more massive southern lumps, Shute Shelf Hill with its sharp outline, Wavering Down and Crook's Peak, all of which enclose between them the Winscombe Valley. At Bleadon Hill the two ridges of Limestone unite again in a massive hill which narrows down to the shapely prow of Brean Down, thrust out into the deeps of the Bristol Channel.

§ v.   *Features of Particular Beauty or Landscape Importance*

Many of the notable features have already been mentioned in connection with the foregoing divisions of the country: again, several are so well known, indeed of national fame, that a description here is superfluous. A list is therefore all that is to be attempted at this stage of the Landscape Survey, in order to act as a reminder of the wealth of the Region.

(a) *The Cheddar Gorge* is the feature of first importance. Its origin is supposed to be that of a limestone cave whose roof has fallen in, and certainly it is difficult to see that there has ever been a watercourse through it, as has clearly carved the Avon Gorge. The most effective way to see the Gorge is to approach it from above; the bare and almost featureless plateau of the Mendip insensibly folds itself, and before one is aware a valley and next the gorge grows upon one: then it continues its winding course, ever increasing in grandeur and fantastic beauty. On the other hand, the entrance from the village below is impressive. It must be remembered that in the South of England this type of grand scenery is rare. The Cheddar caves are equally remarkable.

(b) *Burrington Combe*, on the north of the Mendip range, is nearly as fine as the Cheddar. It pursues a less tortuous course, having a well marked right-angled bend. It has escaped human attentions more than has Cheddar.

(c) *Goblin Combe* enters the limestone area of Wrington Warren from the west. The entrance is wooded and there is no road through it.

(d) *Brockley Combe*, a mile north of Goblin, also pierces the Limestone and is wooded in the lower part: there are sharp turns in the road; beyond the woods is the entrance to the wild country of Wrington Warren.

(*e*) *Bourton Combe*, near Flax Bourton, is in the Red Sandstone. It is shorter than the others and thickly wooded.

(*f*) *Avon Gorge*, *Leigh Woods* and *Durdham Downs*. These three contrasting features, the precipitous gorge, the wooded south bank, and the open downs on the north, are natural features practically incorporated in an urban landscape. It is not necessary to enlarge upon the surpassing magnificence of the Gorge as the water approach to a great city. Like the Limpley Stoke Valley it swallows up and dominates human additions; but human activities in the form of quarryings might well lessen its grandeur.

(*g*) *Shirehampton Park*, *King's Weston Hill* and *Blaise Castle* form an attractive group of features in this division; at Blaise Castle the Limestone gorge and woods are magnificent.

(*h*) *Dundry Hill* has already been fully described: the top is 3½ miles long, with the tower-crowned village at the east end and a camp at the west.

(*i*) *Wick Rocks* have been more quarried and defaced than any of the foregoing features, but they are still remarkable, the more so because of their unexpectedness. The River Boyd which has cut these rocks through a boss of Limestone is tame above it and not remarkable below, in spite of the name, "Golden Valley": it is like a man whose humdrum life flames out for a brief instant into a passionate experience, to resume tamely for the rest of his existence. Such are the sudden unexpected beauties of a Region rich in geological formation.

(*j*) The *Bath country* features. These have been described round Bath and must not be recapitulated, but their bare names may be given: St. Catherine's Valley, Solsbury Hill, Lansdown above North Stoke, Limpley Stoke Valley and others.

(*k*) The *Valley of the Chew* particularly from Publow to Keynsham.

(*l*) The *Valley of the Cam* from Midford to Combe Hay.

(*m*) The *Valley of the Frome*, from Stapleton Park, by Oldbury Court, to Frenchay.

(*n*) *Brean Down* has already been several times mentioned: it is a bird sanctuary; it rises to 320 feet.

(*o*) *Middle Hope* is nearly as wild as Brean, of more varied contour, but not so lofty.

(*p*) There are also several private Parks which enclose and have enhanced natural features, such as *Dodington* and *Dyrham* on the Cotswold escarpment; *Ashton Park* and *Badminton* are examples of highly landscaped pieces of country.

SECTION 3. THE COUNTRY TOWNS AND VILLAGES

A. Country Towns

§ i. *Introductory*

It is not quite easy to say what constitutes a Country Town—what for example distinguishes it from a Municipal Borough on the one hand and from a Village on the other. Some places may resent being placed in this category, but the chief qualification would appear to be that they take their positions as local capitals in the countryside: this is confessedly not a clear means of definition, but the following are the Country Towns, so called, in this Region:—

> Keynsham.
> Chipping Sodbury.
> Thornbury.
> Marshfield.
> Wickwar.
> Axbridge.
> Wedmore.

PLATE 23.

Chipping Sodbury.

Photo: N. L. Webber.

Marshfield.

Photo: N. L. Webber.

Keynsham.

Photo: N. L. Webber.

Thornbury.

COUNTRY TOWNS.

Face page 53.

§ ii. *Keynsham*

Keynsham is a somewhat square-planned Town situated on either side of the River Chew before its junction with the Avon. The main road from Bristol to Bath enters on a sweep by the Church, which is well placed, and then again leaves the direct line of the main street to cross the Chew. The road across the Avon diverges at the Church, it is also the station approach. The main streets are fairly wide and there does not seem any reason for planning a bye-pass. The road to the south, through Burnett and Marksbury, runs parallel with the Chew Valley, which before entering Keynsham is extremely attractive. Building is occurring on the outskirts and an immediate plan is required (see Plates 23 and 38).

§ iii. *Chipping Sodbury*

Chipping Sodbury is a fine old Market and Coaching-day Town on the old route from London to Old Passage. It possesses the typical plan of a street widened sufficiently to form a market place or forum: the sense of enclosure is given by the right-angled fork of the road at the east end of the place and by a narrowing down at the west end. This type of plan might have been invented specially for motor traffic: a sharp check is given to speed on entering the town; perhaps the same problem had already arisen in the days of the stage-coach. An estate road on the south has been used as a bye-pass; it is not, however, suitable for through traffic, although part of it could be incorporated into a modern bye-pass route. The station is some distance away on the road to Old Sodbury. The River Frome passes along the northern side of the town and almost immediately begin large tracts of public common and several disused quarries (see Plates 23 and 40).

§ iv. *Thornbury*

Thornbury has also the typical plan of the widened high street with the forking roads at the north end: here, however, the left-hand road branches off diagonally, forming a triangular Place. The right-hand road, leading to Gloucester, is somewhat narrow.

There is a second street parallel with the main high street, and the terminal railway station faces the main road as the latter enters the town from the south (see Plates 23 and 41).

§ v. *Marshfield*

Marshfield is an austere upland town on the 600-foot contour. It lies along the Bristol to Chippenham (and London) road and it has the typical right-angled bend in it where the northern road branches off to Tormarton. The High Street does not widen out for so great a length as in Chipping Sodbury. The Church stands at the head of the High Street, but set back behind the houses. The appearance of Marshfield in the landscape is very attractive: its grey colour harmonises with the Cotswolds and its compact though elongated form suggests the sense of enclosure of a town (see Plates 23 and 41).

§ vi. *Wickwar*

At Wickwar the widening of the High Street is effected by a similar device at either end (in contrast to the right-angle turn at one end as at Chipping Sodbury, Marshfield and Thornbury): here the approach road from each direction takes a slight curve before entering the straight and wider High Street; not perhaps quite so effective a check on speed—but still clearly indicating the point where the Town proper begins.

Beyond the northern end of the High Street the road branches, the eastern arm (to Wotton-under-Edge) passing along a pleasant valley parallel with the line, which is partly in a tunnel. Beyond the line on the high ground stands the Church, well placed and approached by an avenue. The station is on this road, about half a mile from the centre of the High Street. Near the station is a disused brewery, now making cider.

This loose northern part of the town with its varied levels and trees possesses considerable charm; there is also a little suburb called West-end.

§ vii. *Axbridge and Cheddar*

Axbridge possesses a truly remarkable situation, under the wild trackless slope of the Shute Shelve Hill; it fills the terrace between the 100- and 50-foot contours, below which begins the marsh. The railway just manages to creep between the town and the hill side. The plan is quite different to those of the other towns that have been examined: the main street, which is curved and very narrow, suddenly enters a central square dominated by the Church, set high, somewhat back, in one corner (see Plate 25). This is one of the finest interior town views in the Region.

Axbridge, compact and urban, is in direct contrast to its neighbour Cheddar, which is a sort of unplanned straggling garden village of large extent, creating nevertheless a pleasant impression.

It lies chiefly between the 100-foot and 50-foot contours near the mouth of the Gorge, up which part of it creeps. The G.W. line skirts it on the marsh-ward side. The main road from Axbridge to Wells passes with many turns through the village. The greater part of the place is modern.

§ viii. *Wedmore*

Wedmore's situation is tame compared with that of Axbridge, but it is one of considerable attraction, in an indentation of the outline of the island, a slight rising ground in the prevailing marsh. The entrance roads follow naturally the curves of this indentation, the northern from Cheddar, the southern from Theale (and Wells); the western road (to Blackford and Mark) follows a slight depression: all seems inevitable and right. The town itself is squarely planned and the centre is dominated by the superb Church (see Plates 25 and 40).

B. The Villages

§ i. *A Survey*

There are some one hundred and forty villages and about the same number of hamlets in this Region, each of which has its characteristic form, its special feature and its relation to the future of the Region. A complete Village Survey would be a valuable piece of work and should contain among other things records of the following :—

Physical Features.—Levels and contours; geological formation; rainfall.

Buildings.—The Parish Church, description including Parish Area; other buildings, their number and use, age and condition, architectural character and materials.

Population.—Numbers, distribution of sexes, occupations, vital statistics.

Planning.—Notes on historic evolution of the village: its recent growth; the road plan.

Traffic.—Relation of village to main road; traffic through the village; dangerous spots; service of buses; railway connection.

Public Services.—Water; drainage; electricity; refuse disposal.

Historic.—Events or persons connected with the village; antiquities and objects of interest in the village and immediate neighbourhood.

Open Spaces.—Public open spaces, school recreation grounds, private sports grounds, actual areas available for sports for different age-groups of the population; nature of tenure.

Cultivation.—Area under cultivation in allotments, area of permanent allotments; nature of tenure of temporary allotments; nature of soil and produce; farming in the parish.

Natural History.—Flowers, birds, mammals, insects.

Disfigurement.—(Classified under headings of Chapter VIII.)

This Survey would be illustrated by photographs, plans and, if necessary, models. It would be kept in some accessible place in the village and a duplicate sent to some central spot for comparison with that of other villages.

In the Fourth Part of this Report it is suggested that this detailed study of the villages might be undertaken under the guidance of the Council for the Preservation of Rural England, acting through its local representative.

PLATE 24.

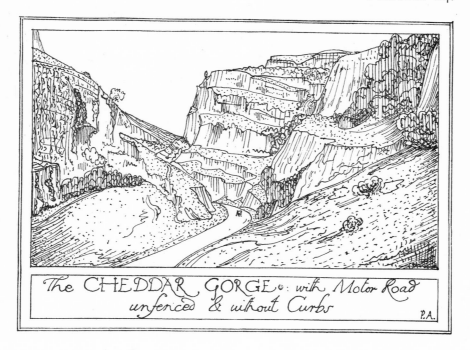

The CHEDDAR GORGE: with Motor Road
unfenced & without Curbs
P.A.

Entrance to CHEDDAR GORGE: colour-
washed cottages of simple form in harmony
with green bank of Foliage & the towering
mass of silver-grey Limestone

It is evident that so complete a study of village conditions is not possible within the scope of this Report, which must content itself with a list of villages and some notes on a few of them which attract attention for one reason or another. Several again will appear in later parts of the Report in connection with proposals which are likely to affect them.

§ ii. *List of Villages and Hamlets*

The dividing line between a village and a hamlet is not always easy to define; generally speaking, a community which has a church, inn, post office and *also* some shops is deemed to be a village, but a collection of houses and cottages without shops, even if it is sheltering under the wing of a parish church, is a hamlet. There are of course other smaller hamlets which would appear in a more detailed survey.

Included in the list are certain villages which have become suburbs of the larger towns: these have only been given a village status where they appear to have preserved their entity. In a few years' time perhaps some of them will have become completely absorbed.

VILLAGES AND HAMLETS

Abbot's Leigh	Churchill	Frampton Cotterell (with Coalpit Heath)	Mark
Abson	Clandown		Marksbury
Acton Turville	Clapton-in-Gordano	Frenchay	Midford
Alderley	Claverham	Freshford	Monkton Combe
Almondsbury	Claverton	Hallatrow	Nailsea
Alveston	Cleeve	Hallen	Nempnett
Aust	Clewer	Hambrook	Newton St. Loe
Backwell	Clutton	Hanham	North Stoke
Badgeworth	Cocklake	Harptree, East and West	Northwick
Badminton	Codrington	Hawkesbury	Norton Malreward
Banwell	Cold Ashton	Hawkesbury Upton	Oldland
Barrow Gurney	Combe Down	Henbury	Old Passage
Barton	Combe Hay	High Littleton	Old Sodbury
Bathford	Compton Bishop	Hillesley	Olveston
Beach	Compton Dando	Hinton	Patchway
Berrow	Compton Greenfield	Hinton Charterhouse	Paulton
Bishop Sutton	Compton Martin	Hinton Blewett	Peasedown St. John
Bishopsworth	Congresbury	Horton	Pensford
Bitton	Conham	Hutton	Pill
Blackford	Corston	Ingst	Portbury
Blagdon	Cross	Iron Acton	Priston
Bleadon	Dodington	Itchington	Publow
Brean	Downend	Kelston	Pucklechurch
Brent Knoll	Doynton	Kenn	Puxton
Brentry	Dundry	Kewstoke	Pye Corner and White's Hill
Bridgeyate	Dunkerton	Kingston Seymour	
Brockley	Dyrham	Langford	Queen Charlton
Burnett	East Brent	Langridge	Radford
Burrington	East Dundry	Latteridge	Rangeworthy
Butcombe	Easter Compton	Lawrence Weston	Redhill
Camerton	Easton-in-Gordano	Little Sodbury	Redwick
Carlingcott	Edithmead	Littleton (Glos.)	Ridgeway
Chapel Allerton	Elberton	Litton	Rooksbridge
Charlcombe	English Combe	Locking	Saltford
Charlton	Engine Common	Long Ashton	Sand
Cheddar	Farleigh	Longwell Green	Sandford
Chelvey	Farmborough	Lower Failand	Shipham
Chelwood	Farrington Gurney	Lower Weare	Shirehampton
Chew Magna	Felton	Loxton	Shortwood
Chew Stoke	Filton	Lulsgate	Shoscombe
Chilcompton	Flax Bourton	Lympsham	Sidcot
Christon		Mangotsfield	Siston

VILLAGES AND HAMLETS—*continued*

South Stoke	Tickenham	Watley's End	Winscombe
Stanton Drew	Timsbury	Weare	Winterbourne
Stanton Prior	Tockington	Wellow	Woodborough (near
Stapleton	Tormarton	Westbury	Winscombe)
St. Catherine	Tresham	Westerleigh	Woolley
Stoke Gifford	Tytherington	Weston-in-Gordano	Worle
Ston Easton	Ubley	West Town	Wraxall
Stoughton	Uphill	Whitchurch	Wrington
Stowey	Upton Cheney	Wick	Yate
Swainswick	Walton-in-Gordano	Wick St. Lawrence	Yatton
Temple Cloud	Wapley	Willsbridge	
Theale	Warmley	Winford	

§ iii.   *Notes on certain Villages and Hamlets*

Mark.   Near Wedmore, a roadside village of open character slightly raised above the marsh.   There is a fine church set back from the road, taking the centre of the village.   There are scattered offshoots, and on the Causeway is ribbon growth strung along the road to the west.

Blackford.   Near Wedmore, a somewhat squared village situated comfortably off the main road on the edge of Wedmore island.   The church is an octagonal building built 1823.

Compton Bishop.   An isolated hamlet in a beautiful cul-de-sac situation well back from the through road in a combe leading up to Crook Peak; the church is well placed on the hillside at the upper end.

Brent Knoll and East Brent.   Practically continuous villages of remarkable form, following the pear-shaped road which skirts the base of Brent Knoll.   The Bristol–Bridgwater road skirts the eastern side of the Knoll, but the villages are chiefly situated on the western loop and so avoid through traffic.

Lympsham.   An irregular marsh village of considerable charm: cottages of modern Gothic design.   The church (Perpendicular Tower) is encircled by fine elms.

Uphill.   A well-marked village becoming absorbed by Weston-super-Mare. The ruined church is situated on the westernmost spur of Mendip, overlooking the mouth of the Axe.   The main road from Bridgwater passes through part of the village and through the woods of Uphill Manor which enclose it on the north.   The G.W. main line is in a deep cutting on the east.

Hutton and Banwell.   Growing villages situated on the road that follows the northern foot of Mendip.   At Banwell several minor roads meet and there is a breach in the escarpment.

Sandford.   A straggling village on two through routes : the road along the northern foot of Mendip and the road between Banwell Camp and Sandford Hill to Winscombe, parallel with the Yatton–Wells Railway (station).   The village is chiefly dependent upon the quarries.

Winscombe.   A large straggling village combining with Woodborough, the G.W. Railway (station) passing through it.   The main road (Bristol–Bridgwater) passes a quarter of a mile to the east.   Winscombe is a growing place and a shopping centre in urgent need of planning.   It is pleasantly situated in a sheltered valley surrounded by spurs of Mendip.   The older part of the village, to the south, on the Mendip slope, is dominated by the fine church tower.

Shipham.   A pleasant but not remarkable village of buff-coloured cottages round a small green, on the 500-foot contour of the west slope of the main mass of Mendip.   The limeworks near by scatters white dust far and wide (see Plate 26).

East and West Harptree.   Villages under the northern escarpment of Mendip; West Harptree, well placed at the junction of six roads : East Harptree, square planned, on lines that appear too large for its needs.   Richmont Castle (remains) stands in a wooded combe between the two villages.

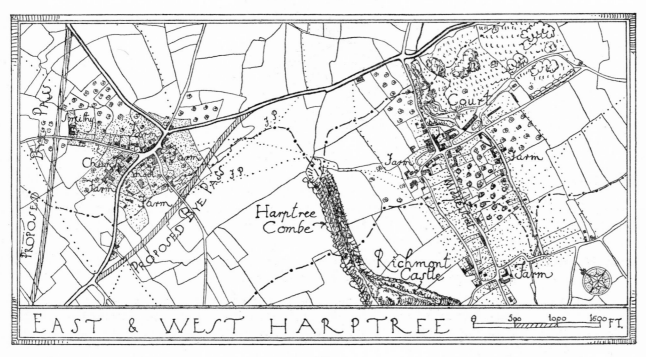

EAST & WEST HARPTREE

Blagdon.   A scattered village covering a large area and growing. It is climbing up the northern slopes towards the plateau of Mendip and overlooks the Yeo Reservoir.   The situation is extremely beautiful.   The contours of the country surrounding the lake are softened and the lake itself (though artificial) appears to focus the irregular lines. The approach from the west is along a road that passes through sweeping woods and glades, following the contours.   The station is the terminus of the branch from Congresbury.

Bishop Sutton.   A straggling village under the brow of Burledge Hill. There is a village colliery near by.

Walton-in-Gordano.   A neat pleasant village on the Portishead–Clevedon road, facing the Gordano moor or marsh. The village also climbs up a combe in the hill behind with good grouping of cottages.

Kingston Seymour.   One of the most attractive of the Marsh villages, quiet, remote and Dutch in feeling. It is somewhat scattered round the head of a branch off the Clevedon–Yatton road.   The church is well placed within a group of trees.

Yatton.   A ribbon village one mile in length with its toes in the marsh and its head towards Cadbury Camp.   The station is on the main line and junction for Wells and Clevedon.   It has been selected as the site for the County Secondary School.

Congresbury.   A developing village of T-shaped plan situated on a right-angled bend of the Bristol–Weston road, just beyond the bridge over the Yeo; the lesser road of the T leads towards Langford.   Congresbury straggles three-quarters of a mile along it.   There are the remains of a cross; the church has a west tower surmounted by a spire (unusual in Somerset).   There is a station (G.W.R.).

Wrington.   One of the finest villages in the Region in a splendid situation in the Yeo Valley, backed by the woods and combes of Wrington Hill.   The village is large and compact and planned on a radiation of four roads.   Several groups of Georgian houses give the village an urban appearance.   The church and its setting are very fine, and the Tower one of the noblest in Somerset (see Plate 25).

Flax Bourton.   Chiefly of ribbon form, one of several on the Bristol–Weston road.   Behind the village is the wooded Bourton Combe.

Long Ashton.   The best example of an old ribbon formation village, and at the same time distinctly attractive.   Ashton Park entrance forms the termination of the vista in the Bristol direction where the main road turns to the right and a hill road mounts to the left (see page 132).

PLATE 25.

Wedmore.

Wrington.

Axbridge.

Chew Magna.

Photos: N. L. Webber.

TOWNS AND VILLAGES.

Dundry. A remarkably situated village at the top of Dundry Hill near its north-west extremity. It is dominated by its lofty church tower, crowned by a rich parapet. The view from the top is one of the finest in Somerset, and the tower itself is a feature of the landscape seen from Bristol.

Winford. A compact double focus village on a through road from which five other lesser roads radiate. There is a market in this village (see page 129).

Chew Magna. Originally a cross-roads village in the valley at a fork of the River Chew, it has now a somewhat complicated plan. The main street has a raised causeway and the village is attractive and spacious, though some of the commercial buildings are disappointing. Otherwise it is an example of an English village at its best: the church is fine, with lofty tower (see Plate 25).

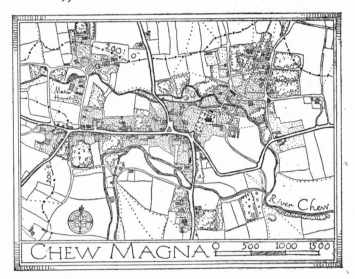

Chew Stoke. Placed on a loop, this village has the through road passing on its eastern side. The church has a tower and small spire: there is a fifteenth-century rectory of great interest.

Stanton Drew. A village on a side road across the Chew from the through route, chiefly remarkable for its prehistoric remains: three stone circles and a large tumulus. There are some good Georgian houses, but the village has probably seen its best days. The church is in a cul-de-sac.

Pensford. An industrial but picturesque village situated on the main road around the bridge over the River Chew. The railway here crosses the valley on a fine viaduct.

Newton St. Loe. A compact, neat and intricately planned village situated a quarter of a mile back from the main road from Keynsham to Bath. The village is closely associated with Newton Park, which contains two lakes following the narrowing valley crossed by the Wansdyke. The church is at the extreme west end of the village at the head of a cul-de-sac.

Stanton Prior. A secluded hamlet half a mile from the main road from Keynsham to Marksbury. Near by are two hills: wooded Stantonbury with camp, and bare Winsbury. The view from Stantonbury is extremely fine and extensive: on the east the Bath country and Bath itself; on the west Dundry and Bristol; to the south-west the long line of Mendip.

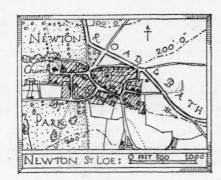

Marksbury.   A village conveniently placed to one side and slightly below the through road. The road passes along somewhat dull country : but Marksbury Vale, a pleasant offshoot from the Chew Valley, runs up to the village.

Farmborough.   Semi-industrial village lying between a V-shaped fork in the main road.

High Littleton.   Greystone ribbon village : roofs chiefly slate.

Timsbury, Priston, Paulton, Hallatrow.   Semi-industrial villages showing signs of growth and at present devoid of systematic planning.

Farrington Gurney.   A cross-roads village, the main route being the Bristol–Wells road.

Peasedown St. John, Dunkerton, Carlingcot, Camerton, Radford.   Unattractive colliery villages and hamlets situated near or in the valley of the Cam. Peasedown St. John is on the Fosseway.

Wellow.   A large village interestingly situated on a cornice road overlooking the valley of the Wellow Brook. A right-angled road mounts the steep hill behind and descends the valley in front under the railway (see Plate 26).

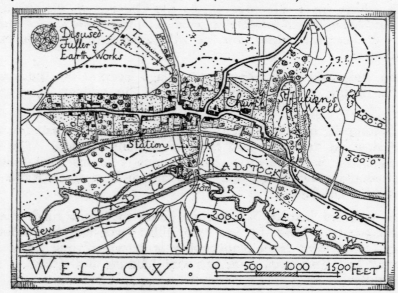

Combe Hay. A closely planned, charming hamlet on irregular ground, enclosed within the valley of the Cam; one of the most attractive places in the Region, remote and unspoilt. The single line from Limpley Stoke to Hallatrow passes near.

Hinton Charterhouse. On the level ground above the Wellow Valley on the road from Bath to Frome via Norton St. Philip. The village is not interesting but there are some ruins reputed to be remains of a Carthusian priory.

Woolley. A hamlet resembling an Apennine hill town on a knoll in the valley opposite the Gloucester road. There is a wooded combe at the back. The hamlet is compact, remote and charming; it has a Renaissance church with a bell turret.

Langridge. A remote roadside hamlet situated on an extremely steep slope on a bye-road from Lansdown Hill. It has a Norman church and manor house.

Cold Ashton. Situated at the head of the combe of St. Catherine's Brook, just off the intersection between the Bath–Gloucester and Bristol–Chippenham roads. The centre point of the village is the Manor House, a typical Cotswold house. Cold Ashton is a model of a well-situated village both in regard to the valley and the cross-roads.

Wick and Abson. Wick and Abson are scattered villages on either side of the valley of Wick Rocks; they are not as attractive as the natural beauty of the Rocks should command.

Pucklechurch. A large village well planned on a quasi-circular road from which five roads radiate. There are two coalpits in the parish, working the Upper Measures. The present village is not very attractive but is of historic interest.

Siston. An isolated small hamlet of great natural beauty with a fine Jacobean Manor House seen from the road, and an interesting church.

Dyrham and Hinton. Hinton is a hillside hamlet on one of the roads that descend the Cotswold escarpment: it has a village green. Dyrham is a square-planned village near by. Between the two is a Camp of eighteen acres. Dyrham House was designed by John Talman, 1698.

Dodington. Under the Cotswold escarpment: a hamlet attached to Dodington Park, one of the most beautiful places and houses in the Region, situated upon the broken ground of the escarpment.

61

Tormarton. A well-placed attractive grey Cotswold village just off the Bath–Gloucester road. It has a complicated irregular plan on a level site.

Old Sodbury. An extremely picturesque village situated just below the bend that sweeps down the Cotswold escarpment from the famous cross-roads. At this point the G.W. tunnel plunges into the Oolites.

Horton. A hillside hamlet dominated by a camp on a spur of the Cotswolds; the fine church and manor house lie half a mile away and form a beautiful group in the charming wooded amphitheatre of the escarpment.

Great Badminton. Badminton is manifestly the village which is an appendage to a great Mansion. It is perfect in upkeep and contains a fine wide street as approach to the House.

Acton Turville. Situated at the point where the road from Chipping Sodbury forks north-east to Malmesbury, south-east to Chippenham. Not an interesting place.

Hawkesbury and Hawkesbury Upton. Two villages in striking contrast: that in the Combe has a wonderful situation, sheltered, remote, wooded. The church is surrounded by a clipped yew hedge cut into square openings (see Plate 20); there are only a vicarage and one or two houses. Hawkesbury Upton, on the plateau, is populous, treeless and cold; it is over a mile from the main road. Near by, well placed on a knoll, is the Beaufort Tower, whence is a superb view of the cornice road, the extraordinary beauty of the surrounding broken country and the plain towards the Severn.

Tresham. A pleasant little village on a V-shaped road, the apex being the head of a combe, rather more than a mile from the Bath–Gloucester road.

Hillesley. A village of complicated irregular plan situated on a wide plateau between the broken country and the plain. It is not very interesting.

Alderley. A beautiful village placed round the foot of a wooded ridge. It contains three large houses and a church in "Strawberry-Hill" Gothic.

Tytherington. A plain village on the cross-roads with a station on the branch line (L.M.S.) to Thornbury. There are remains of a Roman Camp across the line, and limestone quarries to the north.

Alveston. A scattered residential village situated at the junction of the bye-pass road to Gloucester with the road from Bristol to Thornbury.

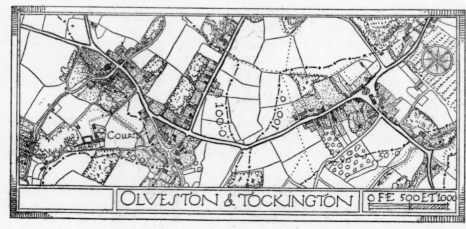

OLVESTON & TOCKINGTON

PLATE 26.

Wellow.

Tockington.

Photos : N. L. Webber.

Olveston.

Shipham.

VILLAGES.

Olveston.   On the former high road from Chipping Sodbury to the Old Passage Ferry.   An attractive village with two foci : at the south end three roads meet on a solid triangle of building ; at the north the church, post office (late Georgian), inn, and rows of cottages form a pleasant group (see Plate 26).

Tockington.   Has a triangular green and central tree ; a junction village, but it retains an atmosphere of quiet charm.   It is on the old coach route (Aust–Sodbury) and the local milestone directs to Sodbury with no mention of Bristol (see Plate 26).

Aust.   A small village a quarter of a mile from Aust Cliff.   The high road to the Old Passage Ferry passes through it.

Almondsbury.   A village of great character partly situated on the brow of the plateau along which the Bristol–Thornbury road passes.   There is an attractive Common, whence are magnificent views over the flats and Severn Estuary.   Upon the Common are two disused quarries which add greatly to its beauty ; an incongruous tower to the cottage hospital unfortunately takes the eye.   Lower Almondsbury and the church (fine lead-covered spire) are on the lower slope toward the marsh.

Severn Beach.   A modern " seaside " eruption of shacks and bungalows on the embankment of the River Severn and the marsh-land behind.

Weare,   Pleasant hamlets in the beautiful undulating country of the Isle of Wedmore ;
Clewer,   they are the largest of several congregated on this rising ground clear of the
Stoughton,   marsh.   A fertile neighbourhood with many orchards and clean yellow
Allerton,   colour-washed houses.
Badgeworth.

SECTION 4.   EXISTING   OPEN   SPACES

§ i.   *Introductory*

The Open Spaces in the Region may conveniently be classified as :—

a. Existing public open spaces, e.g., parks and recreation grounds.

b. Reservations in local town planning schemes for public open space purposes.

c.   (i) Reservations in local town planning schemes as private open spaces.
        (ii) Other private and semi-private lands.

Under the last category are lands, in private ownership, to which the public are allowed access by permission, and lands over which the public have, or are believed to have, partial rights ; they cannot perhaps be termed " existing open space " in the strict legal sense, but it has been thought that this is the most convenient place in which to refer to them.   The lists given below are not exhaustive, some minor items of local character are omitted.

§ ii.   *Public Open Spaces*

These include (*a*) commons and downs ; (*b*) natural parks and nature reserves ; (*c*) formal parks and recreation grounds.

(a) Commons and Downs

Location.	Name.	Controlling Authority.	Approx. Area : Acres.
Bristol	Clifton and Durdham Downs	Bristol Corporation and Society of Merchant Venturers	442
do.	Brandon Hill	Corporation	19½
do.	Redland Green	do.	7½
do.	Horfield Common	do.	33
do.	Penpole Common	do.	10½
do.	Gore's Marsh	do.	5½
do.	Bedminster Down	do.	27½
do.	Novers Common	do.	5
Bath	High Common	Bath Corporation	40
do.	Beacon Hill	—	5
do.	Solsbury Hill Common	Bath R.D.C.	75
do.	Banner Down	do.	80
Mangotsfield	Rodway Hill Common	Mangotsfield Parish Council	35
Frenchay	Common	Chipping Sodbury R.D.C.	32
Hawkesbury	Hawkesbury Common	do.	112
do.	Inglestone Common	do.	135
do.	Assley Common	do.	33
do.	Hareley Common	do	12
Wickwar	The Buthay	do.	7
Hinton	Common	do.	8
Westerleigh	Common	do.	140
Chipping Sodbury	Stub Riding	do.	90
do.	Sodbury Common	do.	300
do.	Colt's Green	do.	11
do.	Smart's Green	do.	1½
do.	Kingrove Common	do.	37
Wapley	Common	do.	18
Winterbourne	White's Hill Common	do.	9
Pensford	Common	Clutton R.D.C.	20
Chew Magna	Knowle Hill	do.	25
Chew Stoke	Breach Hill	do.	24
North Widcombe	Widcombe Common, Bushy Common, Lower Common, Little Common	do.	43
Bishop Sutton	Burledge Common	do.	11
Litton	Shortwood Common	do.	20
Bishopsworth	Highridge Common	Parish Council	20
Whitchurch	Common	Keynsham R.D.C.	5
Almondsbury	Common	Parish Council	10
Charlton	Common	do.	15
Tytherington	Stidcot Plat	—	6
Warmley	Siston Common	Warmley R.D.C.	120

[Continued over

(a) Commons and Downs—continued

Location.	Name.	Controlling Authority.	Approx. Area: Acres.
Bridgeyate	Bridgeyate Common	Chipping Sodbury R.D.C.	16
Siston	Goose Green	Warmley R.D.C.	10
do.	Webb's Heath	do.	25
Hanham Abbotts	Common	Hanham Common Committee	7
Pucklechurch	Lyde Green	Chipping Sodbury R.D.C.	15
Felton	Felton Hill	Parish Council	100
Clevedon	Church Hill	Clevedon U.D.C.	16
do.	Wain's Hill	do.	12
Langford	Havyatt Green	—	27
		Approximate total	2278

(b) Natural Parks and Nature Reserves

Location.	Name.	Character.	Controlled by	Approx. Area: Acres.
Bristol (Henbury)	Blaise Castle	Natural Park and playing fields	Bristol Corporation	190
Bristol (Brislington)	St. Anne's Wood	Natural Park	do.	10½
Bristol	Snuff Mills	do.	do.	8
Bristol (Shirehampton)	Shirehampton Park	Natural Park, now used as Golf Course	National Trust	99
Bristol (Abbot's Leigh)	Leigh Woods	Woodland	do.	127
Cheddar	Part of the Gorge	Rocky Cliff	do.	100
Portishead	Battery Point	Downland	Portishead U.D.C.	5
Clevedon	Salthouse Woods	Woodland	Clevedon U.D.C.	3¼
Portishead (North Weston)	Redcliff Bay	Foreshore and Cliff	Redcliff Bay Estate	15
			Approximate total	557¾

(c) Formal Parks and Recreation Grounds

Location.	Name.	Character.	Controlled by	Approx. Area: Acres.
Bristol	Ashton Park	Formal Park and playing field	Bristol Corporation	25½
do.	Victoria Park	do.	do.	51½
do.	St. Andrew's Park	Formal Park	do.	11
do.	Perrett Park	do.	do.	10
do.	St. George's Park	Formal Park and playing field	do.	38

[*Continued over*

(c) Formal Parks and Recreation Grounds—continued

Location	Name.	Character.	Controlled by	Approx. Area : Acres.
Bristol	Eastville Park	Park and playing field	Bristol Corporation	71
do.	Canford Park	Formal Park	do.	10
Portishead	Foreshore Park	do.	do.	35
do.	East Woods	Woodland	do.	19
Bath	Royal Victoria Park and Lower Common	Park, Botanic Gardens, and Recreation Ground	Bath Corporation	
			do.	70
do.	Institution Gardens	Formal Park	do.	4
do.	Alexandra Park	do.	do.	45
do.	Henrietta Park	do.	do.	7
do.	Sydney Gardens	do.	do.	10
do.	Hedgemead Park	Formal Park	do.	4
do.	Odd Down	Playing Fields	do.	39
do.	Larkhall	Recreation Ground	do.	6
do.	Picnic Park	Woodland Park	do.	$9\frac{1}{2}$
do.	Twerton Round Hill	Recreation Ground	do.	9
do.	Moorfield's Ground	Children's Playground	do.	3
Weston-s-Mare	Clarence Park	Formal Park	Weston U.D.C.	18
do.	Esplanade	do.	do.	24
do.	Ashcombe Park	do.	do.	40
do.	Grove Park	do.	do.	8
do.	Winter Gardens	do.	do.	4
Midsomer N'rton	North Road Field	Recreation Ground	Local Committee	3
do.	Westfield	do.	do.	2
do.	Rackvernal	do.	Mids'mer N't'n U.D.C.	5
Radstock	Southfield	Recreation Ground	Radstock U.D.C.	5
do.	Westhill Gardens	do.	do.	1
do.	Wells Road	do.	Local Committee	6
do.	Roundhill	do.	do.	$6\frac{1}{2}$
Clevedon	Esplanade	Sea Front	Clevedon U.D.C.	12
do.	Salthouse Fields	Recreation Ground	do.	7
do.	Herbert Gardens	Park	do.	4
do.	Alexandra Park	do.	do.	2
Cheddar	—	Recreation Ground	Cheddar Parish Council	$1\frac{1}{2}$
Staple Hill	Page Park	Park	Mangotsfield U.D.C.	20
Pill	Victoria Park	do.	Easton Parish Council	1
Long Ashton	Ashton Playing Field	Playing Field	Ashton Court Estate	5
Backwell	Farleigh Playing Field	do.	Local Committee	5
do.	West Town Playing Field	do.	do.	5
			Approximate total	$662\frac{1}{2}$

§ iii. *Public Reservations in Local Town Planning Schemes*

These comprise lands earmarked under Town Planning powers for acquisition by the Local Authority for Open Space purposes, including allotments and cemeteries. Town Planning in the Region is only in its infancy, and these lands are at present in private ownership, but as they cannot be built upon and will eventually be acquired by the Local Authority and dedicated to public use, they can conveniently be referred to here. The total acreage proposed to be reserved in this manner in the Bristol No. 1 and 2 schemes is 3430; many of them are of purely local character; some of the more important in the Regional sense are listed below :—

Local Authority.	Location of Reservation.	Area : Acres.	Purpose for which Reserved.	Remarks.
Bristol	Westbury	59	Golf Course	Henbury Hill Golf Course
do.	Filton	83	do.	Filton Golf Course
Bristol and Chipping Sodbury	Stapleton, Purdown, and Stoke Park	310	Downs, Park, and playing fields	Now Mental Home
Bristol	Avon Valley (*Shirehampton to Sneyd Park*)	47	Riverside Reserve	River Avon
do.	Trym Valley (*Sea Mills to Combe Dingle*)	38	Riverside Reserve	River Trym
Bristol and Warmley	Avon Valley (*Conham to Keynsham*)	250	Riverside Reserve and playing fields	River Avon
Bristol, Warmley, and Chipping Sodbury	Frome Valley (*Stapleton to Moorend*)	277	do.	River Frome
Chipping Sodbury and Warmley	Winterbourne	165	Riverside Reserve, Park, and Ancient Camp	River Frome, Bury Hill Camp, etc. (*The ancient camp is now being quarried*)
Chipping Sodbury	Winterbourne	112	Riverside Reserve	Bradley Brook
Bristol	Bishopston	15	Sports Ground	The old County Ground
Chipping Sodbury	Wick Rocks	88	Natural Park and Riverside Reserve	River Boyd, *now being quarried*
Chipping Sodbury and Warmley	Golden Valley	182	Riverside Reserve	River Boyd
Warmley	Willsbridge and Oldland	112	do.	Warmley Brook
Warmley and Kingswood	Warmley	49	Extension of Siston Common	
Weston-super-Mare	Worlebury Hill and Cliffs	50	Natural Park and woodlands	Contains Early British Camp

§ iv. *Private Open Spaces*

These fall under two headings :—

(*a*) Land reserved under Town Planning Schemes as *private* open spaces; this kind of reservation is made by agreement with the landowner, who retains possession and agrees (without claiming compensation) not to develop the land for building purposes.

(*b*) Lands over which the public are believed to have partial rights, and lands to which the public are allowed access by permission of the landowner.

(*a*) *Private Open Spaces in Town Planning Schemes*

Local Authority.	Location.	Area : Acres.	Purpose for which Reserved.	Owner.
Bristol	Westbury-on-Trym	26	Nature Reserve and Bird Sanctuary	S. H. Badock, Esq.
do.	Kings Weston	84	Kings Weston House and Park	Dr. Napier Miles
Weston-super-Mare	Ashcombe Park	38	Private Open Space	—
do.	By Sanatorium	46	Golf Course	—

(*b*) *Lands over which the public has partial rights and lands open to the public by permission.*

Riverside (R. *Avon*), Keynsham
Stantonbury Hill and Camp
Kingsweston Hill, Bristol
Purdown, Bristol
Worlebury Hill, Weston
Woodspring Hill, Sand Bay
Dial Hill, Clevedon
Castle Hill, Clevedon
Back Hill, Clevedon
Court Hill, Clevedon
Cadbury Camp, near Tickenham
Cadbury Hill and Camp, near Congresbury
Cleeve Hill and Goblin Combe
Wrington Warren
Brockley Combe
Barrow Gurney Hill and Common
Backwell Hill
Ashton Court
Dundry Down and Maes Knoll
Lansdown, Bath
Bathampton Down

West Littleton Down, Tormarton
Leigh Woods (*extra to the National Trust property*)
Burrington Combe
Dolebury Camp
Rowberrow Warren
Axbridge Hill
Fry's Hill, Axbridge
Callow Hill, Shipham
Wavering Down
Shute Shelf Hill
Crook Peak
Cheddar Gorge
Banwell Hill
Bleadon Hill
Roundhouse Hill and the Knoll, Shipham
Brean Down (*Bird Sanctuary*)
Nailsea Golf Course
Failand Golf Course
Long Ashton Golf Course
Tytherington Hill

PLATE 27.

Kelston Hill, Bath, from Newton St. Loe.

Photos: N. L Webber

Mendip from Brean Down.

LANDSCAPE STUDIES.

CHAPTER VIII. DISFIGUREMENT

SECTION 1. THE LEGACY OF THE INDUSTRIAL AGE AND MODERN DEFACEMENT

NO Region which has reacted to the prosperity of the industrial age during the nineteenth century but must show some scars as a result : and no tract of equal size, unless it be of remote mountain fastness, can be pointed to as having escaped the penetrating defacement of modern enterprise. The old world up to the close of the eighteenth century aimed indeed at changing the face of nature—in fact it seemed hardly to appreciate that nature existed or was worth looking at : but what it substituted was always instinctively or intentionally congruous to surroundings or dominated by an æsthetic motive.

The industrial age and modern times have lost this instinct and have been ready to sacrifice this intention to immediate or apparent economic needs. But this Region has not suffered as severely as have other parts of our country : nineteenth-century industrialism has not been anywhere so intense as it has in parts of the North of England : the coalfields of Bristol and Radstock are not only on a smaller scale than those of South Wales, but the physical conformation of the ground has not induced so crowded a huddle of pit and houses ; some flavour of the old country town or village persists in such places as Midsomer Norton and Warmley : no one would dream of comparing them to the Rhondda Valley or Ebbw Vale. Bristol itself, although it has become a great modern city, has kept much of its former beauty : the Avon Gorge still forms the commercial approach by water : its latest change, the addition of Portway, has not impaired its romantic grandeur. The city itself has not lost its numerous churches and old commercial buildings, and its dock still brings the mystery of the sea into its modern traffic centre. There are large parts, too, of the country in this Region which are unspoilt, owing in most cases to the good fortune of difficult communications.

But while there is much already done in the existing towns that does not come up to the requisite standard of fitness, there are signs of more changes occurring in the country owing to the rapidity of modern transport and means of development.

SECTION 2. THE CHARM OF THE COUNTRYSIDE

It is well therefore to keep before our minds, as a standard, the essential qualities of the countryside, unimpaired by modern alterations : Dr. Vaughan Cornish has thus attempted to define its charm :—

> "The Arcadian charm of rural England depends largely on the fact that form and
> "movement and colour are a decorative scheme which harmonises with the quiet con-
> "tinuity of the least changing of industrial pursuits. Agricultural England is a country
> "of gentle undulations where rivers flow quietly in winding curves, a land well timbered
> "by deciduous trees of rounded form, of fields divided by a bushy fence, all in a climate
> "of soft skies, where the song of birds is heard throughout the year. And we still have

" a wealth of architecture of cob and thatch, of mellow brick and mossy tile, of grey church
" towers, and Georgian mansions calmly classic, all in harmony with the natural scene.
" If this quietude of the senses be broken, as by buildings of harsh form or stirring colour,
" or by clatter of mechanical noise, there is a loss of happiness out of all proportion to
" the material discomfort, for the mind begins to pay attention to imperfections instead
" of dwelling upon an ideal, and we no longer live in Arcadia."

It is true that we no longer live in Arcady : nor can we perpetuate these conditions in their
entirety. We are using the country more than we have ever done before ; it is now possible
to live in it and yet to work in a town every day : or to retire to even remoter spots at week-
ends : or to visit it from the town by means of day or afternoon excursions. It is necessary
to ascertain whether it is possible to provide for this greater use and yet for the country not
to become decountrified—in a word, how much of modern additions it is possible to absorb
without breaking the harmony of the natural scene, by making the utmost use of contours,
tree screens, grouping, congruous colour and suitable shapes.

Wordsworth, in his thoughtful and practical suggestions for buildings in the Lake District
where nature is in sublime mood, suggests that man should be content with a humble rôle :—

" The principle that ought to determine the position, apparent size and architecture
" of a house, viz. : that it should be so constructed and (if large) so much of it hidden
" as would admit of its being gently incorporated into the scenery of nature—should also
" determine its colour."*

In a Region where, with the exception of Mendip, the landscape is beautiful rather than
sublime, architecture may be allowed in places to dominate the scene, as it does in the church
tower of Dundry.

SECTION 3. CLASSIFICATION OF DISCORDANCIES

To lay down the principles of Rural Planning or Landscape Development is outside the
scope of this Report : but the humbler and easier task of classifying discordancies and cataloguing
disfigurements may serve to point the way, though negatively, in a more positive direction.

Broadly speaking, it is possible to classify the discordancies into four main types ; not indeed
that they can be considered in water-tight compartments, but that it is useful to group them
into well-marked types, allowing for shading off from one type to another. The following
is this tentative fourfold classification :—

(*a*) Things which may be necessary or desirable to have in the country, but which are discordant because they are badly done ;

(*b*) Things which are good or beautiful in themselves, but which offend because they are
in the wrong place ;

(*c*) Discordancies which are caused by the newness or rawness of the objects but whose
offence is of a temporary character ;

(*d*) Unwarrantable intrusions which under no circumstances should be allowed and which
are incapable of being incorporated into the landscape scene.

One or two clear-cut illustrations of these types may be given. Of the first, the simplest
example is that of a bad house, of poor design and ugly material, standing in the midst of the

---

* Wordsworth : *Scenery of the Lakes of England* (Third Section).

PLATE 28.

N. L. Webber.

Dundry, from Bristol.

Aerofilms Ltd.

The Severn Plain.

LANDSCAPE STUDIES.

seemly countryside ; it may be possible by dint of tree planting in the grounds and creepers on the walls to make it approximate towards a temporary disfigurement ; but when the very bones of a creature are ugly the covering of flesh can never veil it, or if the body is deformed or grossly repulsive, it cannot be hidden by the most skilful tailoring. The usual petrol station is also a glaring example of this first type.

The second type is much less common than the first and there are some people who say that a beautiful thing can never be out of place. But there are scenes whose characteristic is their remoteness from human handiwork ; it is difficult, for instance, to imagine a building, though the work of an inspired architect, which one would not wish away from the Cheddar Gorge ; but the roadway (equally a piece of human handiwork) has there become happily incorporated into the scene. Misplaced tree planting comes also under this type : there are single conifers or plantations of them which can be beautiful in form and colour, but there are certainly scenes where they are entirely out of place.

The third type, the temporary disfigurement, frequently causes the loudest complaints : everyone has an instinctive and easily comprehensible dislike for sudden change in a landscape which has matured during centuries ; and the change, of course, is at first seen with all the rawness of a gaping wound. A new road is the most usual form of this type : and even more strikingly the widening of an old one and the possible consequent demolishment of hedgerows and trees. It is necessary to be on one's guard before classifying a new road as a permanent disfigurement : one writer (Mr. H. J. Massingham), for example, says :—

"The new motor road, inhuman, unnatural and altogether relentless, drives like a ram
"through the countryside with as much regard for its forms and design as a red-hot poker
"drawn over a carpet."

But one might hazard that the same person may be found to be an ardent admirer of the Roman roads which like the Fosseway must have ploughed just as crudely across this Region. Even railways, that require embanking and cutting in a way that roads do not, have in many places become only a slight disfigurement : no one makes the proviso that the Limpley Stoke Valley *would* have been beautiful if it were not for the railway and the road.

But while optimistically pointing out the passing nature of certain discords, there are other outrages which can never cease to offend. The clearest example is the vulgar blatant advertisement standing in the full view of a country scene. It is an unwarrantable intrusion and the only cure for it is total elimination.

SECTION 4. A CATALOGUE OF EXISTING AND POSSIBLE DISFIGUREMENTS

Introductory

For convenience of study, Disfigurement may be catalogued under a number of headings, some of them consisting of the things subject to disfigurement and others of the disfigurement itself which is inflicted upon the countryside. A few examples are given and the way in which the disfigurement may occur is described. A complete and documented survey might well be undertaken (see page 54).

1. Buildings.
2. Roads.
3. Bridges.
4. Footpaths.
5. Rivers and Watercourses.
6. Commons and Open Spaces.

    7. Planting and Uprooting.
    8. Petrol Stations.
    9. Railways.
  10. Quarries and Tips.
  11. Overhead Wires.
  12. Advertisements.
  13. Litter.
  14. Smoke.
  15. Dust.

It will be noted that of these headings the first seven represent, as said above, objects which are subject to disfigurement, and the last five are actual disfigurements which may be applied to some of the objects or may exist by themselves.

§ i. *Buildings*

(*a*) *Houses*. The disfigurements of which houses in common with other buildings are capable are, broadly speaking, three : α, bad design ; β, discordant materials ; and γ, wrong placing. Sometimes all three are found together.

α. Bad design may consist in a wrong shape or fussy and broken outline where repose is required ; or an attempt may be made, as mentioned by Wordsworth, to dominate the view in an ostentatious manner ; or again, the actual proportion of the parts may be unsatisfactory, the shape of windows wrong and features such as doors badly detailed. Contrasting examples may be found within this Region of houses which face each other and are built of the same materials to illustrate the discordant effect of bad design ; and it will be noted that the bad design is more expensive than the good one (see Plate 35, page 107).

β. The fault of the materials may be inherent or may consist in being discordant with their surroundings or they may be discordantly mixed together. Unpainted corrugated iron and pink diagonal asbestos tiles may be classed as inherently wrong : bright red bricks or tiles may be suitable in some places, but are discordant in a Cotswold village ; a mixture of slates and tiles in roof and ridge is unpleasant anywhere. Sham half-timber work, especially when thrust into a gable, is ugly and adds an unnecessary expense. In materials good and harmonious colour is the most important requirement, but texture is also to be studied. A hard-pressed and almost glazed red brick may not be bad in colour, but it is unsympathetic in appearance and does not accord with rural surroundings. Black mortar has always a funereal look.

γ. The chief danger in the placing of houses is the ribbon along the country road frontages. Well-designed buildings of suitable material can destroy a landscape if they are strung out for several miles along a road. The æsthetic fault is of course that the continuous building up of road frontage is an urban feature of growth, but an urban feature is an unwarrantable intrusion in the open country. (The practical drawbacks of the ribbon development are described on p. 132.)

Many of the faults found in houses occur equally in other types of buildings, but these other buildings also have their dangers.

(*b*) *Public Buildings*. These may legitimately be made conspicuous provided due attention is given to the lines of the landscape and its prevailing colour. But large buildings such as hospitals or lunatic asylums which may of necessity be placed in the country should not draw attention to themselves by lofty campaniles or by sites chosen for their conspicuousness.

(*c*) *Commercial Buildings*. These are more usually found in the villages and small towns than in the open country. Banks and Post Offices are to-day generally well designed and frequently add a new distinction to a street ; but the multiple shop is a usual cause of disfigurement. Vulgar stock designs, a sort of trade mark of the firm, are often erected in charming surroundings, or an old building is brutally disfigured with a new shop front or an outrageous facia board. Messrs. W. H. Smith & Son have shown in many places that it is by no

PLATE 29.

Photos: N. L. Webber.

The beginnings of Shack Building.

Face page 72.

means necessary that a modern and efficient shop front should be out of keeping with its surroundings.

(d) *Factories*. Nor need industrial buildings be discordant. Messrs. Crittall's new works upon the Bristol–Bath road are good in design and pleasant in colour ; they do not inflict any injury upon the scenery. The two most likely causes of offence in industrial buildings are α, a general untidiness or disorderliness, due often to lack of forethought when planning the site, new sections being added piecemeal and from hand-to-mouth in a manner that suggests an equal irresoluteness of policy ; β, the familiar symbol of a tall chimney.

Artists have pointed out that a tall chimney should not be more objectionable on the skyline than an obelisk or those plain brick towers of mediæval Italian cities. But it is impossible to dissociate the tall chimney from the concomitant of smoke. Electric power available at the places where factories are to be encouraged will eliminate both the smoke stack and its black accompaniment.

(e) *Huts and Shacks*. The hut or building made of temporary materials is frequently an eyesore : but it must not be thought that a weather-boarded house is necessarily a disfigurement. There is, especially in the south-eastern counties, many a charming little cottage, weather-boarded, white painted, and with red pantile or slate roof. But there are equally many stock pattern designs that are extremely ugly, and there are botched hovels which should be replaced by more permanent and seemly structures. These shacks have in some places on the coast been put up as bathing huts and gradually get used for week-end residence. These things can be controlled under town planning schemes.

Huts and sheds are also added to existing buildings of good design. There are examples of these defacing the cottages of Cheddar.

§ ii. *Roads*

As has already been said, a new road is frequently only a temporary disfigurement : the new route, particularly when it is fenced with concrete posts and wires, has a bald appearance : the width is sometimes insufficient to allow space for tree planting when traffic requirements have been met : advantage is not always taken by the County Councils of their powers to plant trees which can turn a straight dull route into a stately avenue.

Heavy curbs and channels standing too high out of the ground give a hard and mechanical appearance to a country road, though some sort of curb is necessary. Footpaths, which are loudly called for in the interests of pedestrians, have an urban appearance in the open country ; a grass margin on which the walker can step when a motor passes is probably sufficient where there is no roadside building.

But a more subtle form of disfigurement arises from the placing of the new road out of harmony with the contour of the country. Cutting and embanking have sometimes been used to preserve even gradients and obtain straight roads. The avoidance of these errors calls for an appreciation of landscape effects. It may be safely said that provided a road falls naturally into the lie of the land, it will eventually become an unobtrusive feature of the landscape, however raw it looks at the moment ; there must of course be no discordant detail in the design of the road itself. The Black road is a new note of colour in the country scene ; a writer in *The Times* recently was expatiating upon its beauties of colour and sky reflection, especially when wet ; anyhow, tar spraying has one solid advantage to its credit—see § xv below (Dust).

§ iii. *Bridges*

The worst disfigurement that can overtake an old bridge is its destruction. Widening is frequently done injudiciously, an ugly parapet taking the place of the old one. It is pleasant to be able to record that this type of disfigurement has not occurred frequently in the Region ; on the contrary, there are good examples of the preservation of one side of the bridge and the rebuilding of the widened side in such a way as to harmonise with the old work.

An entirely new bridge may be a grievous eyesore if it is badly designed and especially if a simple engineering structure is garnished with adscititious ornament. The Clifton Suspension Bridge is an example of a bridge which fulfils its function without an unnecessary feature; and it is generally agreed that it adds to, rather than detracts from, the beauty of the gorge.

§ iv. *Footpaths*

Like Bridges, the worst that can befall a footpath is its extinction. This happens through owners, and particularly new owners, wishing to add to the value of their property by removing a right-of-way that may disturb privacy or hamper private use. But there is a more subtle danger in the immediate neighbourhood of towns of footpaths being absorbed by the road plan: there is already a right-of-way and the owner or local authority finds it easy to plan a road along it. But the footpath exits from a town become of increasing importance year by year and should form an integral part of the park and playground system. A footpath intended for pedestrians is disfigured by any use that interferes with their freedom to ramble at leisure; but this freedom must not be abused. Another disfigurement of footpaths, viz., their enclosure by high and unclimbable fences, is the direct result of unlicensed rambling over growing crops or through private pleasure grounds. The unfenced path through fields, park or woodlands is the real desire of a country walker.

§ v. *Rivers and Watercourses*

These suffer disfigurement through pollution (which is not often visible except in extreme cases) and through being used as tips: this is fortunately not common in this Region; but the sudden depression of a valley is apt to be regarded as a dumping ground.

§ vi. *Commons and Open Spaces*

These are most frequently disfigured by Litter (§ xiii) and Uprooting (§ vii) and thoughtless unintentional incendiarism. But there is sometimes another danger due to the over-zeal of their public owners: a piece of wild country or parkland, made public property, is often subjected to the Landscape gardener's dangerous art. One of the London commons—a priceless fragment of wild nature—was a few years ago only snatched at the last moment from the hands of a Parks Committee that wished to turn it into a Petit Trianon.* A pond, for example, in a common should be a place where small boys can fish for sticklebacks and frogs and not an ornamental lake whose trim margins are patrolled by a park keeper.

§ vii. *Planting and Uprooting*

It is not often that planting can cause disfigurement, but there are cases where a bare and austere scene has been reduced in scale by serried rows of conifers; and there are examples of the noble simplicity of glades and forest trees being broken by fussy shrubs. But here again it must be remembered that even a piece of judicious and well-landscaped planting may look unpleasant in its early stages; it would, however, form a temporary disfigurement only.

A more prevalent danger is the opposite one of *Uprooting*. This can take many forms from the chopping down of trees for road widening to the pulling up of primrose roots. The former may be sometimes quite unavoidable, but the latter in a thickly populated district cannot be justified. In modest road widenings of our suburbs and villages it is worth trying to save these hedgerow beauties by giving the full width of the road to carriageway and forming the footpaths outside.

---

* It must be remembered that open spaces in the country are under consideration and not parks in a town.

§ viii. *Petrol Stations*

The disfigurement caused by the Petrol Station in the open country or facing the village green is twofold : the pumps and the buildings.

The pumps individually may be workmanlike objects, like pillar boxes ; they are, however, an urban feature by reason of their bright colour.   But their discordance with the country is emphasised when, unlike pillar boxes, several distinct bright colours are set side by side by the firms marketing different brands of petrol.   No country scene or village can absorb satisfactorily these primary contrasts, which become the dominating colour effect of the scene.

The Petrol Station building is sometimes a worse offender than the pumps ; often it is built of corrugated iron and garnished with glaring advertisements which cannot be controlled by the Advertisement Regulation Acts as interpreted by the Home Office.

There are some shocking examples in the Region of the combined offence of pumps, oil tanks, advertisements and sheds.   The pumps should be taken out of the open and incorporated with the building (where they can be ranged with no more offence than necessary sanitary apparatus) within a loggia or verandah under which the car may drive for filling up.   A simple enclosing form and unobtrusive colour can be given to the whole which is no disfigurement from a distance or near at hand.

Bye Laws under the Petroleum, etc., Act have now been drafted, by means of which this disfigurement can be controlled (see Appendix D).

§ ix. *Railways*

In the past Railways have been a main cause of disfigurement of the countryside.   Their gradients have necessitated in many places harsh forms of embankments which cut across the natural lines of the land : cuttings and tunnels, though equally artificial, are of course unnoticed in the general view, e.g., the Sodbury Tunnel, whose line is only apparent from the ventilating shafts.

It does not seem probable that there will be much new railway making in this Region, so that there is perhaps not a great deal to be feared from this source.

§ x. *Quarries and Tips*

Quarries change the face of the landscape and at times are in danger of demolishing salient features.   But it cannot be said that they are always a disfigurement ; and when deserted they can become picturesque additions to the scenery.   In precious landscape features they should be under careful control : for example, one would not like the Clifton Gorge to lose one of its precipitous sides as a result of quarrying ; actually to avoid this disfigurement the quarries might very well have the vertical wall next the river left as a screen to their operations without incurring financial hardship.

Tips of quarry or mining débris are usually a disfigurement, producing the harsh forms objected to by Dr. Vaughan Cornish.   But much can be done to mitigate this if a little landscape design were employed in the tipping.   Some of the most successful parks of the picturesque school* were formed by creating artificial mounds upon a level field ; shaping and planting have produced results of unexpected beauty.

At the same time there are other places where underground stowage or a wide spreading over low lands are the best methods.

Planting of Tips, which has been done in the Radstock coalfield, can mask the harsh outlines : the chief difficulty and cause of delay in getting results is the lack of surface soil.   If the soil upon the ground where a tip is to go were first removed and stored, to be sprinkled later over the surface of the tip, it would (even though it were much thinner) hasten the clothing of the discordant barrenness which is one of the worst aspects of these tips.

---

* E.g., Birkenhead Park, by Sir Joseph Paxton.

§ xi. *Overhead Wires*

Telephone wires and Electric Power cables are unalloyed disfigurements which must to a large extent be submitted to on account of compensating advantages.

The disfigurement can be completely eliminated if wires are put underground: and it is not yet certain that the economic argument of increased expense is really sound; at any rate, in the case of high-tension cables, when the future of flying is considered.

There are several places in this Region where high-tension cables have been, for practical reasons, placed underground. In one case a first-class disfigurement on the southern escarpment of the Mendips was avoided, the cable passing underground through a hanging wood.

The disfigurement of the skyline is often the result of a direct route settled on paper without regard to amenities: this can often be mitigated by slight deviations in the route made at the instance of landowners, local authorities or societies interested in Rural Preservation (see Part IV).

§ xii. *Advertisements*

A sharp distinction must be drawn between advertisements displayed on hoardings in the town where they often form an attractive episode in the urban scene, and their appearance in the country where they are an unwarrantable intrusion. They are sometimes found painted at large across the façade of a building as on the workhouse at Long Ashton: in other cases offensive signs are affixed to shops in charming villages. Action under the Advertisements Regulation Act should be taken by Local Authorities without delay.

§ xiii. *Litter*

This is a temporary disfigurement but unfortunately it can be a very objectionable one. It may be considered under three headings: (*a*) The casual and thoughtless litter which ranges from the empty cigarette packet to the remains of a picnic with carton plates, paper, and broken bottles. (*b*) The refuse heap of a house or village which has a real difficulty in disposing of cans, broken pots, and other unburnable rubbish. (*c*) The rubbish dump made in the country by an urban authority for convenience, and to save the expense of incineration.

The last is the least defensible and most offensive on a large scale. In certain cases trouble is not even taken to destroy the paper, which is blown over acres of fields, to rest at last in the hedge-bottoms; and when the dump is abandoned, the hedges even when they border on a highway or public footpath are littered with scrap metal, old motor cars, tins, enamel kettles and chamber pots. Fortunately the local authorities of this Region have not been so neglectful of their duties, but it is to be regretted that Burrington Combe, one of the choice places of beauty, should be defaced by tin cans, buckets and broken bottles.

§ xiv. *Smoke*

There is no excuse for the smoke nuisance in the country, and happily it is a disfigurement from which the rural parts of the Region are free.

§ xv. *Dust*

The dust nuisance has disappeared from the main roads, owing to modern methods of waterproof road construction and the practice of tar spraying. When one condemns many of the modern disfigurements it must not be forgotten that this freedom from roadside dust is a solid achievement. There is the greater reason now for planting along the road, seeing that the beauty of foliage can be enjoyed. But there are cases of industrial dust causing disfigurement: lime and cement works in some places powder the country over a considerable area, as at Callow Hill, near Shipham.

CHAPTER IX.   PUBLIC SERVICES

SECTION 1.   DRAINAGE

§ I. *Natural Drainage Areas*

PLATE 30 shows the Region divided into areas of natural drainage or "basins" according to the river system described in Chapter I of this Part. On the diagram each stream is shown in blue and each basin is distinguished by a different colour, the basin of the River Avon and its tributaries being co-ordinated under various tints of green. The main (Avon) watershed is shown by a thick purple line and the other watersheds by thinner dotted lines. The Avon basin is by far the most important as it comprises about two-thirds of the Region ; the next in order of importance are the Axe, Yeo and Kenn basins. A study of the drainage areas in relation to contours will show in a general way the amount and rate of fall which occurs ; for example, the River Yeo emerges from the Yeo Reservoir (some ten miles from the sea) at about 100 feet above Ordnance Datum, but the point at which the Axe enters the Region—near Wedmore, twelve miles from its estuary—is not more than twenty-two feet above Ordnance Datum ; moreover, the ground level of the marsh remains about the same during the whole course of the river. It will thus be seen that in some parts of the Region it would be difficult to plan main trunk sewers, and there is insufficient fall in some of the existing watercourses to deal effectively with untreated sewage effluent.

§ ii. *Existing Sewage Schemes*

The diagram shows by red hatching all the areas in the Region which are now sewered—also the discharge points—distinguishing between crude and purified effluents.

Reckoning Bristol as one, it will be seen that there are 54 drainage areas in the Region ; 6 of them—Bristol, Weston, Clevedon, Portishead, Pill and Redwick—discharge crude sewage into tidal waters ; the others make use of inland streams and watercourses. In only 14 of these inland schemes is the effluent purified, and in the remaining 34 cases crude sewage is discharged direct into the watercourse.

The 14 areas having sewage purification plant, with the streams concerned, are :—

Stream.	Town or Village.	Local Authority.
Avon	Bath	Bath City Council
Little Avon	Wickwar	Chipping Sodbury R.D.C.
Frome	Chipping Sodbury and Yate	do.
do.	Harry Stoke	do.
do.	Filton	do.
do.	Winterbourne (part of)	do.
do.	Mangotsfield	Mangotsfield U.D.C.
Warmley Brook	Warmley and Oldland	Warmley R.D.C.

[Continued over

77

Stream.	Town or Village.	Local Authority.
Wellow Brook	Radstock	Radstock U.D.C.
do.	Midsomer Norton	Midsomer Norton U.D.C.
Ashton Brook	Long Ashton	Long Ashton R.D.C.
River Kenn	West Town	do.
River Yeo	Blagdon, Compton Martin and Ubley	Axbridge R.D.C. and Clutton R.D.C.
River Axe	Cheddar	Axbridge R.D.C.

The 34 towns and villages which discharge their sewage direct into inland watercourses, and the streams concerned, are :—

Stream.	Town or Village.	Local Authority.
River Avon	Keynsham	Keynsham R.D.C.
do.	Saltford	do.
do.	Limpley Stoke	Bath R.D.C.
do.	Freshford	do.
River Hen	Henbury	Thornbury R.D.C.
River Boyd	Pucklechurch	Chipping Sodbury R.D.C.
Wellow Brook	Hinton Charterhouse	Bath R.D.C.
do.	Wellow	do.
do.	Stratton-on-the-Fosse	Midsomer Norton U.D.C.
do.	Chilcompton	Clutton R.D.C.
do.	Ston Easton	do.
Cam Brook	Farrington Gurney	do.
do.	Temple Cloud	do.
do.	Clutton	do.
do.	Hallatrow	do.
do.	High Littleton	do.
do.	Timsbury	do.
do.	Peasedown St. John	Bath R.D.C.
do.	Combe Hay	do.
do.	South Stoke	do.
Conygre Brook	Farmborough	Clutton R.D.C.
Newton Brook	English Combe	Bath R.D.C.
do.	Newton St. Loe	Keynsham R.D.C.
River Chew	Pensford	Clutton R.D.C.
do.	Publow	do.
do.	Stanton Drew	do.
do.	Chew Magna	do.
do.	Chew Stoke	do.
do.	West Harptree	do.
River Axe	Axbridge	Axbridge R.D.C.
do.	Wedmore	do.
River Banwell	Banwell	do.
River Yeo	Part of Yatton	Long Ashton R.D.C.
An unnamed Rhine or Ditch	Olveston	Thornbury R.D.C.

It is interesting to note that whilst the City of Bath discharges a treated effluent into the Avon at Saltford, the local sewage is discharged untreated at a spot about a mile up-river; also it will be seen that there are six schemes on the River Chew, all of them within a distance of about four and a half miles, and all discharging crude sewage into the river.   Similarly on the Cam and Wellow Brooks there are groups of separate schemes within very short distances of each other.

None of the other villages and hamlets in the Region have sewers or sewage disposal schemes; they depend apparently on earth closets, cesspits and other individual arrangements.

SECTION 2.   WATER SUPPLY

§ i.   *Introductory*

Almost the whole population of the Region obtains its water supply to-day through mains fed from springs, catchment areas, and reservoirs situated mainly within the Regional boundary. This elaborate system is controlled by eight Local Authorities, viz. :—

Bath Corporation.	Axbridge R.D.C.
Midsomer Norton U.D.C.	Bath R.D.C.
Weston-super-Mare U.D.C.	Clutton R.D.C.
Radstock U.D.C.	Long Ashton R.D.C.

and eight private Companies, viz. :—

Bristol Waterworks Company.	Clevedon Gas and Water Company.
West Gloucestershire Water Company	Brent Knoll Water Company.
Combe Down Water Company.	Berrow Water Company.
Portishead Water Company.	Downside Water Company.

The whole Region is not supplied with water at the present date, but the *statutory areas* of the above undertakings cover the whole Region except about four square miles of marsh land between the rivers Kenn and Yeo (including the hamlet of Kingston Seymour), and about $5\frac{1}{4}$ square miles on the north of Bath (including Cold Ashton, and part of Charmy Down and St. Catherine's Valley).

The Water Supply Diagram on Plate 31 shows the areas controlled by the different Water Undertakings; it also shows (by brown hatching) the approximate known catchment areas as far as they are ascertainable, and (by brown tint) the areas at present supplied, whether by public service, local spring, or well.   The reservoirs, pumping stations, springs and main pipe-lines are shown in red on the diagram, except that, where these are situated in another Authority's area they appear in blue.

The areas tinted brown as being at present supplied have been taken a quarter of a mile on either side of the water main where the supply is by public undertaking, and have been drawn as an approximation to the actual area served in those cases where the supply is from local springs or wells.

§ ii.   *The Statutory Undertakings*

(a) *Local Authorities*

Bath Corporation obtains its supply from springs thrown out of the Midford Sands and Inferior Oolite by the Lias Clay and from the Great Oolite by the Fuller's Earth.   The water is collected in two catchment areas on the north of the City, viz. :—

(1) Lansdown, and

(2) The hilly country comprising Charmy Down, Holts Down, Solsbury Hill, and extending to Marshfield on the north and Banner Down on the east.

Curiously enough the latter area includes the greater part of one of the two portions of the Region for which there is no statutory water undertaking. The water is stored in reservoirs at Lansdown, St. Catherine's Valley and Chilcombe bottom; the supply is by gravitation. The supply is constant and the quality apparently satisfactory, although there is no filtration.

The statutory area includes the greater portion of the City and part of the Rural District lying to the north (i.e., the parishes of Bathampton, Batheaston, Charlcombe, Langridge, Swainswick, Weston and Woolley).

Weston-super-Mare U.D.C. Until 1914 Weston obtained its water from two wells in the Carboniferous Limestone at the foot of Worlebury Hill, from whence it was pumped to a reservoir on the hill. Additional supplies are now obtained from a spring at the foot of Banwell Hill. This supply gravitates to Weston and is there pumped up to the reservoirs near the upper Bristol Road and on Worlebury Hill. The statutory area includes the whole of Weston, the villages of Uphill, Worle, Kewstoke, the district of Sand Bay, and extends from the River Banwell down to the mouth of the River Axe.

Midsomer Norton U.D.C. The supply is obtained from three sources—Chilcompton, Downside, and Downhead. At Chilcompton the source is a spring from the Dolomitic Conglomerate belonging to the U.D. Council.

Water is purchased in bulk from the Downside Abbey authorities and the Radstock Urban District Council respectively.

The statutory area is the whole of the Urban District, except Downside Abbey and neighbourhood.

Radstock U.D.C. obtains its water from a spring in the Old Red Sandstone at Downhead, outside the Region and about 5½ miles south of Radstock, whence the supply gravitates to the town.

The statutory area is the whole of the Urban District. The Council also supplies the village of Camerton, in Clutton R.D.

Axbridge R.D.C. This Council obtains its water supplies from four sources on Mendip and one on the alluvial plain. The Schemes comprising the Council's water supply system are :—

(1) The Cheddar, Axbridge and Highbridge Supply.

(2) The South Marsh Scheme.

(3) The Winscombe, Shipham and Rowberrow Scheme.

(4) The Blagdon Scheme.

The Burrington Water Scheme is another, but this is administered by a local " Water Committee " and is maintained by subscription only. There is no water rate.

(1) *The Cheddar, Axbridge and Highbridge Scheme* originates in overflow springs from the Old Red Sandstone emerging from the Lower Limestone Shales at Charterhouse; the water gravitates to a reservoir in Cheddar Gorge and supplies Cheddar, Axbridge and parts of Compton Bishop and Charterhouse; there is also a storage reservoir at Brent Knoll, which supplies the town of Highbridge (outside the Region). It is entirely a gravitation supply and very abundant.

(2) *The South Marsh Scheme* obtains its supplies from two springs at the foot of Mendip arising in the Carboniferous Limestone, one at Cross (near Axbridge) and one at Dunyeat (Compton Bishop). The water is pumped to a reservoir on the hillside and supplies the parishes of Badgworth, Biddisham, Brent Knoll, Burnham Without, Compton Bishop, East Brent, Lympsham, Mark and Weare and Chapel Allerton. Arrangements are being made to augment the supply from the Bristol Water Company's new reservoir at Rowberrow.

(3) *The Winscombe, Shipham and Rowberrow Scheme* probably has a similar origin to the Cheddar Supply; it is fed from springs at Rowberrow Bottom, in the Old Red Sandstone; this is a gravitation scheme with a reservoir, supplying Rowberrow, Shipham and Winscombe and part of Churchill; the quantity available from this source is insufficient in drought summers and an auxiliary supply is obtained as required from the Bristol Water Company's main at Sidcot.

(4) *The Blagdon Scheme* is also a gravitation supply with a reservoir; it is fed from springs originating in the Carboniferous Limestone and emerging from the Old Red Sandstone.

The Council's Statutory area of supply is the Rural District excepting Uphill, Brean, Berrow, Brent Knoll and Kewstoke.

Bath R.D.C. This Council has two detached statutory areas covering together less than half the Rural District; one comprises the parishes of Camerton, Dunkerton, and Wellow, the other the parish of Bathford.

The former area has three small but separate systems at Dunkerton, Shoscombe, and Wellow, supplied from springs in the local Oolite formation; the first gets its supply by gravitation, the others by pumping.

The latter area is supplied from a hillside spring out of the Fuller's Earth at Bathford; the water is pumped to a reservoir above the village. This Council also owns two water schemes within the present statutory Supply Area of Bath Corporation, viz., at Bathampton and Swainswick. The Bathampton supply (formerly a private undertaking) is obtained from springs out of the Fuller's Earth; it is a gravitation scheme with a reservoir. At Swainswick part of the village is supplied by a small system fed by a spring from the Great Oolite and thrown out by the Fuller's Earth.

Clutton R.D.C. The statutory supply area of this Authority is the whole of its district plus the parishes of Winford and Dundry (in Long Ashton R.D.). Only the south-eastern corner of this area is at present supplied, the water being obtained in bulk from the Downside Abbey Waterworks for Cameley, Clutton, Farmborough, Farrington Gurney, High Littleton, Paulton and Ston Easton; and from Midsomer Norton U.D.C. for Chilcompton parish.

Long Ashton R.D.C. The statutory area of this Authority contains only one parish— Yatton. The supply is from a well sunk in the Keuper Marls; the water is elevated to a reservoir (200 feet) near Cadbury Camp, from whence it gravitates to the village and neighbourhood.

(b) Private Companies

Bristol Waterworks Company.—This is the most important water undertaking in the Region under survey; its area of supply includes the whole of the City of Bristol, and portions of the Keynsham, Long Ashton, and Thornbury Rural districts. The Company also supplies the hamlet of Upper Stanton Drew (Clutton R.D.).

The Company was established in 1695, the first works being the conveying of water in pipes of elm timber from the Avon at Hanham to a reservoir at Lawrence Hill.

At the present time the Company derives its supplies from the Carboniferous and Mountain Limestones of the Mendip Hills, and the New Red Sandstone at Chelvey in the Nailsea Basin.

The works in the Mendip area include numerous springs and reservoirs, the Great Blagdon Reservoir (formed by damming the valley of the River Yeo) and pumping plant at Cheddar: the latter being planned to deal with 10 million gallons per twenty-four hours. Of the total supply to Bristol, one half has to be pumped from Chelvey and Blagdon, and in the case of the Cheddar supply, it has to be twice pumped before it reaches the City. After the water reaches Bristol a large portion has to be pumped several times before it is finally distributed. At Barrow Gurney there are extensive filter and aeration beds.

West Gloucestershire Water Company.—The statutory area of this Company extends beyond the Regional boundary; within the Region it includes the Urban Districts of Kingswood and Mangotsfield, the Rural Districts of Warmley, Chipping Sodbury (except the parish of Cold Ashton) and parts of Keynsham and Thornbury Rural Districts.

The supply is obtained by pumping from the water-bearing Pennant strata of the Coal Measures, at Frampton Cotterell, Oldland, Sodbury and Whitchurch. There is also a small separate system at North Stoke fed from two springs issuing from the base of the Great Oolite above the 600-foot contour line on the Lansdown Hills.

Combe Down Water Company.—This Company's area of supply includes the southern part of the City of Bath, and a portion of the Bath Rural District.

The supply is obtained from springs out of the Midford Sands at Horsecombe Vale, Midford. It is pumped to a high-level reservoir on Bathampton Down, whence it gravitates over the system.

Portishead Water Company.—The area of supply includes Portishead Urban District and a large part of the surrounding Rural District of Long Ashton. The sources of supply are: (1) The Limestone strata at Failand; (2) Springs at Portbury issuing from the Lower Limestone Shales; (3) Well at Portbury in Upper Keuper Marl; (4) Borehole at Middle Bridge; (5) Borehole at the new Wireless Station.

Clevedon Gas and Water Company supplies the town, the Urban District and part of Long Ashton Rural District; the supply is from a well and borehole in the Marls at the foot of Tickenham Hill; the water is pumped to two reservoirs on Dial Hill.

Brent Knoll Water Company supplies the village of that name and neighbourhood. Brent Knoll itself is a small catchment area, and the water is obtained from the mains of the Burnham U.D.C., and from springs on the hillside.

Berrow Water Company supplies the coastal strip shown on the diagram; it obtains its supply from the Burnham Water Company.

Downside Abbey Waterworks.—This large and important undertaking belongs to the Abbey Authorities, but only a small part of the supply area lies within the Region, including Downside Abbey itself. Supplies are furnished in bulk, within the Region, to Midsomer Norton U.D.C. and Clutton R.D.C. The source is a well at Gurney Slade, fed, apparently, by a strong spring, and the water is pumped to reservoirs at Downside, a distance of about 10 miles from the source. The supply is abundant.

Winscombe village and neighbourhood lie upon the Catchment Area of a Water Authority supplying outside the Region, viz., the Burnham U.D.C., whose reservoirs, pumping station and main are shown on the diagram.

§ iii. *Village Local Supplies*

Several villages are supplied locally by means of small privately owned water undertakings, but there are a large number of villages and hamlets still dependent upon local springs and shallow wells.

The private water schemes include :—

Village.	Owner of Scheme.	Source.	Other information.
Corston	Earl Temple	Spring issuing from White Lias	—
Newton St. Loe	do.	Spring issuing from Midford Sands	—
Stowey	Lord Strachie	Spring in Lias	A gravitation supply with reservoir, 1600 gallons, near the spring
Kelston	Gen. Inigo Jones	Springs issuing from Lias	—
Christon	Mr. G. K. Wainwright	Spring from the Dolomitic Conglomerate	A gravitation supply with storage reservoir 11,500 gallons
Loxton	Mr. E. W. Galton	—	—
Brent Knoll	Mr. G. A. Johnstone	Springs in Middle Lias	Brent Knoll is a small catchment area
East Harptree	Mr. G. Hill	Three springs in Trias and two in Lias	—
Burrington	Parish Council	Spring in Old Red Sandstone, piped to reservoir at Link	Administered by a local Water Committee, and maintained by subscription

A survey of all the village wells would be a formidable undertaking, but the following notes will show the conditions in a number of cases :—

Some villages adequately supplied by local wells or springs include : Ubley, Nempnett Thrubwell, West Harptree, Litton, Hinton Blewett, Cameley, North Widcombe, Stowey, Norton Malreward, Camerton, Dundry, East Dundry, Winford, Clapton-in-Gordano, Weston-in-Gordano, Walton-in-Gordano, Rangeworthy, Dodington, Dyrham and Hinton, West Littleton, Cold Ashton, Little Sodbury, Horton, Hawkesbury, Alderley, Hillesley, Combe Hay, Swainswick, Corston, Kelston, Newton St. Loe, North Stoke, Priston, Stanton Prior.

Some villages having inadequate or unsatisfactory supply are : East Harptree, Chelwood, Publow, Pensford, Chew Magna, Chew Stoke, Carlingcot, Barrow, Kingston Seymour, Bleadon, Littleton-upon-Severn, Elberton, Aust, Iron Acton, Marshfield, Whitchurch, Queen Charlton, Burnett, Compton Dando, Marksbury, Wrington (including Redhill), Congresbury, Wedmore (including Blackford).

SECTION 3. ELECTRICITY

The statutory Electricity Authorities operating in the Region are :—

> Bristol Corporation.
> Bath Corporation.
> West Gloucestershire Power Co.
> North Somerset Electricity Supply Co.
> Weston-super-Mare and District Electric Supply Co.
> Wedmore Electric Light and Power Co.
> Thornbury Supply Co.
> West Wilts Electric Supply Co.

The areas of Supply of these Authorities are shown on Plate 32 ; they cover the entire Region except a small area south of Bath which has not yet been allocated : this, which includes a strip from near Keynsham to Wellow, is to be included in the North Somerset Supply Company's area.

A new super-power Station is in course of erection at Portishead ; this will ultimately become one of the selected super-stations in the National Grid system of the Electricity Commissioners. The main route of the connecting lines of the Grid have not yet been published.

The diagram aims at showing (by orange colour) the actual areas at present supplied from the Transformer sub-stations as well as the maximum areas which they are capable of supplying (orange tint). It will thus be seen that the Bristol, Bath and Weston Companies already supply a large part of their areas, and by means of Low-Tension lines from their present transformers could supply practically the whole.

The North Somerset Company (which obtains its current from Bristol Corporation) has carried a big loop line from Long Ashton through Congresbury, Sandford, Axbridge, and (after a break outside this region) Chilcompton, Midsomer Norton, Clutton, Pensford, and Whitchurch. This route leaves unsupplied the large area from Dundry to the Mendips, which is described in this Report as an area of Special Landscape Beauty. A branch from Winscombe supplies Brent and Burnham.

The West Gloucestershire Company is not yet operating within the Region but has designed Transformer Stations for Wickwar, Sodbury, Yate and Wick.

In some parts the High-Tension lines follow the main roads (Long Ashton to Congresbury) : in other places they cut across country from village to village. Considerable lengths of cables are laid underground ; e.g., from Portishead to Bristol ; from Portishead to Clevedon ; from Flax Bourton to Congresbury ; from Axbridge over the escarpment of Mendip to Shipham (a fortunate thing for the amenity of the landscape) ; from Axbridge to Cheddar ; from Brislington through Keynsham to Saltford ; from Bath through Limpley Stoke ; from Filton to Almondsbury.

PART THE SECOND

THE REGIONAL PLAN

PART THE SECOND.   THE REGIONAL PLAN

CHAPTER I.   ZONING

SECTION 1.   GENERAL OBJECT

§ i.   *Flexibility*

IN the interests of real economy it is essential that land should be put to the best use of which it is capable.   In a Region which contains such diversity as Manufacturing and Business Centres, Residential Towns, Health and Seaside Resorts, Ports, Suburban Settlements, Villages, Country Towns, Mining Areas, normal Agricultural Land, Low-lying Marshy Tracts, and Elevated Hilly Districts, it would be manifestly uneconomic to allow any sort of development to occur anywhere.   At the same time a rigid separation on theoretical grounds is not advisable : a seaside resort, for example, may require certain factory buildings, an agricultural district will need houses.   The forecast of zoning requirements must therefore be made for each area in order to determine :—

(*a*) What is the predominant use to which it should be put ; i.e., what form of development is to be encouraged as wholly appropriate.

(*b*) What may be tolerated with special permission, in order that there may be no undue interference with the predominant use.

(*c*) What is discordant and detrimental to the area and should therefore be disallowed.

Working within these lines of definition a sufficient degree of flexibility should be possible ; and it will be found that a number of zones emerge which have a sufficient sharpness of outline and contrast.   But it must be remembered that Regional zoning is put forward in order to obtain a general conspectus of the problem only : it is left for local authorities to subdivide when preparing their town planning schemes.

§ ii.   *Threefold Object*

In addition to providing for flexibility of definition, it is necessary to define a little more clearly the object of zoning in putting land to its best use.   It is possible to subdivide into three main aspects :—

(*a*) To facilitate the economic development of the Region.

(*b*) To preserve its existing beauty.

(*c*) To safeguard the health of the future community.

In the definition of the objects of Town Planning, the wording and order of procedure is slightly different in the Act, which aims at securing " proper sanitary conditions, amenity and convenience."   From an ethical standpoint this is obviously the right order : the whole machinery of the community exists for the human being, therefore " Proper Sanitary

Conditions" or Health and Happiness are the prime desiderata: "convenience" or economic development subserves the human need. But as regards the technique of planning the requirements of economic development lead the way: Health is dealt with by means of safe-guards. Each list agrees in putting Beauty second, and according to certain methods of calculation this means that it may occupy the first place while the rival claims of the others are being settled.

There need and should be no antagonism between the three aspects of planning for the rightful use of land. But it is necessary at times to decide which shall be given a preponderant place in any one area, in view of the wider issues involved. For example, it might be quite possible to encourage the economic development of the Avon Valley right up to and beyond the City of Bath; but it is doubtful if the industrial gain on a small area would counterbalance the loss to amenity over a wider one. Again, there are places where health considerations would be antagonistic to the opening of a coal-mine in immediate proximity to houses. But generally speaking the separation of Residential from Industrial zones resolves itself naturally along the lines of the zoning plan.

As regards the amenities of rural preservation, it will be found that these coincide com-pletely with economy of development, whether of houses or factories. Thus if houses or factories were allowed to straggle over the whole face of the countryside, some superficial advantages might appear, such as ease of development, absence of all restrictions, perfect freedom to build anywhere and anyhow; but the corresponding disadvantages would soon become apparent: expensive drainage plants; additional mileage of traffic roads; extensions of water supply; distance from schools; and last, but by no means least, the loss to the community of the beauty of the countryside.

SECTION 2.   APPLICATION TO THIS REGION

§ i. *Indeterminate and Omnibus Zones*

There is a tendency in some quarters to put the bulk of the land into Indeterminate or Omnibus Zones. The former is a frank confession that it is impossible to say what is the best use to which the land can be put; and, while bringing it under the ægis of a town planning scheme, to defer definition until some further indication is given of the growth desired to encourage. This may be an advisable course where large areas are included showing little sign of any sort of change at the moment, but which may become animated in an unforeseen manner at any time. The Omnibus Zone appears in certain recently approved Town Planning Schemes: here over very wide areas houses, factories and shops will be allowed, the latter two, however, by consent of the Authority. This type of treatment presupposes that the actual subdivision into definite zones is to be done during the course of development instead of on a plan beforehand: it can only be advisable when the general topography gives no indication of a natural subdivision, and then only with a big authority which has available continual planning advice: but it closely approximates to the old conditions where there was no certainty as to what sort of building was going to be placed next to another. In other words, the stabilising value of town planning is not realised.

§ ii. *Possibility of more Definite Zoning*

In this Region there is a possibility of more definite zoning: though a large part of the area is truly rural, its importance in remaining rural in certain parts, and the likelihood of its change in a clear direction in other parts, is not a matter of abstruse speculation. Again, the topographic indications as to use are manifest: a coalfield under one part; low-lying land unsuitable for residential use in another; bleak hill tops equally unsuited for houses or factories and required for water catchments ; beautiful country surrounding places that live on their attractiveness ; sea fronts inviting development. What signs could be more definite, what indications of growth and sensible use more precise ? The Zoning plan, indeed, is entirely based upon the elaborate studies made in the first part of this Report, and it should be closely compared with the Geological, Contour, Landscape, Watershed, Industrial, Electricity and Road accessibility plans.

§ iii. *Zoning Divisions*

The following list comprises the whole of the land within the Region :—

1. Built up or closely developed areas.
2. Residential Zones.
3. Residential-agricultural Zones.
4. Industrial Zones.
5. Normal Agricultural Zones.
6. Agricultural Zones over Coalfield.
7. Residential Zones over Coalfield.
8. Low-lying Zones.
9. Special Landscape Reservations.
10. Special Landscape Reservations over Coalfield.
11. Rural Reservations.
12. Open Space Reservations.

Of these Nos. 2 to 8 would be described under a town planning scheme as Character Zones, i.e., they would prescribe the character of buildings to be erected ; Nos. 9 to 12 would be described as Reservations under a town planning scheme ; the last two also appear in the section on Open Spaces as well as Nos. 9 and 10, which though not withdrawn from building will nevertheless partake of the nature of open country.

The imposition of Character Zones (when approved as reasonable by the Minister of Health) does not afford any ground for compensation, but there *may* be a possibility of compensation in the case of the Reservations.

SECTION 3.   DESCRIPTION OF THE DIVISIONS

§ i. *Developed Areas*

Before dealing with the actual parts of the Region to which it is suggested zoning proposals should apply, it may be well to amplify somewhat the bald title of each ; and afterwards a table is given showing how the zones can be scheduled upon the lines of the Ministry of Health's formula for Town Planning schemes.

Regional Planning is not primarily concerned with large and continuously developed areas unless some improvement of them has a reaction upon regional growth or vice versa. Built-up towns require more detailed treatment than can be shown in a regional scheme : it has therefore for simplicity's sake been decided to include these areas in the surrounding zones. For example, parts of the developed City of Bristol are included in a Residential Zone (pink on folding map) and other parts of the City are included in an Industrial Zone (purple on map). On the Zoning Diagram (Plate 33) a rough indication of the Built-up areas is shown by black hatching.

This combination of different functions into a single category must not be taken to mean that the various activities should be allowed to flourish in juxtaposition, but that they require to be dealt with outside a Regional Plan.

§ ii.   *Residential Zone*

Similarly areas recommended for residential growth are all coloured alike, though within local Town Planning schemes there will be many gradations, more particularly as applied to the number of houses per acre.   Generally speaking, it will be found that three degrees of density (12, 8 and 4 per acre) will cover the varied needs of such zones.   Twelve is the usually accepted highest average density except where areas partially built on old lines are involved. The maximum permitted on any one acre is governed by the proportion of the site to be covered by building.   Four houses per acre may be regarded as the lowest density usually imposed in suburban districts most suitable for large houses.   It will frequently happen that the gardens to individual houses will be considerably bigger ; but on normal building land 4 per acre will generally secure the erection of detached houses in gardens.

Houses are the predominant type for which the Zone is intended : but other buildings will be allowed by obtaining consent, provided they are not likely to injure the amenity of the area. It is possible, and has been done in one of the Birmingham schemes, to subdivide the Residential Zone according to the manner in which this consent may be given : in one part it is according to discretion of the Local Authority ; in another the authority has to give public notice before giving consent, thus allowing a species of local option to the inhabitants of the neighbourhood.   The consent or refusal is subject to an appeal, preferably to the Minister of Health.

§ iii.   *Residential-agricultural Zone*

The Residential-agricultural Zone is limited to two houses per acre.   The buildings allowed without consent are those (including houses) requisite for Agriculture and Small Holdings.   The density of 2 per acre is imposed with a quite different object to that of 4 under Zone 2 : these areas are used chiefly as a sort of buffer or transitional state between suburb and country.   The houses may be quite small ; but under the machinery of land unit control, it may be possible to group the houses together upon part of a Land Unit, and devote the remainder of the unit to permanently open land.   This zone will require skilful planning in detail and a close co-operation between local authorities and landowners in order that public services may be available at the spots chosen for development.

§ iv.   *Industrial Zone*

This zone may be dealt with in several ways.   One method would be to allow inoffensive industrial buildings as the normal use over the whole zone : all other buildings to be " by consent," including houses at one end of the scale and buildings for offensive trades at the other; relying upon the skill and discretion of the local authorities concerned to see that they are not intermixed.   A second method would be to subdivide the zone, e.g., into

(*a*) General Factory areas, where any sort of trade will be allowed but no houses (this might be suitable to the industrial areas on the low-lying lands which anyhow are unsuitable for houses).

(*b*) Special Factory areas in which houses and other buildings may be permitted by special consent, but no offensive trade.

Probably both methods may be used with advantage in this Region.

§ v.   *Normal Agricultural Zone*

This zone is the nearest approach to undetermined zoning in the Region.   It is designed to embrace all the open agricultural land which, though pleasant as all cultivated ground should be, has no special claims for preservation on account of remarkable landscape beauty.   It differs from Zone 3 (residential-agricultural) because it is more remote from development and its future destiny beyond agricultural cannot be clearly forecasted. A considerable part of it comes under the influence of the coalfield and is dealt with under Zone 6. It might be suggested that it should be reserved permanently for agriculture and its building value finally eliminated by means of compensation. But it is by no means certain that it is undesirable to build upon it, provided it is properly done: nor is it necessary to restrict the density of any groups of building below the normal average of 12 per acre. At the same time it may be used by local authorities to promote satellite rather than the ribbon form of growth.

What is required therefore is freedom to erect buildings required for its present use and a certain margin for unexpected requirements; beyond this there are two methods of dealing with future use: (i) by Supplementary Zoning under which an area when required can as it were be re-zoned; (ii) by a simple permissive use for "other buildings." This latter would probably be the simpler and would mean that whenever anyone wishes to put up a factory, single house or group of houses, application must be made to the Local Authority who would have the power to withhold consent subject to appeal to the Minister of Health. The practice of the Authority in giving or withholding consent would have to be upon a system which meets the Minister's approval as satisfying requirements of density, convenience, amenity and economy. In other words the reasonableness of the zoning restriction will become evident during the working out of the permissive power.

To this end it is suggested that the buildings for which the area is primarily intended are those necessary for farming and agricultural purposes, together with dwelling houses having not less than 3 acres of land attached thereto. The term agricultural purposes should be interpreted in the widest sense: thus a blacksmith and a builder wholly or principally occupied with agricultural work could have houses built for their use.

The buildings which would require the "special consent of the Council" would simply be described as "Other buildings" which would include, e.g., a Church, a School, a shop, a factory, a house or a cottage for week-end use or as a residence for an urban worker. If a group of houses were to be erected, the Local Authority before granting permission should satisfy itself that the houses can be economically drained and that they are not strung out along the highway so as to impede through traffic: wherever possible the group should be planned with its main axis across rather than along the main road.

§ vi.   *Agricultural Zone over Coalfield*

This zone would be precisely the same as No. 5 with the exception that as it falls upon the coalfield it is necessary to make a slight distinction in favour of industrial development. In East Kent it has been suggested in a similar type of zone that a coal-mine may be allowed provided it does not damage existing amenities; but when once established the Pithead would automatically become the centre of an industrial zone having a radius of (say) $\frac{1}{2}$ mile. Within this localised industrial area only a limited number of houses would be allowed for safety men and caretakers. The industrial zone so established would closely resemble the General Factory area described in Zone 4 (with the addition of houses for safety men, etc.): it would also be the natural place in which to group other and ancillary industries, this grouping together being desirable from economic reasons no less than for purposes of amenity. Outside the half-mile radius a residential settlement could be allowed.

§ vii.   *Residential Zone over Coalfield*

Where the residential zone (coloured red) lies on top of the coalfield it is intended that mines should not be allowed except by special consent of the Council, though a glance at the industrial map will show that there are already several mines in the Bristol and Radstock residential areas. Zoning, of course, is not retrospective and what is now in existence is not affected: but future coal-mining development will not be allowed in these areas unless it can be arranged in such a way that it will be of no detriment whatever to the neighbourhood:

i.e., the mine would have to be run electrically and produce no débris heaps, the winding and other machinery being housed in buildings of satisfactory appearance.

But there is one area, the valley of the Cam, where the coal-mining and residential areas are still sufficiently loose to be properly segregated. It is not certain whether any new pits will be sunk here, but if so a similar treatment of pithead industrial zone as suggested under Zone 6 should be adopted. The whole of this Cam valley requires very careful zoning and planning in order to correct the unsatisfactory conditions which are there present and which have not progressed too far to be remedied.

§ viii. *Low-lying Zone*

It is not desirable that low-lying, marshy lands should be used for normal residential use except where expressly zoned for this purpose (e.g., on the sea board) : buildings required for agriculture would, however, be allowed and others at the discretion of the Local Authority. This elimination of general residential building can also be effected by a by-law prescribing the floor level at a figure well above the level of the swampy ground. But there is not the same objection to industrial use, provided this does not unduly interfere with the amenities of the zone itself or of surrounding or neighbouring zones. The erection of a factory building on a flat expanse is not so conspicuous as it may be on higher ground.

§ ix. *Special Landscape Reservation*

The land in this Reservation is meant to be retained in its present form with as little change as is practicable, with the object of conserving the existing landscape character and also of preventing straggling development. It has been chosen because of its manifest beauty, which is a definite asset to the district and to the immediate surroundings ; in certain parts its remoteness of access makes this Reservation comparatively simple : in other parts its nearness to places that depend upon amenity make its reservation essential. It is not, however, desirable over large areas to prohibit any new buildings other than agricultural ; and it is suggested that the Responsible Authority should allow in exceptional circumstances certain types of buildings in this Reservation : but these must be sited so as to drop into the landscape and *all* such buildings must be controlled as to materials and design. This condition must also apply to agricultural buildings in this Reservation.

This area is intended to be treated differently from Zone 5. Here a general freedom to develop is not intended : it is to be to all intents a non-building area, but as it would be hazardous to apply this restriction rigidly to large areas, a limited degree of building is envisaged. The Wheatley Housing Act (1924) described a Rural Area, *inter alia*, as one in which there was not more than one house per 10 acres. This standard might be taken and the Land Unit method of calculation (with possibly a larger land unit) adapted for use in a Reservation in order to allow the placing or grouping of houses under such a density restriction.* An increase also proportional to population might be allowed in all existing villages, which could be zoned (within the Reservation) so as to allow this, and also shops (this has not been included in the table of Zones).

§ x. *Special Landscape Reservation over Coalfield*

Where the Special Landscape Reservation lies on top of the Coalfield and has been hatched purple similarly to Zone 6, the intention is again different. Mining, it is true, would be permitted, but the Pit would not be allowed to become the centre of an industrial zone ; rather it would be an isolated phenomenon in which the characteristics that are inseparable from a

---

* Thus : if four houses were to be put up they might be placed in a suitable site together—but this would render 40 acres adjoining free from subsequent building. The thing would have to be done in a very free but conscientious manner.

mine are reduced to their least objectionable form: the machinery would be run by electricity, the buildings would be properly designed under architectural control, and there would be no unsightly spoil heaps, smoke or noise. A limited number of houses for safety men would be allowed in proximity to the colliery; these of course would also be subject to architectural control.

The coal-mine in the park at Temple Newsome near Leeds proves that these safeguards to surrounding amenity can be adopted without impairing the economic working of the industry.

§ xi. *Rural Reservation*

This is also not a Character Zone, but a Reservation, in which no building or development is to be allowed except possibly that of Quarrying. The object in selecting these areas has been broadly twofold: the preservation of water catchment areas from contamination, and the reservation of certain tracts of wild country which it might not be necessary to purchase as public open spaces but which might profitably be left in private ownership provided that their essential character were not damaged.

§ xii. *Open Space Reservations*

These also figure on the Zoning Map and may conveniently be taken as representing one of the twelve categories into which all land in the Region is subdivided. They are, however, Reservations rather than Zones and will be dealt with in Chapter III of this Part.

SECTION 4.   ALLOCATION OF THE DIVISIONS

§ i. *Zoning Map*

The next thing is to determine to what areas in actuality these twelve Zones or prescriptive land-user regulations should be applied. This can be most conveniently seen by studying the Zoning Map; but it may not be amiss to give some of the reasons for the selection of the different areas, though it is anticipated that the studies in the existing trend of development contained in the First Part will have already given hints as to the appropriate zoning for different places. The twelve categories will not be taken seriatim but grouped in order to give a broad idea of the underlying intention of the scheme. In the Third Part some more detailed account of the probable effect of zoning and other recommendations upon particular places will be given, and also (page 130) it is shown that a wide margin is provided for residential growth.

§ ii. *Built-up and Residential*

It will be seen that nothing startling is proposed in the way of new areas for residential use. A careful examination of the Region reveals that the majority of natural foci of growth have been discovered—there are not many places where an entirely new satellite community might spring into existence. This will not seem surprising when it is remembered that there are no fewer than 150 village centres in addition to the large and small towns. These sites have borne the test of time as to their suitability and it would be unnecessarily experimental to attempt alternatives or to seek out unexplored possibilities. What has been done is rather a matter of emphasis: some sites are shown to be stimulated, others are left stationary or only given what might be called a normal increase of growth. It would be idle to attempt a classification of all these areas, but they might according to the above remarks be grouped under four headings:—

    (*a*) Existing sites planned for normal growth.
    (*b*) Existing sites to be stimulated.
    (*c*) New sites.
    (*d*) Existing sites unlikely to develop.

An example or two of each will suffice to illustrate the principle involved. Under (*a*) will naturally be found the urban areas: Bristol, Kingswood, Bath, Weston-super-Mare, Portishead, Clevedon, Warmley, and villages like Chew Magna, Cheddar, etc. Under (*b*) will be found such places as Nailsea, Bishopsworth, Whitchurch, Portbury and Pill, Winscombe, Combe Down (a Bath satellite). Under (*c*) representing the few new sites may be taken the two sea-side areas of Sand Bay (Woodspring) and Brean, and a small but attractive area in the Loxton Valley. Under (*d*) will be found, as would be expected, the villages in the Special Landscape Zones, in the Low-lying Zone and also in those parts of the Normal Agricultural Zone which do not show any great likelihood of growth. These villages have not been coloured apart from their enclosing zone.

§ iii. *Residential-agricultural*

This zone is fairly well distributed about the Region, usually found in close proximity to the Residential areas. It forms an almost continuous ring round Bristol, Kingswood, Mangotsfield and Warmley, on the north of the Avon, from Henbury to Bitton. A similar ring, though not so continuous, is found on the south of the Avon. Bath is also almost encircled. In several places it will be found forming links between neighbouring villages, where coalescence is not desired but where a certain amount of growth more intensive than agricultural may be expected (e.g., Congresbury and Yatton).

The chief extended area of this zone is to be found south-west of Thornbury where a loose form of growth is already taking place which appears to be both likely to continue and to be desirable so long as it continues on somewhat similar lines.

§ iv. *Industrial*

This is not primarily an Industrial Region, and it has not been thought advisable or desirable to schedule large areas for primarily industrial use, though certain of the other zones (e.g., Normal Agricultural No. 5) can take individual factories or be subdivided to contain factory areas.

The largest of the Industrial Zones are situated on the Channel Front north and south of the mouth of the Avon. There is a suggested industrial area on the low-lying land in connection with the Nailsea Coalfield and a similar one on the Bristol Coalfield in the neighbourhood of Coalpit Heath. The Radstock Coalfield being already well developed, there does not appear to be a need for a new industrial area of any extent: but probably a more detailed planning of the Clutton district would result in a subdivision of several portions of this area. The industrial zone in the Avon valley, it will be noted, stops at Bitton.

The large area covered by the Coalfield and hatched with narrow purple stripes represents those parts of the Region where industrial conditions may be allowed to assert themselves. For the most part these hatchings are found in the Normal Agricultural Zone, but special attention is drawn to the places where the purple hatching occurs over the Special Landscape Reservation (No. 10).

§ v. *Normal Agricultural*

A large area is scheduled under this description, corresponding with the recommendations of the Landscape Survey. Roughly speaking, a broad band, occupying the centre of the Region from north to south, is given up to this zone, qualified by the industrial influence of the Coalfield. Other areas outside the Coalfield are in the neighbourhood of Tormarton, south of Wrington (the valley of the Yeo) and the Isle of Wedmore.

§ vi. *Low-lying Lands*

The situation of lands included under this zone explain themselves: the extent of the zone is not so large as might be expected from a purely topographic survey as it is impinged upon by coastal residential areas, industrial areas, and by agricultural zones.

§ vii.   *Special Landscape Zone, Rural Reservations and Open Spaces*

The positions occupied by these are practically identical with the area of Special Landscape Beauty and the Wild Country of the Landscape Survey.   It will be seen that in spite of the Coalfield (the limit of the Lower Measures of which passes through the centre of Bath), a large sweep of this zone encircles the city, following, on the west, the limit of the Upper Measures. Unfortunately, on the other hand the same band of Lower Measures cuts across the stretch of beautiful country from Winford and Chew Magna to Litton.   It would be worth while ascertaining if these Measures are likely to be productive (they are already worked in a village colliery or two): for it would be gratifying to the lover of beautiful country if no colliery development were to be allowed on this special Landscape area.   But it is perhaps impossible, in the absence of a place like Bath whose amenities require protection, to prohibit exploitation of natural resources: the part therefore which lies on the productive Coal Measures has been hatched over to allow mining as described in Section 3, § x, under careful and stringent restrictions.

SECTION 5.   SCHEDULE OF CHARACTER ZONES ON THE FORMULA OF THE MINISTER OF HEALTH

§ i.   *Regional Recommendations and Town Planning Scheme Zoning*

It is not always wise in a Report upon a large Region to attempt to reduce the general zoning recommendations into the precise form in which they can be incorporated into all the Town Planning Schemes of single or joint local authorities.   There may be within the Region itself a certain amount of variation in the interpretation of a zone; for example, the Residential: its meaning in a semi-industrial area such as Kingswood or Warmley may be slightly different from what it is in a residential town like Clevedon.   The following Table is therefore put forward in order to give an idea of how the requirements, described at length in Section 4, could be reduced to the formula for a Town Planning Scheme.   The table is based upon the Ministry of Health's Illustrative Table of Character Zones in the Model Clauses for Town Planning Schemes, but it is hoped that these will not become stereotyped and included in every Town Planning Scheme without due regard to local conditions.

§ ii.   *Table of Character Zones for Local Schemes*

Zone.	Buildings for which the respective areas are primarily intended.	Buildings proposed to be allowed with the consent of the Council subject to appeal to the Ministry.	Buildings not to be erected.
A. RESIDENTIAL (*Various densities*)	Dwelling houses and residential buildings	Other buildings not likely to injure the amenity of the area	All industrial, unless run by electricity and free from noise, smoke and dirt
B. RESIDENTIAL AGRICULTUR-AL	Agricultural buildings or dwelling houses to give an average density per unit of not more than 2 houses per acre	Other buildings not likely to injure the amenity of the area	Buildings for noxious trade or industry *[Continued over*

c. INDUSTRIAL			
(a) General	Industrial buildings and business premises	Other buildings	Buildings for noxious trade or industry
(b) Special	Industrial buildings and business premises	Buildings other than industrial and business premises, but not dwelling houses except such as are essential for the purpose of providing dwelling accommodation for timekeepers, caretakers or persons the nature of whose employment necessitates their presence continuously in immediate proximity to their place of employment	—
(c) Pithead	Industrial buildings	Buildings other than industrial buildings but not dwelling houses or residential buildings except such as are essential for the purpose of providing dwelling accommodation for safety men employed at the colliery or ancillary factory	—
D. AGRICUL- TURAL			
(a) Normal	Agricultural buildings, and country houses	Other buildings (excepting buildings for noxious trade or industry) provided they are grouped to allow of economic development	Buildings for noxious trade or industry
(b) Special (over Coalfield)	Agricultural buildings, and country houses	Other buildings; but collieries and noxious trades and industries must be segregated under Supplementary Zoning	—

E. RESIDENTIAL SPECIAL (over Coalfield)	Dwelling houses and residential buildings	Other buildings	Buildings for noxious trade or industry except coal-mines, with approved surface buildings, run by electricity, and not causing unsightly heaps of débris in the Zone
F. LOW-LYING LAND (a) General	Agricultural buildings; also industrial buildings other than buildings for noxious trade or industry	Dwelling houses; special buildings; buildings for noxious trades or industry if segregated	—
(b) Special	Ditto	Special buildings, buildings for noxious trade or industry if segregated	Dwelling houses

NOTES ON THE ABOVE TABLE :—

(1) Under the Town Planning Act of 1925, closely built-upon areas may not be included in a Statutory Scheme, except in special circumstances, and the above table would not therefore apply to " built-up " areas of large extent.

(2) In giving their " *consent* " to the erection of any building the Town Planning Authority would have power to impose conditions ; the procedure is intended to assist in the preservation of amenity and the method is set forth in the Model Clause No. 29. Zones A, B and E come under the normal sub-clause C of Model Clause 29 ; and in the case of Zones D and F in this Region, the sub-clause might be amended to read :—

> " In the case of any building proposed to be erected in Zones D and F, which may
> " be erected only with the consent of the Council, the Council, in giving or withholding
> " their consent or imposing any conditions, shall have regard to the suitable grouping
> " of buildings, in order to secure proper sanitary conditions and economy in respect to
> " sewage disposal, convenience and economy in respect to communications, and amenity."

(3) The term " *country house* " in the table means a dwelling house having a curtilage comprising not less than three acres of land.

(4) The term " *agricultural buildings* " in the table is intended to include all buildings for agriculture and husbandry, cottages for small holders and poultry farmers, and buildings for ancillary trades connected with these occupations.

(5) The regulations controlling the areas numbered 9, 10, 11, and 12 on pages 92 and 93 cannot be dealt with under a table of Character Zones as they are Reservations. They are dealt with in Chapter III of this Part.

§ iii. *Business Zones*

It will be observed that in the above Table of Zones there are no Business Zones : this is merely the result of regional preoccupation with the broad lines of planning. The Special and General Business Zones given below are extracted from the Table in the Ministry of Health's Model Clauses, and they might well be used in detailed Town Planning :—

Zone.	Buildings which may be erected without Council's consent.	Buildings which may be erected only with Council's consent.	Buildings not to be erected.
SPECIAL BUSINESS	Shops and business premises	Dwelling houses, residential buildings, public buildings and special buildings	Industrial buildings not included in the definition of a shop, and buildings for noxious trade or industry
GENERAL BUSINESS	Shops, business premises, dwelling houses, residential buildings and places of assembly	Schools, institutions, industrial buildings, not included within the definition of a shop, and special buildings	Buildings for noxious trade or industry

Either of these zones might be applied to the Village Centres and to limited areas in parts of the Residential Zone where it is thought desirable ; or even in the Normal Agricultural Zone and the Special Landscape Reservations the villages might be picked out and zoned thus, provided that the elevations must be controlled by means of the Model Clause (see Section 6 below) for architectural control.

The Special Business Zone forbids industrial buildings and is a tighter form of control than the General Business Zone ; it would be suitable for a relatively small portion in (say) the centre of a village where there would be no difficulty in deciding upon the policy of development. The General Business Zone would be suitable for larger and more remote areas, the only prohibition being " Noxious Industries." In course of time parts of such a Zone might be transferred to " Special Business " by Supplementary Zoning, in order to encourage a concentration of business activity into well-defined shopping centres.

SECTION 6.   ARCHITECTURAL CONTROL

The survey of existing features has emphasised the large number of good buildings which there are in the Region, in town, village, and isolated farm and cottage : it has also shown that the amenities can be damaged by the erection of buildings which are bad in design or in colour of materials. This is recognised by the Town Planning Act which gives Local Authorities power to protect their districts from building outrage. It may be said without exaggeration that there are considerable parts of this country where the maintenance of a certain standard of design and particularly of materials is the most urgent need of the moment.

This applies to essentially rural areas where the single building, whether attached to a village or standing alone, may be built to-day : that building can damage the amenities of a large surrounding area by its unsightliness.   There are Rural District Councils in parts of England more remote from general probability of growth than any in this Region that are embarking on Schemes under the Act with this control of building as their primary object, though they have not the incentive of immediate commercial advantage in preservation which should animate many parts of this Region.   The method is by the insertion in the Town Planning Scheme of an appropriate clause based upon the model clause prepared by the Minister of Health.   The Clause can be made applicable to a whole Scheme or to certain zones or reservations. It is by no means safe to say that it is not necessary to exercise control over the appearance of buildings used for manufacturing purposes, though of course such control must not interfere with efficiency (and it will be very rarely found that amenity and efficiency are in antagonism). But it may be desirable to establish a higher standard in certain areas.   The Model Clause, the working arrangements of which are described in Part IV, Chapter IV, provides for the setting up of an Advisory Committee to pass elevations of buildings : the submission to this committee is left to the discretion of the Local Authority.   In certain areas, e.g., Zone B (see Table on page 95) and the Special Landscape Reservation, it would be in the interests of amenity that all building went automatically before the Advisory Committee.   As these are not areas in which much building is contemplated, there would be no undue delay involved.

In Part IV, Chapter IV, details are given of supplementary assistance in carrying out the objects of the Model Clause for control of architectural design which would greatly assist intending builders and preserve a high standard of design and materials.

A TOWN SQUARE (AXBRIDGE)

CHAPTER II. COMMUNICATIONS

SECTION 1.   ROADS

A.   Proposals for Road System

§ i.   *General Description*

THE Road proposals in the Regional Scheme fall into six divisions, viz. :—

    (i) Ring roads round Bristol.
    (ii) Coastal road in Somerset.
    (iii) Proposals based on the projected Severn Crossing.
    (iv) The approaches to Weston-super-Mare.
    (v) The exits from Radstock Coalfield area.
    (vi) Other roads.

These are shown graphically on Plate 34, and in detail on the folding map; they have been planned to follow as far as possible existing roads and tracks, and they are described seriatim in the next paragraph.

§ ii.   *Details of the Road Proposals*

(a) Ring Roads round Bristol.

An Inner and an Outer Ring are proposed, both making considerable use of existing roads. The route of the *Inner Ring* (No. 1 on Map) includes Portway, Winterstoke Road, Vale Lane, a new road skirting Nover's Hill and Knowle to Arno's Vale; thence to St. Anne's; and a new bridge over the Avon at Crew's Hole; after proceeding up Troopers Hill Road to Air Balloon Hill, a short length of new road connects with Kingsway, and so along Kingsway and Thicket Avenue to Staple Hill Road. From this point a new road is proposed crossing the Downend Road and Cleeve Hill to connect with the Bromley Heath Road; at Bromley Heath a short length of new road leads to a new bridge over the River Frome, and thence, passing north of Frenchay Village to Woolfactory Road and along the existing road leading to Filton; at Filton another short length of new road across one of the City of Bristol estates leads to the north end of Southmead Road; thence a new road passes round the north of Westbury to Canford Road and Sylvan Way, Sea Mills, completing the Ring at the Portway end of Sylvan Way.

The *Outer Ring* (No. 2 on Map): Commencing at the Avonmouth end of Portway, the route is via Portway to Shirehampton, and down the lane under the railway by the Station; a new road leads to the River Avon. The proposal then is to cross the River by a new bridge, possibly on the bascule principle; the route then passes through Pill village and a short length of new road leads into Easton-in-Gordano; thence an existing lane is followed, with minor diversions, to the Upper Clevedon Road; then after proceeding down Belmont Hill for some distance, a new link road connects direct to Cambridge Batch where the Ring crosses the Weston Road; about 150 yards along the Barrow Gurney Road a new road branches across the "Wild Country" and connects with the Bridgwater Road, which it crosses, and proceeding eastward it bye-passes Bishopsworth village on the south, via Highridge Common; after utilising the existing lane between Bishopsworth and Whitchurch, it effects another bye-pass at Whitchurch and crosses the Wells Road. A little way up the Queen Charlton Road the route branches as a new road down Charlton Bottom, joining up with a lane leading to Keynsham. The existing road and river bridge (widened) at Keynsham is used with a minor diversion across one corner of Messrs. Fry's Somerdale estate (to cut out the present level crossing) and later a diversion to the right, passing under the L.M.S. Railway embankment at Bitton, makes direct connection with the road through Oldland, Webbs Heath and Siston. At Shortwood Hill it continues as a new road to Cosgrove Hill which is incorporated in the route; after passing under the L.M.S. Railway bridge at the bottom of this hill, it continues in a direct line as a new road across Lyde Green to the existing road to Kendleshire, where it crosses the Badminton Road. From here it continues as a new road passing under the railway viaduct and over the River Frome, to the Fish-pond at Winterbourne. From this point existing roads with minor diversions carry the route to Trench Lane; this is incorporated and connection made (by a short length of new road) with the Gloucester road south of Almondsbury. The route is here deflected to the south-west as a new road connecting with Cribbs Causeway; it passes along the Causeway and over the railway bridge by Henbury Station and continues as a new road by way of Lawrence Weston to Avonmouth and Portway, so completing the circuit.

The first and last portions of this road will serve not only as a ring route but also as outlets from, and approaches to, the important docks and industrial area at Avonmouth.

(b) *Coastal Road in Somerset* (No. 3 on Map).

The object of this route is to connect the coastal towns with each other and with Bristol; such a route will not only be of great mutual benefit to the coastal towns in their development as recreative centres, but also is expected to be of great value to the Region as a scenic route for motors, motor coaches, and tourists generally.

The route may be said to commence as a tangent from the Outer Ring Road (described above) at Easton-in-Gordano, using the existing road as far as Portbury, then, branching from the lane beside the Priory, it strikes across the fields in a direct line to Portishead. Incidentally this will effect a great improvement in the approach to Portishead and will shorten the distance and avoid two rail crossings; this part of the route is recommended to be treated as a Parkway. The road then passes by the Light Railway Station to High Street, and thence by way of the existing road past the Golf Links (where the coastal scenic route may be said to commence) and the Royal Nautical School it continues via the road over Weston Down and Walton Down to the point where the lane turns south towards the village of Walton-in-Gordano. At this point a new road will strike across the shoulder of Back Hill, through the Golf-course to Walton Road by Castle Lodge. Walton Road and other existing roads through Clevedon are incorporated and the southern exit from Clevedon is by way of Pizey Avenue, which is to be extended to Colehouse Lane Halt on the Light Railway; from this point the road will run beside the Light Railway to Worle. Near the gas-works at Worle a new length of road proceeding in the same general direction, crosses the G.W.R. loop line and passes behind Weston roughly parallel to the G.W.R. main line. It then climbs the northern slope of Uphill by an easy curve and at the summit it crosses the Weston–Bleadon road, and passes down by an easy gradient to Bleadon Level and, crossing the River Axe, effects a junction with the northern end of the existing road beside the sand dunes of Brean. This latter suitably widened and improved carries the route to Berrow and Burnham, so completing a spectacular coastal touring route which will be a valuable addition to the attractions of the Region.

(c) Proposals based on the Severn Crossing.

Although the proposals in regard to the crossing of the Severn do not appear to have made much progress recently, it has been thought advisable, whilst a Regional Scheme is under review, to include in the Report some recommendations as to routes to and from the point of crossing. At the time of writing the balance of opinion seems to be in favour of Aust Cliff as the actual site of the crossing, and the road proposals shown on the Map and described below are designed accordingly; it should be understood, however, that this road scheme is dependent entirely on the location of the crossing at Aust, and that it will need to be modified in the event of another location being selected or the crossing scheme being definitely abandoned.

The proposal is to plan a new road (No. 4 on Map) direct from the Avonmouth end of Portway, parallel to the shore and distant about one mile therefrom, incorporating the road bridge over the G.W.R. at Pilning and passing on the west of Aust Village to the assumed location on Aust Cliff.

South of Aust Village another road (No. 5 on Map) would branch eastward to Red Hill Lane; this, widened, would carry the route to Elberton, which would be bye-passed and a length of new road leading north-east would connect with the lane on the north of " Kyneton " (alternatively a new road could be planned to the north of this property) crossing Kington Lane and entering the outskirts of Thornbury near the vicarage. From here an existing road would be utilised to connect with the main Gloucester Road, which would be crossed by the smithy, and a short length of new road would cut out the loop round Upper Morton, the route being finally merged in the Gloucester Road at Knap.

The planning of a route from Aust in the direction of Chippenham and London has been a matter of difficulty on account of the awkward levels between Elberton and Ridgeway. Perhaps the solution of the problem will be found by utilising the existing road (No. 6 on Map) from Elberton to Alveston Down, suitably widened, cutting a new road through the Allotment gardens and behind the Council's quarry at Alveston Down, and proceeding southward across the main road and joining the Earthcott Green Road (old coaching route) to the east of St. Helen's Church. This lane widened and straightened by means of minor diversions shown on the map carries the route to Iron Acton which would be bye-passed on the north, and the existing road utilised to Yate. At the junction opposite the Aircraft Works a new road would branch to the right in order to bye-pass Chipping Sodbury, and the route would merge into the main Chippenham Road near Chipping Sodbury Station.

(d) The approaches to Weston-super-Mare.

The Bristol-Weston road (see traffic census diagram) carries an enormous and rapidly growing volume of traffic, and the question of planning a duplication of this route must receive careful consideration; in the future the coastal road should go a long way to attract tourist traffic from the Weston Road in addition to serving its normal function of providing inter-communication for the coastal towns generally. The northern approach to Weston, therefore, is to be via the existing road as improved or duplicated and the new coastal road described in *(b)* above.

The approach to Weston from Bath (No. 7 on Map) is via the existing road through Marksbury and Blagdon; this should be widened as may be necessary, and the villages of West Harptree, Compton Martin, Blagdon and Banwell bye-passed as shown. West of Knightcott the road forks, the northern arm (No. 8 on Map) leads to the village of Locking, which should be bye-passed as shown, and thence via the existing road, over Locking Bridge, to the Weston–Bristol road.

The main route (No. 7) proceeds westward for about ¾ mile, and just before the road turns south to skirt the shoulder of Elborough Hill the route branches as a new road leading north-west over the G.W.R. main line and along the site of the original Weston loop-line to the centre of the Town. The existing road through Hutton (No. 9 on Map), bye-passed at

Oldmixon, leads to Uphill and the southern end of the town.   An improvement and duplication of the approach to Weston from Wells along the southern base of Mendip, bye-passing Cheddar, Axbridge, Shiplake and Bleadon (as planned by the County Surveyor), is shown as No. 10 on the Map.

(e) The exits from the Radstock Coalfield area.

This part of the Region suffers to-day from the fact that (except the Fosseway) none of its roads were ever made as " turnpike " roads, and so it has had to make the best of what is little more than a network of local lanes.   The contours are very difficult in this neighbourhood ; the valleys of the River Somer and Wellow Brook are narrow and precipitous, and as a result rivers, roads and two lines of railway converge and meet at one spot in the centre of Radstock ; also the road crosses both railways at rail level, and finally between the two lines of railway is the terminus of the road leading to Frome.   The accumulative effect of this is paralysing to the development of the town, and little can be done by way of palliative measures until the level crossing is abolished.

The possibility of planning a direct connection from north to south on the line, approximately, of the old Roman road has been explored but has been abandoned on account of the steep gradients which would be involved ; there appears indeed to be no bye-pass possible, nor any route from north to south other than the existing road, and every effort should be made to improve this by abolishing the level crossing.

It has been found possible, however, to plan east to west bye-passes on both sides of these twin towns, viz. :—

No. 11 on Map.   Proceeding from the main Wells Road at Farrington Gurney along the existing approach road, a minor diversion is planned commencing near the Farrington Colliery rail crossing and ending at the junction by Old Mills Colliery ; then after ascending Buxbury Hill to the corner in Monger Lane, a new road across the fields carries the bye-pass to Bince's Lodge Lane.   After proceeding along this lane to the top of Old Millard's Hill, it branches north-east as a new road over Kitley's Hill and connects with Pow's Hill ; this lane carries the route by Clandown, and from that point a new road bearing to the right brings the route into communication with the Bath Road.   Alternatively a slightly longer and more hilly termination to the bye-pass could be planned to continue from Clandown along the lane and in front of Camerton Farm to the Bath Road near the seventh milestone.

No. 12 on Map.   The Southern Bye-pass branches from the Wells Road by the new Housing Site, runs down the shoulder of South hill, by St. Nicholas' Church, crosses the railway to the shoulder of the opposite hill and joins the Frome Road via the lane by Ludlow's Colliery cottages.   This bye-pass with its long railway bridge and difficult levels would be expensive and not very remunerative ; it is not considered to be so essential as is the abolition of the level crossing referred to above.

A more important proposal from the Regional point of view, is the planning of a new road (*No. 13 on Map*) down the River valley to Midford and the Bath Road, with a branch through Hinton Charterhouse (*No. 14 on Map*) to the Trowbridge Road.   Route No. 13 branches left from the Frome Road at Fir Tree Inn, passes along the lane to Green Parlour, and from there it strikes across fields down into the valley at Foxcote, and follows the course of the valley by Stoney Littleton to Wellow, where the stream is to be crossed by a bridge ; thence in a short distance the existing Wellow–Hinton road is reached and utilised.   At the bottom of Hinton Hill the route branches ; No. 13 (the main route) runs straight on between the stream and railway, past Hankley Wood to Midford.   The remainder of Route 13 to the main Bath–Warminster road is outside the Region ; it is however shown on the map and may be described as following the Midford Brook partly as a new road but using an existing lane at each end.   Route No. 14 leads up Hinton Hill and branches to the right at the top to avoid Hinton Charterhouse village and joins the Trowbridge Road west of Farleigh Hungerford (outside the Region).

(f) Other Roads.

No. 15, *Bristol to Pilning (for Aust)*, uses the Westbury Road to Nazareth Home; it then proceeds as a new road bye-passing Westbury Village, goes along the inner ring road to Passage Road and proceeds along that road through Brentry, Cribbs Causeway and Easter Compton, to Pilning, where it joins Road No. 4 (to Aust).

No. 16, *the northern exit from Bristol (for Gloucester)*, is planned to bye-pass Filton Village, from Horfield Common to the south-eastern corner of the Aerodrome. It then proceeds along the existing main road through Patchway (where a short diversion including a new railway bridge is recommended), Almondsbury, and Ridgeway. At St. Helen's Church (Alveston) a diversion, partly new and partly using an existing lane, cuts out the corner by the Ship Inn and shortens the route. The existing road via Milbury Heath is then followed and a minor diversion at lower Buckover Farm cuts out another bad corner (this last proposal is just outside the area of the Regional Survey).

No. 17. This is an improved *eastern exit from Bristol*, planned to encourage traffic to use the shorter route to London, etc., via Marshfield and Chippenham; most of it is included in the Bristol Town Planning Schemes. The Route commences with Speedwell Road at the eastern termination of which a new road will commence, passing by the Chequers Inn, across Soundwell Road at Hopewell Hill and proceeding to a lane leading through New Cheltenham, across Siston Common, through Goose Green and Webbs Heath. From here a new road, along the line of a footpath, connects with the road to Holbrook Common. At the commencement of the Common a new road strikes across fields to join the main Chippenham Road at Wick. East of Wick a diversion cuts out two right-angle bends and eases the ascent of Tog Hill. From the summit of Tog Hill the existing road carries the route out of the region except that Marshfield is recommended to be bye-passed as shown.

No. 18. This road from Bristol (through Wapley and Codrington) to Acton Turville was a turnpike road in 1820; it is now unclassified. It only needs widening, however, to convert it into a good route to Malmesbury, Cirencester, and Oxford, etc.; also it would then form an attractive tourist route from Chippenham to Bristol as it runs through typical local rural scenery.

No. 19, *the Kingswood Bye-pass*. Most of this is included in the Bristol Town Planning Scheme; it is planned to relieve congestion through East Bristol and Kingswood. Commencing near Lawrence Hill Station the road will cut through to Pile Marsh and along Beaufort Road, at the end of which it strikes across as a new road past Troopers Hill farm to Kingsway, which is crossed, and carries on to Blackhorse Road (Kingswood). It then proceeds along Whittuck Road to Hanham Road, and then as a new road past Mount-Hill Brickworks; from here an existing lane is used, and later a new length of road carries it forward to Grimsbury Lane, along which it proceeds and joins the main road by Warmley brook.

No. 20, *Kingswood, via Mangotsfield to the Badminton Road*. This is planned to provide a much needed northern exit from Kingswood and incidentally to improve the access between Kingswood and its nearest Railway Station (Mangotsfield); it is included in the Bristol Town Planning Scheme.

Commencing at a point opposite the Kingswood Council Offices (where a Town Square is recommended in order to initiate a new civic centre for Kingswood) a new road passes northward across New Cheltenham Road and Pound Lane to Station Road. From here a branch leads to the south side of Mangotsfield Station. The main route follows an existing lane passing under the Railway, and then strikes off as a new road up the valley beside Rodway Hill; it crosses Mangotsfield Road and connects with the road past Hooper's Farm, thus bye-passing Mangotsfield village. This lane carries the route across Road No. 18 at Blackhorse; then it continues along Blackhorse Lane to the point where the lane turns westward, where the route proceeds straight on as a new road and joins the main road south of Wick-Wick Farm.

No. 21.   This is a useful connection from the Bristol–Bath road to the Inner Ring Road at St. Anne's, Brislington.

Commencing at the junction west of Brislington House, a new road is planned to proceed northward over Broom Hill to Birchwood Road; this, when widened, will carry the route through the Corporation Housing Site to the Inner Ring Road (No. 1).

Nos. 22 and 23, Local Roads at Sand Bay.   These are intended as the skeleton of a local road system in the development of this coastal strip into a Seaside Resort.   No. 22 connects the northern part of Sand Bay with the Coastal Road (No. 3), bye-passing Wick St. Lawrence *en route*, and proceeds down the coast along the existing road (which should be widened and converted into a promenade or esplanade) to the south end of the bay; from here after a sharp turn (unavoidable by reason of the contours) the existing road through the woods completes a delightful route into Weston-super-Mare.   Much can be made of the coastal part of this route as a most attractive feature in the development of the neighbourhood if the long view is taken and generous provision for an imposing parkway or boulevard is made in the earliest stage of development.

No. 23 connects Sand Bay with the main Bristol–Weston road.   Commencing at the branch road near Apple-Tree Farm, it strikes across as a new road on the north-east of Worle village to the existing road near Newton's Farm; after proceeding some way along this road, it later continues in the same direction as a new road to the centre of Sand Bay, and joins the sea-front promenade near Myrtle-Tree Farm.

No. 24 is an extension to the south of the Weston sea-front boulevard; it passes behind the Sanatorium and along the seaward edge of the Golf-links, by Shinbridge Farm, and then follows the course of the River Axe, across Uphill Pill to join the Coastal Road.   This road should be considered as part of Weston's development scheme together with the acquisition of the Golf Links by the municipality; both proposals are intimately related and are recommended to be included in the programme of Town-improvement which is proving so real a method of attracting visitors to this town.

Nos. 25, 26 *and* 27, at Berrow, are planned to form, with the Coastal Road (No. 3), the skeleton of a Road System in the development of Berrow and Brean as a seaside resort.   No. 25 connects the central portion with the Weston–Brent road, passing to the north of Lympsham; most of it is new, but a small length of the existing tortuous lane is incorporated near the railway. No. 26 does similar service for the southern portion and connects with Middle Street, Brent Knoll.   No. 27 follows the line of railway from Brent Knoll to Uphill; more than half exists, and the connecting link shown will complete a route of value to the locality.

No. 28 is planned to improve the access to the town of Burnham-on-Sea, which is outside the area of the Region under survey, but nevertheless the value of such improved access to Burnham-on-Sea is sufficiently great to warrant its being included in this Report.   The actual position of the road would be a matter for consideration by the Axbridge and Burnham Councils, and it is suggested tentatively that it might follow the route shown on the Map (No. 28) and lead direct to the centre of Burnham from Edithmead, thus short-circuiting the longer route through Middle Burnham.   The portion within the Region would be an entirely new road.

No. 29.   This is a cross-country connection from the Weston–Banwell road to the Winscombe–Loxton road; following the depression between Bleadon Hill and Banwell Hill, it is planned to facilitate the access from Winscombe Vale to Weston; the new road commences at the Banwell Road near Hillend Farm, skirts the western spur of Banwell Hill, passes near Yarborough, and joins Barton Lane near Barton Farm.   From this point it continues as a widening to Winscombe Village.

Nos. 30 and 31, the Harptrees to Hallatrow and Farrington Gurney.   These are planned to open up a route from the road along the north of Mendip to the Cam district and Radstock Coalfield. No. 30 commences at West Harptree (which is bye-passed on the south) as a branch from Route No. 7.   The existing road past East Harptree Park is followed to the mouth of a lane leading north to Sherborne hamlet; here a new road strikes across the fields and across Whitehouse Lane to the upper end of the Litton Reservoir; proceeding it passes near Short-wood Common to the south end of Hollow Marsh Lane, which is followed until it turns sharp left when the route continues in a straight line as a new road to Pitway Lane. The route here divides into two: No. 30 carries on in the same north-easterly direction as a new road to the main Wells Road opposite the turning leading to Hallatrow and the other townships in the Cam Valley; No. 31 follows the existing Pitway Lane to Farrington Gurney, and thence to Midsomer Norton and Radstock.

Several other routes have been investigated, but it has not been considered desirable to include them in the recommendations for various reasons. The most important of these are a bye-pass road from Bathampton to Batheaston, and a connection from Congresbury via Sandford and Loxton to the Bridgwater Road near East Brent. The former is omitted as it is understood to be the desire of the civic authorities at Bath to attract visitors to their City rather than to provide facilities for bye-passing. The latter was intended to provide an alternative route to the main Bridgwater Road via Redhill. The suggestion was attractive as the gradients would be easy and the opening up of Winscombe Vale appeared desirable, but its effect would be to throw a great volume of traffic on the already burdened Bristol–Weston road, and for this reason it has been omitted from the Scheme.

B. General Road Suggestions

§ i. *Introductory*

As has been commented upon earlier in the Report, the Region is covered with an intricate network of indirect routes, and the policy adopted in the foregoing proposals is to include as many as possible of the existing roads in the improved Regional Road System. It follows that there are no Regional proposals for many of the existing roads, and it is suggested that these should be maintained largely in their present state to serve local needs; they will thus assist to conserve rural amenity and charm.

The arterial roads, on the other hand, will become frankly utilitarian like railways, and will rely upon tree planting as their amenity.

§ ii. *Arterial Road Design*

Arterial Road design is based upon a unit width per line of traffic, and the unit of width recommended by the Ministry of Transport is *ten feet*. For the most of their length the principal arterials pass through open country, planned in the Scheme to remain as such, and here it is suggested that an overall width of 60 feet between fences is adequate. On such a road present needs will be served by devoting half the width to carriageway, i.e., three units of traffic, since there will be no stopping traffic, and the three-unit width will permit a fast moving vehicle to overtake whilst passing another travelling in the opposite direction, and on one (or both) sides of the metalled surface there will be a footway (say 4 feet in width) and the remainder of the 60 feet will be left as grass verge. The grass verge will form a present amenity and will be available for further widening of the metalled portion, should future developments in transport render it necessary to do so.

Those parts of the arterial roads, however, which pass through developed, or developing, areas, or areas planned in the Scheme for future development, will need different treatment. In developed areas the incidence of vested interests is usually found to be so great that the cost of creating an adequate traffic artery by widening becomes prohibitive, and a great danger lies in the natural tendency of local authorities to curtail their programme and to be satisfied with something which may serve for the time but which is after all only a palliative. The

PLATE 35.

Example of a local road added beside an

Arterial road (Bath).

Photos: N. L. Webber.

Inexpensive and well proportioned.   *Expensive and fussy.*

BATH: A CONTRAST OF BUILDING.

Face page 107.

better course, and the least expensive in the long run, in such cases is to plan a diversion or bye-pass of the traffic artery through lands as yet undeveloped, and to provide that if and when building development occurs along the new route, a new *local* road must be added along-side the traffic road at the cost of the developing owner, much in the same way as railway undertakings keep their main lines for their through traffic and provide additional local lines and sidings alongside as required.   A typical cross-section of such a road is shown below (see also Plate 35) :—

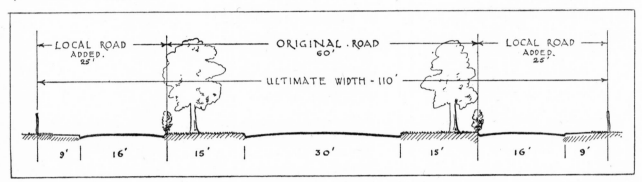

The "local" road will communicate with the traffic artery at intervals, and the Ministry of Transport recommend that such communications should be made at intervals of not less than half a mile ; it appears likely, however, that in the more closely developed areas it will be difficult at the present stage of public opinion to carry out this part of the programme in its entirety, although it should be possible to get a quarter-mile minimum without great difficulty.   But at any rate there must be provision for three lines of through traffic on all main roads in addition to whatever width is required for local traffic.

It will be noted that in the "local" portion of the road shown in the cross-section the 10-foot traffic unit has been reduced to 8 feet.   This is suggested as a minimum ; it would serve where expense is an object, for slow-moving traffic or traffic passing stationary obstacles, but wherever possible the 10-foot unit should be adopted.   The "local" sidewalk can be treated as (say) 5 feet of walking way, and 4 feet of grass verge against the fence ; also where there are these "local" roads with their sidewalks, the necessity for pathways on the arterial portion disappears, and this would give opportunity for effective tree planting or the strips might be furnished with groups of shrubs at intervals.   There is in fact great scope for the provision of valuable amenity in the scientific laying out of these road margins.

In submitting the above suggestions, it is not the intention to recommend a Standardized Cross-Section ; with roads as with other things, there is charm in variety, and the construction of a number of regional arteries to similar cross-sections would result in a road system which lacked interest.   Different portions of the same road might receive different treatment in accordance with local conditions ; it may be an easy matter to obtain additional width in some places, and these extra portions should be laid out to gain amenity along the road itself.

Beyond a certain point (say 60 or 70 feet) the additional width of a road is mainly a matter of amenity, except where the frontage is developed for building and where there are trams ; the amenity of the district through which a road is passing, and certain other circumstances (e.g., whether the road is to be a " Parkway " or an " Industrial Route "), will to a large degree determine how far it is necessary by extra width to provide increased amenity along the road itself.

In urban areas it may sometimes be found difficult to provide a road sufficiently wide to allow of proper furnishing with grass verges and trees.   It is considered that tree planting should only be undertaken, in these areas, on roads where footpath and grass verge together has a minimum width of 12 feet.   Thus in an urban area no tree planting should be done on a 50-foot road, but if tree planting is desired an extra width of at least 5 feet per line of trees should be provided.

In areas which are and will remain definitely rural in character the minimum width of carriageway may safely be less than in urban areas, the most obvious reason being that there is little or no stopping traffic to be provided for.

In some parts of the Region it will be desirable to provide riding tracks alongside the road; it should not be an expensive matter to include an extra width of (say) 12 or 15 feet of grass verge in rural areas, and this provision would not only be an immense boon to hunting people, but would facilitate the movement of cattle, etc., clear of the roadway itself. It may also be desirable to provide cycle tracks; these could be placed in the grass verge, and would take the place of the footpath on one side of the road in open country. (The amenity aspect of Road Design is further dealt with in Chapter III.)

Plate 36 illustrates various examples of Road Design.

§ iii. *Road Junctions*

The proper arrangement of road junctions and the planning of adjoining building lines are matters of great importance and are worthy of more attention than they usually receive at the hands of either the Local Authority or the Landowner. Large sums of both national and private money are being spent on highways at the present time, but, unless careful attention is given to these details, adequate results for the expenditure will not be obtained. On the other hand, proper planning will ensure speed with safety, the general improvement of values, and a saving in the annual cost of supervision—the last resulting from reduction in the need for traffic control.

The most important points for the consideration in the proper planning of road junctions are :—

(*a*) *Frequent entrances to main roads from bye-roads should be avoided*; the interval between junctions should be as long as possible; an interval of half a mile is the standard (see § ii above), but it will vary with local conditions (i.e., urban or rural); it should not, however, be less than a quarter of a mile anywhere. Where the artery passes through a developing or developable area the local roads should be planned to radiate from these junction points. At the same time—

(*b*) *Multiple junctions should be avoided.*

(*c*) *Buildings at corners should be set back* to a sufficient distance to ensure a clear view of traffic approaching on the other road, from a point along each road fifty yards from the actual junction.

(*d*) *Minor roads crossing arterials should be staggered* in order to impose a definite check upon the traffic intending to cross the arterial road. The " stagger " should always be planned so that traffic has (before crossing) to turn *left* on entering the arterial road.

(*e*) *At major road crossings* the gyratory principle should be enforced by the interposition of a large circle which may be planted with shrubs.

(*f*) *Shopping centres* should not be placed at important road junctions on account of the stopping traffic which they bring. At all shopping centres extra width of carriageway should be provided to allow a " bay " for stopping traffic.

An exhaustive report on this subject has been prepared by a Committee of the Town Planning Institute and has recently been published under the ægis of the Ministry of Transport.

§ iv. *Building Lines*

The term " Building Line " is often used locally as meaning the fence line or boundary line of the street, but this is obviously wrong, as the term is intended to apply to " buildings " not " fences." The correct meaning is " the distance from the fence or boundary line of the street, in front of which no building may be erected."

PLATE 36.

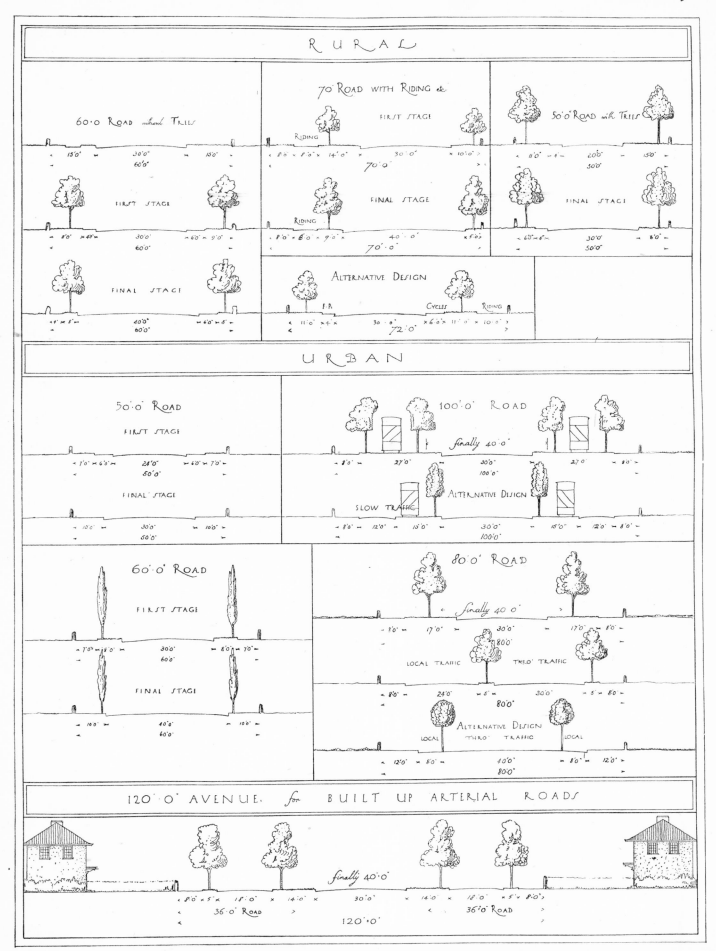

RURAL

60.0 ROAD without TREES

70' ROAD WITH RIDING etc.
FIRST STAGE
RIDING

50'0" ROAD with TREES

FIRST STAGE

FINAL STAGE
RIDING

FINAL STAGE

FINAL STAGE

ALTERNATIVE DESIGN
F.P.   CYCLES   RIDING

URBAN

50'0" ROAD
FIRST STAGE

100'0" ROAD
finally 40'0"

FINAL STAGE

SLOW TRAFFIC   ALTERNATIVE DESIGN

60'0" ROAD
FIRST STAGE

80'0" ROAD
finally 40'0"

FINAL STAGE

LOCAL TRAFFIC   THRO' TRAFFIC

ALTERNATIVE DESIGN
LOCAL   THRO' TRAFFIC   LOCAL

120'0" AVENUE for BUILT UP ARTERIAL ROADS

finally 40'0"

36'0" ROAD   36'0" ROAD

120'0"

ROAD DESIGNS.

The building lines adopted by the Ministry of Transport, viz. :—

30 feet for first-class roads
25 feet for second-class roads

are recommended generally, and it is urged that immediate steps should be taken to lay down building lines on the developable portions of all the important through routes under the powers contained in the Roads Improvement Act of 1925.

It is suggested, however, that careful investigation should be made as to the character of the expected development where the route lies through developable areas. The *raison d'être* of building lines is threefold : (i) a "factor of safety" in case untoward events should make a further road widening necessary at some future time, (ii) to ensure adequate sunshine and light to all ground-floor rooms, (iii) to preserve the amenities of residential development by setting the houses back out of the dust and vibration (and, to some extent, the noise). The general building line should always be maintained, not on the question of amenity, but in order to provide the sites for "bays" at the roadside to accommodate stopping traffic, and thus leave the full width free for through traffic.

§ v.   *Ribbon Development*

One important objective of the Regional plan is the curbing of indiscriminate scattered building, and particularly the stringing of houses along the main roads in the form of Ribbon Development.

The principal main roads are intended for through and fast traffic ; there should be as few cross-roads as possible and the traffic stream should not be hampered with slow-moving or standing vehicles ; it has been stated earlier that if used only for through traffic a carriageway wide enough for the passing of three vehicles is sufficient for all but the most heavily loaded routes, but if houses are to be built alongside an additional 8 feet is required on each side for the local traffic ; this is discussed in detail in Part the Third, Chapter III.

As to the remedy—it is suggested that a salutary check would be given if the Local Authorities could require all developing owners to provide their own roads ; if then an owner insisted on building along the main road, he would have to provide his "local" road alongside (as outlined in § 2 of this sub-section). Such a policy, allied to that of the institution of agricultural and semi-agricultural Character Zones wherein residential development would be permitted only on condition that the houses are suitably grouped, would go a long way to cure this evil of Ribbon Development.

SECTION 2.   RAILWAYS

It will be seen from the Accessibility Diagram (Plate 12) that the principal areas not served by railways are the Cotswolds, Mendip, Chew Valley, and the plain south of Mendip. Reference to the Zoning Plan, however, will show that for the most part these districts should not become extensively developed, and so no railway extensions are there suggested.

It only remains to refer to the railway proposals in connection with the crossing of the Severn ; these include a branch from the South Wales line, commencing near Pilning and proceeding parallel to the shore to Aust, and a branch from Aust to connect with the existing L.M.S.R. at Thornbury. Other local branches for industrial purposes will follow as development proceeds, e.g., in the factory areas north and south of Avonmouth.

SECTION 3. AIR TRANSPORT

§ i. *Present Facilities*

The only existing Aerodromes in the Region are at Filton, near Bristol, and at Yate. The use of the former is to be restricted shortly to the military authorities (as a Royal Air Force Aerodrome) and for the private use of the Bristol Aeroplane Company; it is now used temporarily by a civilian Aeroplane Club, but their occupation will cease when the Aerodrome is closed to general and commercial Air Traffic. The Yate aerodrome is restricted to the private use of Messrs. Parnall & Co.

§ ii. *Expected Development*

The Region is remote from any present National Airway, but Bristol will become of increasing importance as an Air Station when commercial and private flying become more general; it should also form a junction for the chain of Air Ports which would be formed between London and Ireland, and Plymouth and the North, when Transatlantic or Irish air mail services become an established fact.

The other towns in the Region will require smaller Aerodromes as ports of call, and for housing and refuelling purposes; it would not, however, be an economic proposition at the present stage of aerial development for every town in the Region to establish local aerodromes now, but the more important of them would be well advised to seek out and reserve in their Town Planning Schemes suitable sites for this purpose.

In addition to the planning of local air parks for the more important towns, every town and large village will require its " Landing ground," and the more of these there are available the quicker will be the growth of this new form of transport. If there were a number of small landing grounds near all the centres in the Region it would become in air parlance " good flying country," and all this would tend to foster and encourage aerial development. These local landing grounds can be started in a very cheap way, as is done on the Continent, where at small towns the necessary land is acquired by the local Council and used for grazing and sports, in addition to the primary use as a landing ground. The local postmaster or garage proprietor is put in charge, and his duties are to collect landing and housing fees, serve out petrol and oil to the aviators, and collect rent from the sports clubs renting pitches, and the farmer renting grazing.

§ iii. *Bristol—the Headquarters*

The case of Bristol, however, is very different; it is expected that it will be not only an air junction and landing ground, but the headquarters of civilian flying for the West of England; it will be the place where repair shops, service stations, etc., will be established for all types of aircraft operating within a wide radius; and it will collect and distribute meteorological data and reports to the smaller aerodromes and landing grounds at other towns in the locality.

The Corporation of Bristol are fully alive to the possibilities, and have acquired a site within 3 miles of Temple Meads Station for the establishment of a civil Air Port, which is to be opened early in 1930.

§ iv. *Public Service or Private Enterprise*

Whether the aerodromes of the future are to be run by the Local Authorities or by private enterprise is a matter for careful consideration, but it is significant that the Railway Companies are now seeking Parliamentary powers in this direction. It is felt, however, that while the maintenance of an air " Port of Call " at a small town may be a matter for discussion, the establishment and maintenance of a main Air Port at Bristol, where eventually wireless and meteorological stations, beacon lights for night flying, and Customs will be required, should be looked upon as essentially a Public Service.

Another point is that early development of civilian flying in this part of England is coming in competition with private cars, taxis and even charabancs. All machines will require their local landing grounds and housing accommodation, and those not permanently located at Bristol will make occasional use of the workshops and service stations which will be established there by commercial aircraft companies and others, for the purpose of repairs, overhauls and refitting. Those machines plying for hire will also need to make daily use of the services of a Ground Engineer whose duty it is (under Air Ministry Regulations) to inspect and certify each machine each day, before it is allowed to be used for passenger carrying; the most economic arrangement would be to have stationed at Bristol Headquarters a Ground Engineer who would be available to do this for all machines operating in the locality.

§ v. *Conclusion*

The Air Navigation Act, 1920, empowers any local authority to establish and maintain aerodromes, and to carry on any ancillary business connected therewith; also the Air Ministry will advise any local authority on the suitability of any proposed site, and scheme of maintenance. It is not within the scope of this Report, and it would perhaps be unwise, to delineate on a map sites which may be suitable, or to dogmatise on the question of maintenance, but it is certain that the local authorities who show foresight in making provision for aerial development will be well rewarded in the not far distant future.

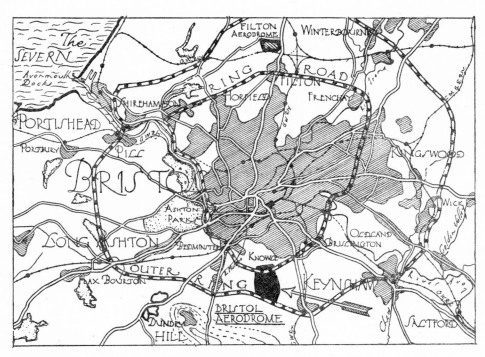

LOCATION PLAN OF THE BRISTOL AIR PORT

CHAPTER III. OPEN SPACES: RESERVATION AND PLANTING

SECTION 1. A REGIONAL PARK SYSTEM

§ i. *A Comparison*

THE object of a Regional Plan, as regards Open Spaces, is to direct attention to the wider aspects rather than to deal with purely local needs. It would not, for example, be reasonable or sensible to take the Zoning Map and, on the basis of the possible population there adumbrated in the residential areas, to pick out and schedule sufficient land for the playing fields required by the hypothetical inhabitants. Those essential accompaniments of urban and rural existence, Local Open Spaces, must be provided, and would wisely be provided *in advance*; but the Regional Plan leaves too wide a margin of populous zones for the detailed playing fields to be selected so far in advance of actual requirement.

But there are certain salient features of the Region, certain areas declared by nature as fit and desirable for reservation, whatever the population. The Regional Park System depends chiefly on this natural disposition: the places most necessary for preservation as open spaces may be in the areas of local authorities sparsely populated and not likely to reserve them themselves, and it may be the duty and privilege of one or other of the more important Authorities in the Region to take steps to acquire some of them. Be that as it may, it is the function of the Plan to consider the Region as a whole and to work up a Park System which is suited to it as a whole.

§ ii. *Agricultural Reservation*

One of the chief features of the present plan is an attempt to preserve large areas of agricultural land as a form of open space or reservation. Not that it is suggested that the public should have any more access to the fields than at present they have by country roads and established fieldpaths: but the existence of unthreatened country occupied by " the least changing of industrial pursuits " is in itself a first-rate recreator of urban existence, which tends to become more rapid and restless every year. The gift of farm land to the City of Birmingham by Mr. Cadbury and of the Langdale Valley Farms to the National Trust by Professor George Trevelyan are examples of the full acquisition by the public of land which is not to be used by them for rambling over. Here public ownership is not aimed at, but only a permanent reservation for farming and similar use. If such types of reservation are included in a Regional Scheme it is manifestly impossible to work out any basis of acreage per head of the population.

§ iii. *A Standard of Local Open Spaces*

For local purposes, on the other hand, it is very necessary to have certain standards as to acreage and distribution: these are here set forth with the object of putting forward a common basis to local authorities in the preparation of their Town Planning Schemes. Where possible they should at once reserve land up to the required amount: where the area is still too undeveloped to be able to locate all the open spaces which the population will require, the Local Authority should keep the standard before them and endeavour to attain the full complement at the earliest possible moment.

The minimum area of open space per head of the population has been generally agreed upon, not only in this country but on the Continent, as 5 acres per 1000 of the population, or 1 acre for each 200 persons.   But there is a wide difference of opinion as to how this space should be allocated, more particularly as between sports grounds and ornamental parks.   One German authority, Dr. Martin Wagner,* allots :—

> One-fifth to Sports.
> Three-twentieths for Ornamental Parks and Parkways.
> Thirteen-twentieths for Woodlands.

This would appear in this country as far too low a proportion for Sports ; further, Woodlands, representing regional open spaces, are apparently included in the total.   In the computation recommended for this Region, the large natural Reservations, whether woods or hills, are to be considered as *additional to* and not part of the local minimum of 5 acres per 1000 people ; for it would be manifestly absurd to suggest that the needs of Bristol for parks were met by the reservation of vast tracts of land on top of Mendip.

The following is the allocation recommended† :—

> Three-fifths to Play Space for games.
> Two-fifths to General Park space.

Of the 3 acres thus given to games it has been further laid down that for children under 14 there should be ½ acre which should be so distributed that no child should have to walk more than ¼ mile to reach a playground.   The 2½ acres for the remainder of the sports-playing population could be more irregularly distributed, the necessity for level ground and a large area in one playground being frequently a prime determinant of location.

There is now an estimated population of 683,000 in the Region, which at the above rate should have 3415 acres of local open spaces ; of this figure 2050 acres should be playing fields.

§ iv.   *Areas of Local and Regional Open Space*

It is not meant to be inferred by the above paragraph that none of the open spaces shown on the Regional Plan are to be counted as forming part of the Local Standard of 5 acres per 1000 persons.   The open spaces in the form of river valleys, woodlands, etc., in the immediate neighbourhood of Bristol, Kingswood and Warmley, etc., and falling within their Town Planning Schemes, may well be allowed to form part of the two-fifths of General Park space. But the more distant and larger Reservations are to be considered as additional to the quota of Local Open Spaces.   In seaside towns the presence of a foreshore would modify the calculation.

The Local Open Spaces will require to be increased *pro rata* with the growth of the population : the area of Regional Open Space may be considered as approximately fixed.

SECTION 2.   DESCRIPTION OF PROPOSALS

§ i.   *Threefold Division*

The Regional Reservations are illustrated on Plate 37, they are divided into three classes :—

> *a.* Special Landscape Reservation.
> *b.* Rural Reservation.
> *c.* Open Space and Special Feature.

These have already been briefly described under Chapter I (Zoning) as forming Nos. 9 and 10, 11 and 12 of the categories into which all land in the Region is subdivided.   It will also be

---

* International Town Planning Conference, Amsterdam, 1924.
† See an article by G. L. Pepler, F.S.I., *Town Planning Review*, vol. x, p. 11.

found that the three classes very closely correspond to three of the divisions of the Landscape Survey, namely, the areas of Remarkable Landscape Value, the Wild Country, and specially Beautiful or Remarkable Features. It is not therefore necessary to go over in detail again the particular areas affected; but it may be remarked that these types of Reservation are accessible to the public in three differing degrees : (*a*) The *Special Landscape Reservations* are for the most part highly cultivated farm land and the public access to it is by means of country roads and footpaths; (*b*) The *Rural Reservations*, consisting chiefly of wild country, either uncultivated or used only for grazing, can be made more accessible, though the requirements of water catchment may limit the use; the land may be public property, but its openness is only incidental; (*c*) The *Open Space Reservations* are intended to be public property specially acquired for the purpose; they may belong in some cases to the National Trust (as Shirehampton Park), in other cases to the Local Authority (as the Clifton Downs).

§ ii. *Special Landscape Reservations* *

The principal areas of this type of Reservation have already been described. It will be noted that Bath is practically surrounded by this protected scenery. Bristol has protection for the high ground immediately adjoining Clifton across the Avon on the west; it is of great importance to the city that this attractive and unspoilt country, so near, be preserved. Approached in several directions from the south of Bristol is the largest tract of this type in the Region, leading uninterruptedly to Mendip; it should thus be possible to walk from Bristol near Ashton Park to the top of the Mendip plateau through permanently safeguarded beautiful country.

Weston-super-Mare has protection in the plan for the broken western extremities of the Mendip ridge, from whence it is possible to walk continuously to the main plateau.

§ iii. *The Wild Country*

There are five principal areas of this type : Mendip; Backwell Hill and Wrington Warren; Dundry Hill; Lansdown; and Charmy Down and St. Catherine's Valley. All are further protected by being practically surrounded by the Special Landscape Reservation.

§ iv. *Open Space and Special Features*

In addition to the Remarkable Features such as Cheddar Gorge, Burrington Combe, Goblin Combe, Brockley Combe, Leigh Woods, Wick Rocks, etc., enumerated in the Landscape Survey, there are a large number of comparatively narrow parkways, largely using the river valleys and acting as radial connections from Bath and Bristol into the country. This is in many ways the most useful form that public parks can take. In other places they take the form of encircling belts.

§ v. *Other Areas not shown*

It must not be supposed that the above constitute the only open ground that will be left in the Region; they are the portions selected to be specially safeguarded as such. But of course there is the Normal Agricultural Land, which will to a great extent remain unchanged, and there are the vast tracts of Low-lying Land, much of which has considerable charm near at hand and is of great landscape value as seen from the heights. If the Zoning recommendations are adopted neither of these two types of country will be defaced or urbanised except in well-planned groups.

There are also the Local Open Spaces—more especially the Playing Fields already alluded to. These cannot be shown at this stage, but in contemplating this Plan the spectator must imagine to himself the 3415 acres which should be there already and the additional amount which will be added according to the growth of the population.

---

* For definition see page 92.

Finally, and of great importance in the local schemes, are the Private Open Spaces in the form of Golf Courses, Cricket, Football and Tennis grounds. Large numbers of the community provide their own playing fields in this way whether as groups of individuals or members of business firms. Every effort should be made to safeguard the permanency of these Private Open Spaces under Town Planning Schemes.

SECTION 3.   FOOTPATHS, PARKWAYS, ROADS AND TREE PLANTING

§ i.   *Amenities of Means of Communication*

Means of communication, in addition to satisfying the needs of traffic, must also be considered as forming part of the open spaces of a region. There are indeed those who think parks, apart from playing fields, can best be provided by adding the amenities of verdure and trees to routes required for traffic, whether pedestrian or vehicular. Railway companies, after the initial defacement caused by their cuttings and embankments, and although safety prevents the admission of the public to their property, are usually careful to see that it is neatly kept; in some cases they have gone to the trouble of planting trees and shrubs along the grass margins, but generally they have left the grass-loving wild flowers to establish themselves and have enclosed their property with a well-trimmed hedge.

But the routes to which the public is admitted present greater opportunities, of which the most use is not always made.

§ ii.   *Footpaths*

Public rights-of-way on foot through private property provide in a great measure the enjoyment of free rambling. If one is a real walker there is not much temptation to stray from the unfenced path leading through fields, though doubtless the naturalist, loiterer, or picnicker would prefer to wander freely in all directions. It is chiefly as a means of enjoying the country while proceeding from place to place, free from the perils of the road, that the Footpaths are to be considered as part of the Regional Park System. For this purpose they should be mapped and rendered as continuous and efficient as possible by exchanging, duplications, and filling in missing links. A footpath map of the Region should be published* and in preparing their Town Planning Schemes Local Authorities should be careful not to merge too many footpaths in roadways.

Such footpaths should be imbedded in a 60-foot strip of grass, and the aim should be to use the footpaths as means of exit from the towns and as connecting links between the Open Spaces: the walker, after being confined to the path, would be able to ramble at large on reaching the Public Open Spaces.

§ iii.   *Parkways*

A Parkway may be described as an elongated park strip, one essential of which is that it contains a "way" leading through it. It is more than a footpath which consists of the right of passage over private property; the Parkway includes both the land for the "way" and a strip of land on either side of varying width. There are, roughly speaking, three types: (*a*) the Riverside Parkway in which the stream is the connecting feature; (*b*) the Footpath or Pedestrian Parkway; (*c*) the Road Parkway. The dividing line between the Road bordered by trees and grass verge, commonly called a Boulevard, and the Parkway in which the road passes through a narrow belt or strip of Parkland is not very definable.

---

* This might be undertaken by the local branch of the C.P.R.E. (see Part IV) in conjunction with the Footpaths and Commons Preservation Society. The Wirral Peninsula in Cheshire has for years had 3-in. maps with the footpaths and open spaces shown in colour available to members of the local Footpaths Preservation Society.

As pointed out in Section 2, there are several Riverside Parkways in the Regional Park System ; a Pedestrian Parkway is proposed from the corner of Ashton Park to the Landscape Reservation in the direction of Barrow.   Road Parkways might well be laid out in connection with some of the new arterial routes.

The formation of the Road Parkway is facilitated by the Roads Fund and Development Act 1909, which enables the Ministry of Transport to purchase land 220 yards (i.e., 1 furlong) wide on either side of a main road ; this land can be partly resold for building purposes, if so required, nor of course need the full width always be bought.   The powers might well be exercised where a new road, leading from a town, is passing through an attractive piece of country and where otherwise the owner would naturally be inclined to develop the building frontage.   A park strip thus provided would be fully used and seen, and the amenity of a dignified approach to the town secured.

§ iv. *Roads*

No one would be inclined to suggest that when the traffic requirements of the road are met, the matter is ended.   In the chapter on Communications, various suggestions are made for additions to roads for the purposes of amenity ; it is not intended to repeat these.   But it may be worth while to take the minimum Main Road through open country which has been given as 60 feet between fences with a 30-foot carriageway and to show different arrangements, including extra width, in order to produce variety of effect and to serve different purposes.

(*a*) The simplest arrangement : the 30-ft. carriageway in the centre with 15-foot grass strips on either side and a hedge or other fence without trees.   This would be suitable where nothing should interrupt the full view of the country.

(*b*) The addition of a single row of trees on either side, well set back to allow of future widening, is the next step.

(*c*) It may be desirable to provide a wider grass strip on one side for riding, or driving of cattle : 10 feet grass on one side and 20 feet on the other would allow trees within the fences.   The pathway in the wider strip need only be a gravel one; it would probably also be used for hacking.

(*d*) Double rows of trees and an ample treatment in general, entailing extra width.

By the addition of extra width, it would be easy to add further variations of the Road having a 30-foot carriageway.   In more urban areas the isolation of tram track and the provision of fast and slow traffic tracks give opportunity for many fine treatments.   (See Plate 34).

As regards footpaths they should be paved even in rural areas to the extent of 5 feet, as if not paved, pedestrians will always choose the road, to their own danger and that of motor traffic.

§ v. *Tree Planting*

This requires careful study if the best results are to be obtained.   It will be remembered that the County Council have powers to plant trees and the Roads Beautifying Association exists for the purpose of giving advice as to the most suitable sorts of trees for different soils and landscape effects.   The Roads of Remembrance Committee of the Association encourages the planting of trees in commemoration of outstanding events, whether of public or private significance.

The arrangement of trees is as important as their species.   There are places where the hard line of an avenue is discordant with the lines of the landscape.   Groups of trees can be planted where the grass verges are wide enough, e.g., in cases where the road approaches the character of the Parkway.   The contrast of open stretches with these groups, if skilfully managed, can be very effective.   A list of suitable trees is given in Appendix B.

SECTION 4.   AFFORESTATION

§ i. *Suitable Areas*

There are several districts in the Region where afforestation might usefully and profitably be undertaken, but there are also some areas, such as the Mendip plateau, where it would be altogether out of place.   Areas suggested as suitable for this treatment are portions of the following :—

> The Cotswold slopes and plateau.
> The combes around Bath.
> The " middle terrace " west of the Cotswolds.
> The Gordano ridges and Failand.
> The Barrow—Backwell—Wrington Warren area.
> The Cam Valley.
> The slopes of Mendip, Banwell and Bleadon.
> Low-lying lands (parts of).
> Spoil heaps of Collieries.

§ ii. *Species and Varieties*

The following species and selected varieties are recommended :—

Generally (except low-lying land and colliery tips).—

Common Name.	Species.	Variety.
Oak	*Quercus*	*Robur ; Cerris ; Palustris ; Coccinea*
Beech	*Fagus*	*Sylvatica*
Larch	*Larix*	*Europæa*
Sycamore	*Acer*	*Pseudo-platanus*
Pine	*Pinus*	*Austriaca* * ; *Sylvestris ; Laricio*
Chestnut	*Castanea*	*Vesca*
Elm	*Ulmus*	*Campestris ; Montana ; Cornubiensis*
Ash	*Fraxinus*	*Excelsior*
Birch	*Betula*	*Alba*

* *Pinus Austriaca* is hardy and is suitable for sheltering purposes.

Selected Areas.—The above list and, in addition—Spruce (*Abies excelsa, Abies Douglasii, Abies grandis,* and *Abies Menzesii*) and Pine (*Pinus Benthamiana* and *Pinus excelsa*) might be planted in sheltered positions on the Cotswold and Mendip slopes, Gordano, Backwell, Cam Valley.   Spruce is not recommended for exposed positions on the Cotswold plateau.

§ iii. *Low-lying Lands*

Planting of low-lying lands and sewage farms with Willow, Alder and the Swamp Cypress is another suggestion : this can be made very profitable if the right varieties are selected. For example, the Huntingdon Willow (*Salix alba cærulea*) which is used for the making of cricket bats, fetches excellent prices at maturity.* The golden-barked, scarlet-barked and silver-leaved Willow, also the *Salix diaphanoides* and *Salix purpurea*, have an especial value to the basket-maker when grown as osiers.

Short List of Suitable Trees for Low-lying Lands

Common Name.	Species.	Variety.
Willow	*Salix*	*Alba Cærulea* (Huntingdon Willow); *Babylonica*; *Ramulus Aurea* (golden-barked); *Caprea* (tricolour); *Regalis* (silver-leaved); *Vitellina* (golden willow); *Vitellina Britzensis* (scarlet-barked); *Diaphanoides*; *Purpurea*
Alder	*Alnus*	*Glutinosa, etc.*
Swamp Cypress	*Taxodium*	*Distichum*
Poplar	*Populus*	*Fastigiata; Canadiensis; Abele; Tremula*
Marsh Oak	*Quercus*	*Palustris*

§ iv. *Colliery Spoil Heaps*

In the Cam Valley afforestation has been found useful for the treatment of colliery spoil heaps, where several varieties of the Conifer family appear to thrive under conditions which would be thought to be unfavourable. At the disused Greyfield Colliery near High Littleton, two spoil heaps have been successfully planted with larch, spruce and pine; the trees are now well established, and are not only valuable as an improvement to the amenity of the neighbourhood, but will in time yield a monetary return for the outlay.

§ v. *Forestry Commission*

The Forestry Commission, Whitehall, London, offer grants for approved afforestation schemes: sums up to £4 per acre may be granted for planting oak or ash, £3 for beech, chestnut or sycamore, and up to £2 per acre for other hardwoods, and for conifers: additional grants are available for clearing scrub-areas.

---

* We are informed by Mr. H. P. Hutchinson, of the Research Station, Long Ashton, that fifty such trees of about twenty years' standing fetched £1100 recently in Somerset.

CHAPTER IV.   PUBLIC SERVICES

SECTION 1.   SEWAGE DISPOSAL

§ i. *Introductory*

IN the Survey of Sewage Disposal Works now in operation in the Region (see Part First, Chapter IX), it was pointed out that the fifty-four existing schemes comprise :—

> 6 discharging crude sewage into tidal waters.
> 14 discharging purified effluent into inland streams.
> 34 discharging crude effluent into inland streams.

Any proposals which are to be put forward in the Regional Scheme must naturally take these existing conditions into account, and it may be well to discuss the merits and faults of the existing state of affairs.   On the shores of the Bristol Channel and in the estuaries of the rivers, the great rise and fall in the tides and the consequent scour produced allow crude sewage to be discharged satisfactorily at certain stages of the tide ; there is, therefore, no occasion to make any suggestions for treatment of sewage in the case of towns having access to tidal waters.   The treatment of effluents discharging into non-tidal rivers is, however, a very different matter, and such effluents should always be rendered as innocuous as possible.   That no fewer than 34 of the 48 communities depending upon inland waters for their drainage should be discharging crude effluent at the present day is a far from satisfactory condition of things.   It should be noted also that in some cases crude sewage is being discharged at more or less regular distances down the same river valley ; and there is other evidence of lack of co-ordination not only between local authorities but between different villages under the same local control.

Natural conditions as to river basin, contours, rate of fall, etc., are of primary importance in considering a drainage system for the Region : also the zoning proposals outlined in Chapter I of this Part of the Report will materially influence the planning.

§ ii. *Policy*

The following suggestions form an attempt to reduce the matter to some kind of system :—

1. Crude sewage should be discharged only into tidal waters.

2. Where two or more outfalls of crude sewage occur in reasonable proximity on the same watercourse, a trunk sewer and a sewage treatment plant should be planned to deal with the combined sewage of the various communities concerned.

3. Areas zoned in the Scheme for growth into new residential districts should have their main sewer and disposal plant planned without delay, and as far as possible the sewer should be laid down and some portion of the plant constructed ahead of development.

4. Existing Villages not expected (under the Scheme) to develop into residential areas should put in hand as soon as practicable small filter beds, etc., to suit their local needs.

119

§ iii. *Application*

The detailed application of the above is beyond the scope of this Report, but subject to confirmation—after local surveys as to levels, etc.—it may be suggested that :—

Bristol and the coastal towns will discharge crude sewage into tidal waters ;

The Chew Valley villages will find it an economy to provide a combined plant and outfall east of Publow ;

The Cam Valley communities—Clutton, Temple Cloud, Hallatrow, High Littleton, Timsbury, Peasedown-St.-John, and Paulton (the last being at present without sewers)—should combine ;

In the Wellow basin, Midsomer Norton and Radstock would probably find it economical in working to set up a single plant below the combined towns, and perhaps to include Farrington Gurney and Chilcompton into their system ;

On the Avon, Saltford, Bitton and possibly other villages would appear to be favourably placed for connection to Bath's disposal plant by arrangement with that City.

There are also a number of growing communities and new residential areas at present without drainage, but for which the planning of detailed schemes should be put in hand without delay ; they include *inter alia* :—

Thornbury

Old Sodbury, Chipping Sodbury and Yate—Combined system.

Iron Acton, Frampton Cotterell, Coalpit Heath. Winterbourne . } Combined system.

Charlton . Brentry . Henbury } Combined system.

Whitchurch

Portbury . Easton-in-Gordano } To combine with Pill, to discharge into tidal Avon.

Nailsea

Congresbury

Brean

Locking Woolvers Hill } Combined scheme (including Hutton if levels permit).

Winscombe . Shipham . } Combined scheme.

The importance of planning and partially constructing systems for the above places *ahead of development* is that it will be a great stimulus to that element of persuasive planning which is discussed in Part III of this Report.

SECTION 2.   WATER SUPPLY

§ i. *Introductory*

This subject falls naturally into two main divisions : collection and distribution. In the Survey (Part I, Chapter IX) the present sources of supply and arrangements for distribution were discussed, and the comments and suggestions which follow should be read with that section.

§ ii. *Catchment Areas*

The principal sources of supply in the Region are the catchment areas. The water supply is the vulnerable point in the modern community and it should be safeguarded at all costs, so that it is of the utmost importance for a Region with a large population that the catchment areas should be maintained free from possible pollution. An undrained community on a catchment area, even though it consists only of a few isolated farm-houses, may be a menace to the health of thousands, and local authorities which permit building upon their catchment areas are running a grave risk. The difficulty, especially in a limestone country, is to find the actual areas of water catchment : careful and constant vigilance is necessary. The ascertainable areas are shown on Plate 31, but their control in order to ensure purity of supply is a matter of difficulty. It is better to be on the safe side and allow no building when there is a chance of the area being a catchment.

Mendip and Cheddar.—This area is not easy to define with certainty : the policy of the Bristol Water Company is to purchase the strategic points such as swallet holes, and to rely on their By-laws for the remainder. It is expected that the zoning proposals in the Regional Scheme will be of assistance in the preservation of this catchment area.

Yeo Valley.—This is subject to rigid control of development by means of special By-laws of the Bristol Waterworks Company : the villages are drained by a sewer running south of the lake with an outfall below the dam, and the outlying farms have each a special filter bed for their sewage, the innocuous effluent being discharged over the surface soil. The Water Company are buying up as they can the land in the area, especially that round the lake ; they find the process of acquisition slow and costly. They consider themselves protected to a very large extent against pollution by reason of their By-laws, which are applied with stringency. Doubtless the Water Company would welcome a zoning plan aimed at preserving the area, and it is suggested that they might be expected to assist in meeting the compensation (if any) which may result from its reservation under the Regional Scheme. Further drainage works are in contemplation by the District Council, and there is some expectation that with the co-operation of the Water Company and other landowners in the valley a comprehensive sewage scheme will be achieved.

Bath.—The top of Lansdown Hill and the St. Catherine's Valley and downs on both sides would appear to be natural catchment areas, and the above remarks apply equally in this case.

Winscombe Vale.—Though Burnham is outside the Region, the catchment area of this town's supply is within the Region, i.e., in the Valley of Winscombe, where there is a growing community that at present has no sewage scheme. This does not appear to be a satisfactory arrangement, though the water supply is probably not fed directly from the surface ; the area has developed too far for effective control as a catchment area, and it appears best to suggest that Burnham will have to look elsewhere for its supply.

Banwell Hill.—Weston's supply is obtained from a spring at the foot of this hill, the catchment area of which is the northern slope of Mendip, including probably portions of Sandford Hill, etc. The abundance of the spring appears to indicate that the catchment area is very extensive and as the neighbourhood is now developing residentially it may be imperative to impose regulations over a wide area in order to safeguard the purity of the supply emerging from the hill itself.

The catchment area north of Axbridge and the crown of Banwell Hill are almost uninhabited ; they are both zoned in the Scheme similarly to the Mendip area, and the system of control in vogue on Mendip should also be applied to these areas.

*   *   *   *   *

It would be worth investigating whether a catchment area does not exist under Wrington Hill and Backwell Hill : this is an almost uninhabited limestone area similar to parts of the Mendip, having a considerable surface exposed to surface rainfall. Increase of population makes it advisable to tap all possible sources of supply.

§ iii. *New Development*

It appears from the diagram that whilst there are large areas yet unserved by the statutory undertakers, some parts of the Region which are zoned in the Scheme as " agricultural " have water services ; there is of course a necessity to provide a water supply for the whole Region, but the various water authorities will no doubt find it advisable to study the Regional Scheme in planning new developments of their systems in order to ascertain the spots where intensive development is to be expected and vice versa.

It is interesting to note that the statutory areas of supply do not run with the areas of local administration. It may result in economy for authorities to combine to form a Joint Water Board or Boards, although it should be noted that the cost of distribution in rural areas is frequently found to be in excess of the cost of independent local Schemes even after allowance is made in the local schemes for cost of pumping. The working out of a scheme of Regional water supply is beyond the scope of this Report, but it is suggested as a fruitful field for detailed enquiry.

SECTION 3. ELECTRICITY

§ i. *Method of Distribution*

Before proceeding to discuss proposals for electrical development in the Region, it may be of use to explain that Electricity is generated " in bulk " and is conveyed by means of " High Tension " mains over the countryside, but that these mains are not available for tapping indiscriminately at all and every point of the route ; the " High Tension " main carries electricity at high pressure (usually 11,000 volts), and this needs to be reduced to a pressure of about 200 volts before it can be available for domestic or 450 volts for normal industrial use. The reduction of pressure is effected by the setting up at selected spots of " Transformer Stations," and the effective range of the transformed current is limited to a radius of about 1½ miles from the Transformer Station. Thus the fact that a High Tension line traverses a given stretch of country does not necessarily mean that electrical development will inevitably spring up all along the route, and herein lies a most important aspect of electrical planning in relation to the Regional Scheme.

§ ii. *General Proposals*

The existing H.T. lines are shown on Plate 32 ; these will no doubt be added to in the evolution of the National Grid Scheme now being prepared by the Electrical Commission, and in this connection attention should be drawn to the necessity of locating the best sites for Transformer Stations (and consequently the areas of local use) in conformity with the zoning proposals in the Regional Scheme. Unfortunately, in some parts (e.g., along the Bristol–Weston road as far as Congresbury) continuous low-tension service cables have been laid already, thus encouraging that obnoxious form of development known as ribbon, to curb which is one aim of the Regional Scheme. If, however, there is the element of co-ordination between the electrical authorities and the local authorities of the Region, it will be of material assistance in stimulating growth in the right places and discouraging it in areas zoned for use other than residential or industrial.

§ iii. *Position of Power Lines*

One other recommendation is made—an æsthetic one : it is concerned with the fact that both the titanic pylons (or lattice steel masts) and the smaller posts carrying these high-pressure mains across the face of the countryside can completely upset the scenic qualities of

the area.   These masts, which are usually about 80 feet high, can easily be placed, thought-
lessly perhaps, in positions where they will dominate the landscape ; whereas by the exercise
of a little care and thought they might just as economically be placed so as to minimise such
injury to the amenities.   The Commissioners and Electricity Companies have shown themselves, when their attention has been drawn, ready to consider alterations in the route when
these are practicable.   Local Authorities, Landowners, Rural Preservation Societies and others
can do much by meeting the Electricity representatives and putting forward workable alternative suggestions.   The Advisory Committee (Part Fourth, Chapter II) would be the body to
arrange these conferences ; *it is therefore strongly recommended that no individual Local Authorities
or Landowners in the Region should agree to any new route before referring the matter to the Regional
Committee (or the Advisory Committee if it is set up).*

The æsthetic questions involved are not simple : electric companies may be acting upon
certain principles which are not agreed to by others : for example, the advisability of taking
lines parallel to, but some distance away from, roads.   In one part of the county the electricians
had avoided this so as to preserve the view for motorists, but in so doing had carried the
standards along a skyline to the damage of the distant prospect.   Straight lines or curved or
angular ones are also debatable.   Sharp angles in the direction add to the cost and the
emphasis of the posts, as those at the angles require additional strutting.   These are some
among many points which may require to be settled by joint conference.

IN THE CAM VALLEY (COMBE HAY).

123

PART THE THIRD

THE EFFECT OF THE REGIONAL PLAN

PLATE 38.

a

b

Two Impressions of the Mendip.

(a) The rounded southern slope.
(b) The long line of the northern escarpment.

Facing page 127.

PART THE THIRD.   THE EFFECT OF THE REGIONAL PLAN

CHAPTER I.   ACTIVE AND PASSIVE

§ i.   *Persuasive Planning*

THE main object of a plan is to provide a reasoned basis for future growth, founded upon the varied factors which exist to-day. It is of necessity a forecast, an attempt to visualise the future, and it sets forth the means by which this line of growth is to be organised or directed. But it is clear that the less compulsion that is necessary, the better : a plan which interferes at every point with natural tendencies and which requires vexatious rules and regulations would not only meet with opposition, but would stand small chance of being adequately realised, unless in the hands of a Dictator. What is required is to stimulate natural tendencies in the right direction, only opposing a flat negative where public health or general convenience or paramount claims of amenity demand it.

The stimulation of tendencies which are in the right direction has been called Persuasive Planning : a moment's reflection will show how this may be done. Take a district which, now agricultural, is shown as a future residential area : to mark it as such on a Zoning Map will not necessarily have any immediate effect, except the important one of a label which has a subconscious effect upon the public mind. But strictly speaking, the showing on the Zoning Map of a residential area at this point means that if and when a change takes place, this is what is anticipated will be the most suitable use to which the land can be put, and certain regulations as to how this change shall be carried out are given, i.e., the number of houses per acre, etc. The Zoning Plan, therefore, is in a sense negative or at any rate passive. But the use of Persuasive Planning consists in taking steps to bring this change about so that a residential area will spring up whether there is a zone shown or not. What steps could be taken ? The greatest number would result from the co-operation of Private Owners and Public Authorities or Statutory Companies. In the first instance, the Landowner, by offering and advertising land at tempting prices ; a development company, constructing roads in advance so as to open up the property ; a railway company, opening a new station or improving a train service, or/and a bus company making a feature of the new place ; the Local Authority improving road communication, putting in a sewage scheme (or connecting up) ; the Water Company laying down a new main ; the Electricity Company taking a branch and transforming from their nearest high tension cable.

If all these were to act in concert a very powerful stimulus would be given, first to a change in the use of the agricultural land ; secondly to a change in a definite direction. As is well known, this intensive and interadvantageous co-operation very rarely does take place, as there is no plan, prepared without a selfish end in view, upon which so many varied interests can heartily concentrate their efforts.

A Regional Zoning Plan provides this basis of action : it must be assumed that the active means of stimulation will be directed towards its realisation. It would, of course, have been attractive to attempt to plan the actual lines of these various stimulating agencies—to show for example the extended electric power lines, water mains, sewers; to suggest new train services, electrification of sections of lines, new bus routes, etc., all in conformity with the Zoning Plan. But this would be pushing the planner's zeal too far; it would be impossible even to approximate to a working arrangement. What therefore has been done is to give accurate plans of these various activities as they at present exist and leave it to be assumed that they will be scientifically and co-operatively extended in accordance with the requirements of the Zoning Map.

With this Persuasive Planning inherent in it, the Zoning Map becomes a real power, not of compulsion, but of constructive growth. A close study of the zoning tables show how carefully any harsh restriction has been guarded against: but at the same time they give the general directions which are not only desirable but also likely.

§ ii. *Antagonistic Planning*

Without a Zoning Map, Persuasive Planning is frequently indulged in sporadically and even antagonistically to the great damage and loss of the community. For example, one authority will be widening a road for through traffic, obtaining the maximum width possible with a view to industrial or pleasure traffic having a rapid and unimpeded flow between two places. At the same time a statutory company is laying down low tension electric cables on either side of this road in order to stimulate continuous building development along its frontages,* the result of which, by causing standing or slow-moving vehicles, will be to nullify by exactly one half the work of the traffic authority. For if the road can only be widened to take four widths of rapid traffic, this possibility will now be reduced to two of rapid and two of slow-moving. And here, it will be noted, it was not a question of rival private enterprises each striving for its individual gain; but of two public bodies honestly attempting to serve the public but without any plan to direct their common action. It is perhaps not frequent that such direct conflict occurs: but lack of co-operation is of common, or one might even say usual, occurrence.

Again, the above-mentioned services, which should be a means of promoting development, are often merely camp-followers—they are provided by their respective authorities only when they are asked for, thus losing their formative rôle.

§ iii. *A Limit to Stimulation*

It is obvious that there must be an obverse to the stimulation to develop applied to certain areas. The total amount of space required for urban growth has been estimated in the next chapter, and a very large margin has been allowed in order to permit full scope for selection and to avoid cramping. It is therefore desirable in the interests of economy to limit the services so far as is possible to these areas of anticipated growth, leaving the remainder with only what is necessary for present requirements.

Roads offer the most obvious instance of the need for a limitation of services. With the overwhelming growth of motor traffic a policy appeared to be growing up that it was desirable to open roads in all directions so that Traffic might dash backwards and forwards whether there was any objective or not: any patch of country not intersected by a main road should be " opened up " at once; traffic in ever-increasing density and at ever-increasing speeds must be flowing in all directions as an end in itself.

This locomotor obsession has fortunately brought about its own reaction, and people are beginning to remember that there are times when one is not in a car, and that a piece of country which has no motor track across it may possess advantages in another direction—at any rate that it is a waste of money to create new main roads unless there is a need for them. The

---

* This is actually occurring on the Bristol–Weston road from Long Ashton to Flax Bourton.

local inhabitants must be able to get about their business without delay or danger, but the improvements which they require are on an entirely different scale to those necessary for through traffic.

The same reticence is recommended for other services and for other types of area : there would not then be inducements held out to develop by one body and repressive measures adopted by another to keep things as they are.

§ iv.   *The Object of this Part*

It is therefore worth while going over the ground of the Region again, in the light of the scheme that has been prepared, in order to show what effect is aimed at in the different parts of it.   This has been done, from a different angle in the Zoning section (Part Second, Chapter I). *There* the objective was to take zone by zone and show what areas were included in each : *here* the places are taken as entities and described in relation to the zoning, traffic, open spaces and other services by which they are affected.   It is impossible so to describe every town, village or parish separately ; on the contrary, as much grouping as is possible has been aimed at, and striking effects of growth, change or reservation portrayed rather than instances of normal development.   Individual places that are not mentioned must not therefore take it amiss.

In the first place, however, it is necessary to consider the relation of Zoning to the future population.

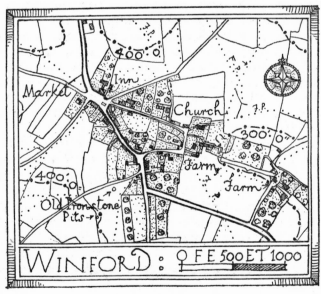

A DOUBLE-FOCUS VILLAGE

CHAPTER II.   POPULATION AND ZONING

THE Population of the Region in 1921 (the date of the latest census) was 662,517, and the estimated population in 1930, based on the average rate of increase in the two decennial periods 1901–1911 and 1911–1921, is 700,080. At the same average rate of growth (see Part the First, p. 41), it is estimated that the population in A.D. 1980 will be about 950,600, and in a further fifty years, i.e. A.D. 2030, it may reach 1,292,000. Not all of this population will be located in the towns and villages, but as it is impossible from the available figures to separate the population figures for farms and hamlets, and as this part of the population represents only a very small percentage of the whole, it is sufficient for the purpose of calculation to assume that the whole is located in the towns and villages ; also this course provides a margin for contingencies.

The figure given above for A.D. 2030 represents an increase of 592,000 in the hundred years ; assuming that this new population is all housed in the towns and villages at an average density of about 40 persons per acre (based on an average of 9 houses per acre and about 4½ persons per house) it follows that 14,800 acres will be required for their accommodation. To this figure may be added areas for local industries, open spaces and the re-housing of people from congested areas ; it is unlikely, however, that unless some unexpected impetus sends up very materially the future rate of growth, more than 17,000 acres will be required for all new urban development in the Region in the next hundred years.

The areas zoned as Residential in the Scheme comprise about 61,000 acres of which less than 20,000 acres are now developed, and thus there are about 41,000 acres available for new development within these Residential areas ; which is more than twice the estimated acreage required to meet the needs of the next hundred years. It is obvious, therefore, that the provision in the Scheme of land for residential development is more than sufficient to meet all reasonable expectations, and there is no necessity to encourage residential development on any areas but those provided in the Zoning Scheme.

To put the matter in another way—the areas zoned for residential purposes will allow of an increase in population of 1,640,000 (say 1½ millions) on the 1930 figure, which (at the past rate of growth) will not be reached for more than 180–200 years. In addition there will be a certain, though very much smaller, population housed in the small residential groups that will probably be allowed in the areas scheduled for agricultural purposes, and in face of these figures it can hardly be said that the Scheme imposes any arbitrary limitations upon the growth of towns or villages or that it interferes unduly with freedom in the selection of building sites. It should be noted that the allocation of land for urban and village development has been effected in the Scheme without any great departure from the principle of grouped development separated by large open areas.

CHAPTER III.   METHODS OF DEVELOPMENT: GROUP OR RIBBON*

§ i.   *Group Development and Through Traffic*

IT may be useful to summarise the gist of remarks that have been made in the earlier parts of this Report as to the best form for building development to take. The Zoning Map indicates that the scheme favours a form of growth in grouped building : this grouping to consist either of additions to existing masses, or of satellites either entirely new or nucleating round existing village centres. It was further pointed out that as this Region is exceptionally well supplied with village centres, many of them capable of expansion, it will be rather a stimulation of certain existing foci than the foundation of new ones which will be the economic method to pursue. Finally, it is clearly the modern practice, wherever possible, to free the residential areas, and particularly the central focus, of through traffic, by means of special bye-passes planned to divert the main stream. Where, however, the residential tract is continuous, as in the suburb of a large town, and the main traffic route must pass through, then the road must be treated with additional carriageway for slow-moving traffic and screens for the protection of the houses (see Part the Second, p. 107).

This then is a clear and logical form of development : the building in groups, compact so far as modern standards of density will allow, and the Through Traffic free to flow unimpeded.

The advantages of this method to the individual, whether at home or *en route*, are manifest : at home he is quiet though not remote, and on the road he can get about with ease and safety to himself and others. There are many other advantages in this form of growth, but perhaps an analysis of the disadvantages of the opposite method, the Ribbon Development along the main roads, may be a more effective way of bringing them out.

§ ii.   *The Natural Ribbon*

It must be at once agreed that the building of houses along road frontages is the normal method of *urban* growth : and the more continuous these frontages, as in the Roman and mediæval and modern town, the more complete and satisfying the purely urban effect : continuity of frontage does not necessarily mean high density, as the mediæval town had large garden space within the building blocks. An elementary community, like a village, naturally begins with some form of ribbon growth, sometimes as in Long Ashton it is markedly strung along a main road. But more often various causes, economic, practical, and probably social, combined to prevent its abuse : possibly distance from the village well was as much as any-thing the cause why offshoots from the main road occurred, also the tendency, when once a village is established, for paths to radiate out in various directions. So that in place of one continuous strip, the community becomes a knot or bunch of short lengths of ribboned ends : in other words, it assumes a compact instead of an elongated form.

The modern prolongation of the Ribbon is therefore simply an abuse of a normal urban growth, just as cancer is merely a morbid and uncontrolled cellular extension of the method

---

* The Council for the Preservation of Rural England has issued a valuable Memorandum (No. 5) on Grouped Building Development.

that creates and re-creates the human body. Sound development for the town run into a malignant growth over the country is therefore the definition of the Ribbon.

§ iii. *Disadvantages and Advantages*

The disadvantages of this malignant growth may be roughly grouped under four heads :—

> Practical.
> Social.
> Æsthetic.
> Financial.

These will be more fully expanded later. The immediate advantages may be disposed of at once : they are sufficiently obvious and are largely the result of motor-mobility. The car and bus open up the country continuously as compared with the railway which only gave accessibility at fixed and rather wide intervals. The line of least resistance is therefore for houses to be built along the main motor routes, nor can the owner be blamed for realising, though in a shortsighted way, a suddenly enhanced frontage value. The other great advantage results from the singular anomaly of English Law which decrees that if a man builds a new house on a new road he must pay the cost of half the road in front of his house though the community will use it one hundred times more than he will himself : whereas if he builds a house on an existing road, however much he thereby alters the character of that road (turning it from a country road to a town street, with consequent footpaths, etc.), he need not contribute one penny. Clause 30 of the Public Health Act of 1925 appears to aim at the deletion of this anomaly ; for the first time the principle is there stated that an existing country Highway is in fact converted into a *New Street* as a consequence of building operations which have been or are likely to be undertaken in the vicinity. Hitherto this free road frontage and the obvious accessibility of the bus service have between them accounted to a great extent for the sudden outburst of Ribbon growth. Other subsidiary reasons, such as the post-war difficulty of finding houses in towns, the growing desire for space in surroundings, etc., need not be enlarged upon.

§ iv. *Practical Disadvantages*

(*a*) *The Traffic disadvantage* has been explained in the Chapter on Communications. If the normal main road suitable for the undeveloped country-side becomes suddenly built up, the through traffic becomes impeded to the extent of two units of slow-moving traffic, one on each side. Thus the 30-foot carriage way constructed for three units in width of quick-moving traffic becomes reduced to 14 feet : in other words local and through traffic get inextricably involved.   The alternative of course is to widen the road : this can be done in two ways, by adding an 8-foot strip to each side of the 30-foot carriageway, making it 46 feet wide ; *and this widening must be done in the expensive material and heavy specification of the main road* ; whereas if the same width had been constructed in a new settlement off the main route, it could have had a cheap specification suitable for local traffic.   The second method of widening is by means of adding a separate local traffic road on each side of the main route, separated by a grass strip and trees.   This type of road is recommended for new main roads in continuously built tracts (*see* Part the Second, p. 107), but there is the expense of two light roads where, if they had been at right angles instead of parallel to the main road, one would have sufficed.

(*b*) *The Drainage disadvantage* is as marked as the traffic.   In the early days of such a growth the houses, isolated or in occasional groups, are drained into cesspools ; gradually the rows become continuous and then the demand or need for drainage becomes apparent.   In only one conceivable and rare occurrence of natural circumstances can this scattered community be easily drained, i.e., where the road follows an even slope in the ground, which will give the sewer its requisite fall.   If the road is level the sewer will have to be sunk to a costly depth to maintain a continuous fall* : or if the road undulates (as is the condition of the greater part of this Region) the sewage will have to be raised, or separate disposal schemes installed at frequent intervals.

(*c*) *Public Services disadvantage*.   It is a growing practice that in order not to disturb the expensive surfaces of main traffic routes, the pipes and cables of public services are duplicated on either side instead of being laid down the middle as they can be in less important roads. For a given sum a larger area of land could be provided with these services if it were developed adjacent to the arterial road instead of alongside it.

§ v.   *Social Disadvantages*

These also may be considered under three heads :—

(*a*) There is the *danger to children* who emerge from their front gardens on to the ever-increasing speed of through traffic.   There can be little real ease of mind to parents who live on these main roads unless the expensive method of separate tracks for local and through traffic is adopted.   Even then there will be the crossing to pay a visit to the house across the road.

(*b*) *Noise and disquiet*.   Through traffic tends to become more noisy and there is a disquiet caused by swiftly moving and multicoloured vehicles.   Dust has perhaps been eliminated, but there is certainly a considerable amount of smell from petrol and oil.

(*c*) *No focus of community life*.   This is the most serious of the social drawbacks.   A new district spread out thin in this way cannot weld the community into an entity.   The school, the church, the meeting place, even the shop and bank, are at a maximum distance.   The ribbon can produce nothing to correspond with the village green or the civic centre.

§ vi.   *Æsthetic Disadvantages*

It is loosely thought that the æsthetic disadvantage arises from the ugliness of the houses ; this may be, and frequently is, the obvious defect.   But it is more deep-seated and it depends

---

* The comparison between the average depth of a sewer 500 yards long in a single line on level ground and the same length radiating from a centre point in 10 directions—

Average in single length	. .	15 feet.
„ „ group of 10 lengths	.	6 feet.

upon the fundamental morbidity of the Ribbon, which is an urban growth thrust into the country. Whereas a row of trees stretching for miles may be suited to the country landscape, a row of houses of similar length is certainly not. It is sometimes said that the disadvantage is chiefly felt by the motorist who is shut out from a view of the country: but the drawback is just as acute as seen from the fields. The same number of houses formed into a group or groups may actually enhance the landscape if skilfully placed and harmonious in colour. The principles which govern landscape design are distinct from those of urban design: in the former Nature is dominant, in the latter Artifice. The town should preserve its urban character, the country its rural character. This is a subject that can only be touched upon here, but it is fundamental to the right appreciation of artistic treatment.

§ vii. *Financial Disadvantage*

The financial disadvantage to the Community has been stressed already: if there were no zoning restrictions the Region would in time become dotted with numerous individual houses, strung continuously upon the high roads and straggling about at random on the local roads with which the Region abounds. The cost with which the local authorities would eventually be faced to cope with this unregulated growth, for public services including lighting and policing, would probably outweigh any economic advantage which the actual increase had brought to the Region.

It is doubtful if the value of the Ribbon to landowners is more than superficial. The increased value given to land by the presence of an arterial road is due to accessibility to urban areas rather than to frontage potentialities. If the frontage is built upon (without expensive widenings) the accessibility is diminished by the check on through traffic from standing and slow-moving vehicles.

The Ribbon is an artificial screen to the land behind it: the public passing along the arterial road will be repelled by the continuous wall of building. An estate is closed rather than opened by the Ribbon.

§ viii. *The Grouped Community and Free High Road*

By contrast with the above, the virtues of the Grouped Community may be gauged. It is worth while examining one or two examples of the old villages which have been built in grouped form and adjacent to but not on the main road. There are several in this Region, of which Tormarton and Cold Ashton are good examples; other villages are seen on either side of the Gloucester Road which is unimpeded by buildings for miles.

Welwyn, near London, is an example of a modern Grouped Community placed off the traffic artery; it is on a larger scale, and displays the advantages of compactness and good architecture.

§ ix. *Requirements for Grouped Building*

There are several means which can be used to encourage the grouping of new building. The chief is to be found in the Zoning and Reservation scheme here put forward. In the Normal Agricultural Zone the Local Authority is given power to group the buildings which it permits to be erected: this power if used with discretion need not cause any hardship. Several suggestions from the owners' point of view are given in Part the Fourth, Chapter III.

Local authorities can also help in the question of Road costs: where an owner seeks to develop a group off the main road with houses facing on purely local roads, the local authorities should meet him as to light construction and narrow carriageway (which of course does not necessarily mean narrow roads between fences).

All the powers of Persuasive Planning should be brought to bear to encourage this right type of growth. And there is little doubt that when once its benefits have been felt by residents, no one will wish to live in a Ribbon House.

CHAPTER IV.   EFFECT ON AREAS IN DETAIL

SECTION 1.   THE BRISTOL GROUP

§ i. *The Conurbation*

IN the Zoning Plan the coalescent areas of Bristol, Kingswood, Mangotsfield and Brislington, and also the still distinct communities of Warmley, Oldland, Hanham, Bishopsworth, Henbury, Charlton, Filton, Stoke Gifford, Hambrook and Frenchay have been treated as one huge urban area, or " conurbation."   This treatment is dictated to a large extent by existing conditions : it may be urged that a conurbation of this size exceeds the bounds of economic growth and might be considered too large for effective local government, but the cancerous influence of ribbon development has gone so far to link up the various Communities that it is difficult, if not impossible, to prescribe any other treatment.

An attempt has been made to ensure that the citizens of the central portion of the conurbation shall not be deprived of reasonable access to green fields and open skies, by the provision in the Scheme of wedges and bands of open space reservations ; it is hoped that in the working out of the local Town Planning Schemes more of these desirable features will be added.

The principal Industrial Zone in the conurbation is that on low-lying land by the Avon from Hotwells to Crew's Hole ; this is already largely industrialised, and it is proposed to extend the industrial area by including the greater part of Bedminster, together with room for further industrial development in the valleys on either side of the Bedminster Down ridge.

The second, and largest, industrial zone has Avonmouth Docks as its centre ; it extends north and south of the Docks on the low-lying lands fringing the bank of the Severn from Portishead Dock to the Severn Tunnel.   North of the Avon the zone is served by a railway along the shore—perhaps not the best position to serve a zone of this character and location. The proposed new road from Avonmouth to Aust traverses the whole length of the Zone.

An agricultural belt on the marsh-land to the east of the industrial zone is planned to act as a buffer between the industrial zone and the residential areas of Lawrence Weston, Hallen, etc., which lie pleasantly facing the Channel on the rising ground culminating in the ridge-like eminence of Kingsweston Hill (300 feet) and the steeply escarped plateau north of Henbury, known locally as Mount Skilham and Spaniorum Hill (200 feet).   The former eminence is planned to be reserved as an Open Space, and the latter is zoned for special control in order to preserve its landscape amenities (see Plate 33).   South of the Avon the zone is well served by the Portishead Railway, and this district will no doubt go ahead when the proposed river bridge at Shirehampton renders it more easily accessible.

Another area lying between Knowle and Whitchurch is zoned for industrial development, for which it is eminently suitable, being situated on a promising coalfield and well served by road and railway.

Another industrial zone has Mangotsfield railway junction as its centre ; this, together with a smaller area near Pucklechurch, will serve the needs of the north-eastern part of the Conurbation.

The mixture of industrial and residential now existing throughout East Bristol and Kingswood presents a real difficulty in any attempt to define industrial zones there in a proper manner, and the matter may be left to be worked out as well as possible in the local Town Planning

Schemes by the provision of small zones based upon what is now in existence (e.g., the Speedwell and Deep Pit colliery area). Also small local industrial areas might be allocated along the route of the main L.M.S. Railway through Fishponds, etc.

The Avon Valley from Keynsham Hams (where Messrs. Fry and Messrs. Robinson have commenced the industrialisation of this low-lying area) to Swinford is also planned as an industrial zone; it is well served by road and rail and water.

An attempt has been made to surround the Conurbation with a fringe of semi-agricultural land (see Zoning Table in Part II, Chapter I). This is intended to act as a buffer between town and country; its use will be to provide market gardens and small holdings for the supply of fresh vegetables, etc., for the townsfolk, and in the more choice portions of the zone quasi-country houses with large grounds will be encouraged, but any development of a suburban character in this zone must be rigorously discouraged, forbidden on roads crossing the belt and strictly controlled (by grouping) in other parts of the zone.

If there is any slackness in the administration of this zone the result will be fatal to the whole zoning scheme of the Conurbation, as it will cause satellite communities to be inevitably absorbed with consequent loss of identity to themselves, and the spilling over of the Conurbation into a yet more unwieldy mass.

Beyond the semi-agricultural fringe lies the normal countryside, punctuated with the satellite communities described in the next section.

The area of the Conurbation (including the industrial areas referred to above) is about 24,660 acres; there are about 15,000 acres yet to be developed, i.e., 5000 as industrial and 10,000 as residential (including open spaces), and at the present rate of growth the scheme is expected to provide accommodation for at least the next 130 years.

§ ii. *Satellites of the Conurbation*

Many of the districts mentioned in the previous paragraph as being included in the Conurbation would, if the problem of zoning had been tackled earlier, have been planned as "satellites" and encouraged to preserve their separate identities. True it is too late to do this for them, but there remain others, and it is possible to consider the following as genuine satellites :—

> Easter Compton.
> Almondsbury.
> Winterbourne and Frampton Cotterell.
> Coalpit Heath.
> Warmley and Oldland.
> Wick.
> Bitton.
> Keynsham.
> Whitchurch.
> Long Ashton.
> Pill and Portbury.
> Flax Bourton.

These are all now physically separate and distinct communities; it is the object of the zoning scheme to assist them to preserve their identity by the prescription of a series of belts of land to be kept permanently open (see Plate 33).

A width of at least half a mile is desirable to effect this purpose, and this has been planned wherever practicable. It is of the greatest importance to insist that these belts are kept permanently open and are not allowed to be frittered away by nibbles here and there. The need here is for an awakening of public opinion to support the Local Authorities in their efforts to implement the Scheme.

The satellites vary in character, being mixtures, in varying degrees, of the dormitory satellite

PLATE 39.

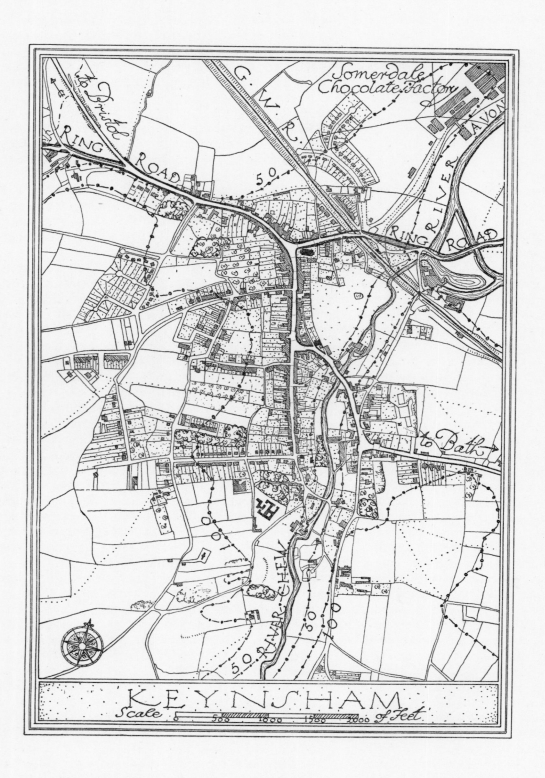

KEYNSHAM
Scale 500 1000 1500 2000 of Feet

and the industrial; Almondsbury, Easter Compton, Wick and Long Ashton will be pre-dominantly of dormitory character, the rest will probably become industrial satellites, housing the population working on the adjacent industrial areas.

Only the open spaces of Regional character are referred to below; others of local character, e.g., playing fields, parks, etc., are left to be planned in connection with the local Town Planning Schemes.

The *Easter Compton* satellite is an oval-shaped area on the edge of the Severn flats, lying on the Bristol–Aust road; its nuclei are the hamlets of Easter Compton and Compton Greenfield; the area zoned in the Scheme is 150 acres, estimated to take a population of 6000 when fully developed.

Almondsbury is on the Bristol–Gloucester road at its junction with the outer Ring Road; it comprises an upper and a lower village, and is flanked north and south by a " special Land-scape " zone. The temptation to allow ribbon development on the main road north and south of the village proper (which is already commencing) should be resisted; the area zoned is 200 acres, estimated to take a population of 8000 when developed.

Winterbourne and Frampton Cotterell. This satellite includes Watley's End and Winterbourne Down in addition to the main nuclei; there is already some loose development (apparently on no plan), and the whole needs to be rigorously pulled together if it is to develop into an ordered town. The outer Ring Road passes through the village, and this should assist its development; belts of open space on the west, south and east are suggested in order to help define the town, and a semi-agricultural belt to cut it off from Frenchay and Stoke Gifford. Acreage 1330; room is given for growth to a town of 53,000 population.

Coalpit Heath. Separated from Winterbourne only by the open space planned along the course of the River Frome; this satellite is a twin town with Winterbourne. The shape is roughly a square extending from the Railway to Frampton End and bounded on the east by an important industrial zone. The acreage zoned is 560, which when fully developed will accommodate 22,500 people.

Warmley and Oldland. A rectangle 3 miles long by 1 mile wide, this satellite includes a number of hamlets loosely strung together, extending from Willsbridge on the south to Goose Green on the north and from Cadbury Heath on the west to North Common on the east. It is almost surrounded by semi-agricultural belts which are, however, curtailed to a minimum width, and it is vital to the separate existence of this satellite that these belts should be preserved intact.

Wick. A triangular shape is suggested, surrounding the remarkable gorge (now being disfigured by quarrying operations) through which runs the River Boyd. Acreage zoned in scheme 400, i.e., room for a population of 16,000 when developed.

Bitton. This interesting village, the site of a Roman Camp, or settlement, is threatened with absorption through the creeping of ribbon development along the main road, and the object of the narrow belt on the west of the village is to check this tendency. There is a railway station named " Bitton " which by location should be called Willsbridge or Oldland; if the station were re-named, Bitton would stand to gain in the end more than she would appear to lose.

Delightfully situated at the bottom of the pleasant Golden "Valley," watered by the River Boyd, and sheltered on the east by the Lansdowne Hills, this village, if not spoilt by thoughtless planning, should develop into a charming satellite town. The site of the Roman Camp and the fringe of the River Boyd are planned as Open Spaces. The area included is 200 acres, providing accommodation for 8000 people.

Keynsham is already a small country town. Ribbon development along the main Bristol–Bath road should be checked on the west at the Cemetery, and on the east at the Avondale estate. There is also a tendency to extend along the Burnett Road which needs to be carefully watched. Generous provision for growth into a compact town of roughly circular shape is provided in the Scheme; the Chew Valley southward from the Gas Works is shown as an Open Space, and this reservation could with advantage be extended northward to the main road as the actual valley has little building value. The town stops abruptly at the line of the railway, to the north of which is low-lying land planned as industrial.

Surrounding the town on the west, south and east is a semi-agricultural belt.

The area (not including the industrial zone) is 830 acres, which will accommodate a future population of 33,000.

Whitchurch. The straggling village is wholly included and provision is made for ample extensions in all directions. There is an important industrial zone on the north which will influence the growth of this community. The Outer Ring Road passes to the south of the existing village centre. A very large area of undeveloped land is included in the residential zone, affording an excellent opportunity for good site planning and the creation of a model satellite town. A semi-agricultural belt is provided towards the Dundry uplands, which are zoned for the special preservation of their landscape amenities, with Maes Knoll Camp as an open space reservation on the summit.

The area zoned as residential is 600 acres, providing for a future population of 24,000.

Long Ashton. This, as its name implies, is little more than a patch of ribbon development lying along the Bristol–Weston road; the original reason being, no doubt, the steepness of the ground on either side of the road. Recently some development of the hillside has taken place and this should be encouraged. The plan shows an elongated satellite bounded on the south by the G.W. Railway and on the north by the upper portion of Ashton Hill, which latter is proposed as an Open Space. A small industrial zone for local purposes is provided beside the railway, and the low-lying lands of Ashton Vale together with the greater part of the Ashton Court grounds are set aside as open spaces; these in reality appertain to Bristol, but they will doubtless add to the amenity of life in this satellite.

Situated as it is on the southern slopes of a hill, hedged in citywards by open spaces, and having a glorious southern prospect over country zoned in the Scheme for preservation of landscape amenity, this village has every chance of developing into a first-class residential satellite.

It will be necessary, however, to check further ribbon development north of the Vicarage and west of the Cider Institute.

The area zoned in the Scheme is 500 acres which will accommodate 20,000 people.

Pill and Portbury. The three villages of Pill, Easton-in-Gordano and Portbury form the nucleus of this new town, which is planned to serve the new industrial zone on the marsh-lands south of the Avon. Interposed between the factory and residential areas is a belt of open space which should be a valuable asset to the community.

The Outer Ring Road crosses the area and the Coastal Route commences at the Portbury end of the town. On the east is an open space following the course of the River Avon from Ham Green; and on the south a belt of semi-agricultural character leads to the wilder Failand and Wraxall uplands, which are zoned for the special protection of their landscape amenities, thus ensuring a pleasant southern prospect for the inhabitants of this satellite.

The acreage is 860, and the estimated future population when developed is 34,400.

Flax Bourton. This is planned to combine with Cambridge Batch into a rectangular-shaped satellite, lying on the Bristol–Weston road and having at its east end the Outer Ring Road. To the north the lower slopes of the hillside are zoned as semi-agricultural, and the upper levels, together with the district south of the village, are zoned as " Special Landscape " areas.

SECTION 2. BATH

The distinction between Bath and Bristol is markedly brought out on the Zoning Map: no better instance of the utility of Regional Planning could be discovered than the different treatment meted out to these two sister cities in conformity with their essential requirements.

A superficial glance at the road map might make anyone unacquainted with Bath imagine that it was one of those reservoirs of unexploited country which were to be left un-opened up by new roads; for while Bristol is furnished with rings and radials, suggesting streams of traffic racing in every possible direction, Bath is left with its present system almost unchanged. But here a closer scrutiny reveals that it is not only a case of different character in the towns but different physical conformation. Bath has already used all the routes that are possible; external additions are practically impossible—like the Brahmaputra flowing through the Himalayas, neither new channels nor extensive widenings or bye-passes are possible—the current must flow through the narrow defiles. Some distant external improvements in order to allow industrial traffic to get direct to Bristol have been devised, e.g., Tog Hill, and Bath itself has in hand a series of internal improvements in order to prevent an absolute stoppage in the streets; otherwise the traffic plan remains practically unaltered.

Again, as the eastern limit of the coalfield passes through the centre of the City of Bath, it might, by one unacquainted with the city, be supposed that a large factory area would be shown to the west, including Kelston, Corston, Newton St. Loe and English Combe, and filling in the level valley bottom of the Avon. Nothing would have been more alien to the real economic interests of the neighbourhood.

In contrast to new roads and factory areas, Bath is shown as a compact city in a setting of beautiful country, specially to be preserved. Considerable scope for growth is shown, but in the form already adopted as natural, namely, the satellite, cut off where the steepness of the ground naturally suggests it by open country, and in other places by a band of the " Semi-Residential " zone in which natural features can be maintained. The two largest areas for satellite growth on the south are at Odd Down and Claverton Down: Bathampton, Bathford and Batheaston are suggested on the east of the city, and on the north a small satellite is proposed on the near end of Lansdown Hill.

The other villages in the surrounding country, which form so characteristic features of Bath's topography, are *not* shown as satellite communities of foreshadowed growth: some increase in their actual buildings is of course to be expected; but the meaning of the plan here is that steps are not to be taken to stimulate their growth. They are a series of country villages in the neighbourhood of Bath. The complete ring of open country with which the city is to be surrounded is made up of the water catchment areas, a wide belt of the Special Landscape Zone and two long strips of Public Open Space, in the Avon Valley below and above the built-up area. The famed Limpley Stoke Valley, with Claverton in its midst, is thus shown permanently protected. Though not so directly associated with Bath, the valley of the Cam falls within this area; it too is protected from Midford to Combe Hay.

Without attempting to pretend that the boundaries shown to these different types of areas can be taken as final, it is suggested that this plan indicates the lines upon which a scheme for safeguarding the special character of Bath should be framed. The essential feature is the sharp contrast between fully developed and highly organised urban and unspoilt and largely wild country of great landscape beauty.

SECTION 3.   THE AVON VALLEY

The Avon Valley is the connecting link between Bristol and Bath. As it is at present it is a succession of sharp contrasts, and it would seem that this character, changing suddenly from one part to another, must continue. The river side towards the east end of Bristol is probably the most acutely industrialised part of the city: a sudden turn towards Conham and all is changed. Here are steep banks, in places resembling a wild common, at others wooded; residential extensions of Hanham and Brislington here seem natural, and the unbuildable steep slopes, a public open space.   Next follow areas on either side where mining may occur : then Keynsham where the Outer Ring Road crosses, using the line of the existing bridge.   A large area of flat land on both sides of the river opposite Keynsham and extending to Bitton is clearly industrial.   From Bitton eastwards there is added to the valley the two lines of railway, the L.M.S. on the north, the G.W.R. on the south. Keynsham would naturally form the southern residential area for this industrial zone.   At Saltford a new phase is reached : this place is already growing (not very attractively) as a residential and boating place, and from here to Bath the river and its immediate flats (possibly including some of the woods of Kelston) will flow through a public park with specially protected country on either side.   This last reach, if the preservation of its beauty is to be done, will require immediate handling.

One would have liked, perhaps, a simpler and more continuous treatment of a River Valley ; but the conditions are complex, and much has already been done to determine the character of certain portions.   There is a great deal of natural beauty along this part of the Avon Valley which it is not too late to conserve.   And though there is railway proximity, the steep banks on certain sections do not encourage industrialism.

SECTION 4.   THE COASTAL TOWNS

§ i. *Weston, Sand Bay, Brean and Berrow*

Weston-super-Mare occupies the middle bay between two undeveloped ones.   Enclosed on the north by the massive Worlebury Hill, its easiest extension is southwards towards Uphill. The principal object of a plan should be to prevent indiscriminate straggling over the low-lying hinterland : the through line of the G.W.R. appears to suggest a limit in this direction. The great inland asset of Weston is the proximity of Mendip, Bleadon Hill being the nearest mass.   Every effort should be made to prevent these hill slopes from becoming continuously dotted with unsightly ill-coloured houses.   The Zoning Plan suggests continuous building as far as Bleadon, but only satellite growth beyond.

Sand Bay, to the North, enclosed by the promontory of Middle Hope, has a future before it owing to the well-marked bay and the remarkable beauty of the Limestone promontory ; unlike Weston, it is access both by road and rail that is lacking here, if it is to grow as something more than a northern overflow.   This, then, is clearly an area requiring Persuasive Planning in the form of the co-operation of interests and agencies.   The zoning proposed is extremely simple—a large residential area and the Middle Hope retained as some form of open space with the historic remains of Woodspring Priory in contiguity.   The chief agencies of development would be (i) road access, from the proposed Coastal Road ; (ii) railway connection, probably by motor bus from Puxton Station ; (iii) electric power.

Brean and Berrow have a longer sea front than either Sand Bay or Weston Bay, but it is less marked in shape.   The chief characteristic consists of a long narrow continuous strip of sandhill.   Access by road is already in existence from Burnham to Brean ; there is railway connection by road from Brent Knoll Station to Berrow (1 mile).   What is required to stop the straggling haphazard development at present taking place, is combined estate planning and a local town planning Scheme to direct development upon right lines and to prevent the danger of the sea frontage being continuously built up to no plan.

The proposed Coastal Road from Bristol to Burnham, with a crossing of the Axe south of Uphill, would link up Weston with its northern and southern neighbours ; it would also greatly stimulate their more rapid development.   The large margin of residential land behind Sand Bay and Brean and Berrow is shown because these places have not yet " found themselves " ; they are therefore given ample space in which to turn.   The map also shows some new roads which will feed the new resort and act as the skeleton of its local road system.

§ ii.   *Portishead and Clevedon with Nailsea*

Portishead and Clevedon are neat compact places hemmed in by low-lying land, over which they would not wish to extend residentially, with the exception of the high piece of coast line between them.   The straggling building that tends to connect them along this coast should not be encouraged.

Each of these places has an industrial area shown in contiguity : from Portishead Dock to the mouth of the Avon ; and south-east of Clevedon, comprising Kenn Moor.   But these two are in a very different category as regards likelihood of development ; the Portishead area comes within the Bristol sphere and with the new Power Station in operation it will be at once available.   It is hoped that steps will be taken to prevent the waste gases from the new Power Station damaging the vegetation in its neighbourhood.

Road connection with Bristol at present is difficult and it would damage an attractive neighbourhood to improve the existing roads adequately for industrial use ; but the projected bridge at Pill (the connecting link across the Avon for the north and south sections of the Coastal route) would bring this Portishead area into direct connection with Avonmouth and (by means of the new Portway) with the commercial centre of Bristol.

The Kenmoor factory area, on the other hand, is problematical and depends upon the future of the Nailsea Coal Basin.   The object of the Plan here is to show (i) how the Nailsea coal area should be zoned in order to reserve the most suitable land to residential use, Nailsea, Congresbury and Yatton ; (ii) to allow a wide margin for ancillary industry while at the same time giving adequate protection to the attractive southern slopes of Court Hill and Tickenham Hill (east of Clevedon) and the northern slopes of the Wrington Warren area.   Clevedon is also given a special series of " cut-off " zones.

SECTION 5.   MIDSOMER NORTON AND RADSTOCK

These two places suffer from complexities of Local Government areas ; from duplicity of drainage schemes ; and from violent contours which have so far offered an invincible resistance to the utmost efforts to impart coherence to a road plan.   The Local Government areas and sewage disposal difficulties would be perhaps amenable to treatment.

On the plan the two towns have been treated as one entity, but a dividing line has been made by the introduction of an Open Space reservation filling the hollow between the two railway lines east of Midsomer Norton and Welton and passing up the hillside, across the Wells Road (including the site of the abandoned Wells Way Colliery) and down into the next valley.   This reservation and a smaller one beside the G.W.R. Line from behind the Brewery to Thicketmead Bridge are to a large extent riverside parks ; another open space on the west includes Underhill and Folly Woods.

The principal area of definitely industrial character is apparently becoming established at the east end following the railways along the valleys : this appears to be sound, and here an Industrial Zone is shown on the plan.   In an area where the mining industry looms so large, it is difficult to dogmatise on character zoning, but it has been thought that it will best meet the case to show the rest of the district as " primarily residential " in order that such collieries as may occur there may be subject to control in the matter of smoke, and other disturbance to the amenities.   The present population is taken to be about 11,500; room for extensive growth to about 60,000 is provided for, in the expectation that these towns will continue to function as the capital of this part of the coalfield in its development (which is expected to be mainly towards the south-east, beyond the Regional boundary : see Part the First, Chapter IV).

On the north, west and south is an encircling belt of semi-agricultural character intended to assist in defining the limits of growth in these directions.

Two new road proposals affect these towns ; they are described in detail in Part the Second, Chapter II.

SECTION 6.   COUNTRY TOWNS

§ i. *Axbridge and Cheddar*

Axbridge and Cheddar show a tendency to coalesce, but the proposed new reservoir to the east of the former may be taken as a convenient cut-off. They should not be allowed to extend indefinitely along the connecting road, but as they are also hemmed in between the mountain slopes and gorge on the north and the marsh on the south, the plan provides a considerable area available for extension of each town, with a belt of low density and an agricultural tract in between them.

A new road proposal on the edge of the marshland provides a bye-pass on the south of Axbridge and the south-west of Cheddar. Some internal improvements might be made in the garden village looseness of Cheddar. The mountain slopes are zoned as " Special Landscape " ; this will prove to be a great asset in the future destiny of these towns as tourist centres.

§ ii. *Winscombe*

Winscombe with Woodborough and Sidcot (population 4000) is shown as having a considerable future before it ; when fully developed the residential area shown will accommodate a population of about 25,000. It lies snugly in a favoured valley, the only enclosure within Mendip, which is, however, part of the water catchment area of Burnham. The zoning proposals in the Scheme are thus antagonistic to an existing Public Service, and it is suggested that the Burnham water supply should be rearranged.

§ iii. *Wedmore*

Wedmore (population 2400) is provided with ample area for expansion on the higher ground north, west and south of the town, to a population of 20,000 ; surrounding the residential area is a zone of low density, and on the moor below a permanent open space is suggested. Other growth might take place satellite-wise in the numerous hamlets on the Isle.

§ iv. *Chipping Sodbury*

Chipping Sodbury will probably grow considerably if the northern coalfield revives and if the proposed industrial area on the coalfield between Yate and Coalpit Heath develops. Chipping Sodbury, just off the Coal Measures, is the natural capital of the northern area. The present population is about 2000 ; provision is made for growth to about 25,500. Surrounding the residential area on the west, south and east is a Semi-Agricultural Zone, whilst on the north are extensive commons which are proposed to be " rounded off " by the reservation of several fields apparently filched from the common at some time or other. The town has a fine wide main street, and would be on a traffic route of first importance if the Aust crossing were carried out. A length of new road from the aircraft works passing to the south of the poor law institution and connecting with an existing road (widened) is proposed in order to provide a bye-pass for through traffic on the Aust–London route.

§ v. *Marshfield*

Marshfield is an agricultural town on the Cotswold plateau, situated in a " Special Landscape " zone. It does not appear likely to grow to any great extent : it is on a first-class traffic route, but the traffic runs through. There is a kink on the main road which could not and should not be straightened ; it is a useful check on traffic speeding through the town. But if the volume increases greatly, a bye-pass could be made on the northern side of the town, as shown on the Map.

§ vi. *Thornbury*

Thornbury is the capital of what appears to be a large area of loose residential growth. It is another example of a town having a kink at the end of its main street ; it is fortunately already

PLATE 41.

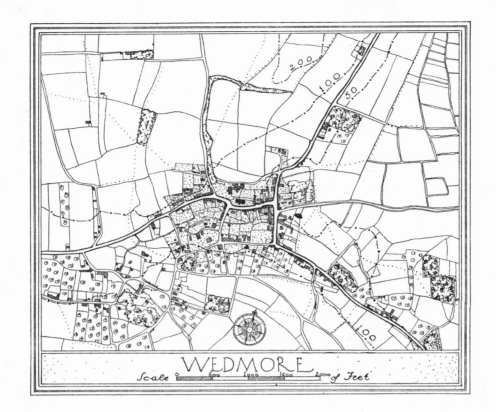

WEDMORE

Scale 0   500   1000   1500   2000 of Feet

WICKWAR

Scale 0   500   1000   1500 of Feet

CHIPPING SODBURY

Scale 0   500   1000   1500   2000 of Feet

PLATE 42.

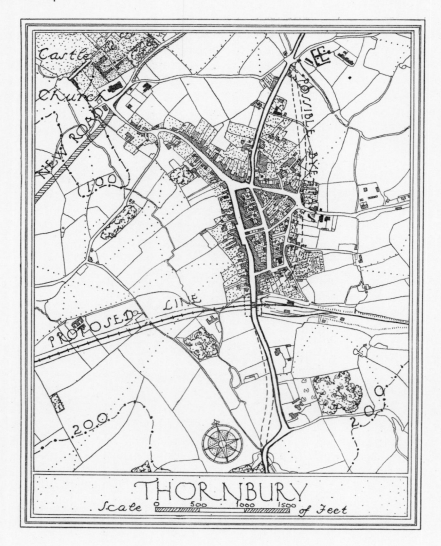

THORNBURY

Scale 0 500 1000 1500 of Feet

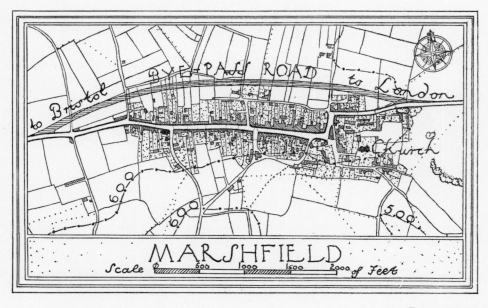

MARSHFIELD

Scale 0 500 1000 1500 2000 of Feet

Face page 143.

furnished with an external bye-pass via Milbury Heath which should free its streets of through
heavy traffic.   A new road running through the northern part of the town and utilising nearly
a mile of an existing lane passing on the south of Thornbury Park forms part of a connection
from Aust to the main Gloucester road.   The Scheme also envisages an extension of the
railway in the direction of Aust and the Severn crossing and the rail level at the existing terminus
will apparently allow a bridge crossing over the main street.   The present population is about
2000, and when fully developed as per plan it would accommodate about 40,000.

§ vii.   *Wickwar*

Wickwar is a purely agricultural town which does not appear likely to grow to any great
extent.   Provision is made for growth to a population of about 7500.

SECTION 7.   THE VILLAGES

In addition to the villages enumerated earlier in this Part as members of a conurbation or
on account of their connection with some particular feature, e.g., the Avon Valley, there
is of course a large number of other villages.   Every village will be affected by the Regional
Plan in a more or less degree, but it is not necessary or desirable to burden the Report with
detailed accounts of every one of them, and it will suffice to pick out a representative few and
to describe in detail the effect of the plan upon these.   The ultimate populations mentioned
may appear very large; but they represent the wide latitude of growth within which the
residential areas may expand.

AUST.—The destiny of this village is dependent upon the location of the Severn Crossing;
at present it is a small agricultural community, and but for the advent of the new Bridge it
would be likely to remain so.

The Plan provides the skeleton of a local scheme including road and rail proposals, residential Zoning and open space Reservation, for a town of about 25,000 population.

This should be amplified into a Statutory Town Planning Scheme immediately the decision
as to the Crossing is announced (assuming of course that this is the chosen spot).

BLAGDON.—The present village is built just on the edge of the Water Catchment area, and
for this reason further residential development there should be discouraged; but there is
immediately adjoining a suitable area which is off the Water Catchment reserve; here the
plan shows a new residential district large enough for an ultimate population of 12,000 if it
were fully built up, having Combe Lodge at its centre, bounded on the north by the sweeping
curve of the light railway, on the west (at Rickford) by a low density Zone (to separate the
new town from Burrington) and on the south by an open space Reservation and special landscape Zone designed to preserve the beauties of Blagdon Combe.   The main road is planned
to be bye-passed on the lower slopes of the hillside on the north of the old village.

BURRINGTON.—This village is planned to develop residentially in a northerly direction with
the definite object of protecting the district south of the village, including the famous Burrington
Combe.   The Combe itself is shown as a permanent Open Space, and between the Combe
and the village are a belt of low density, and part of a Special Landscape zone; whilst beyond
the Combe lies the Mendip reservation.   North of the village is the Yeo Valley, a countryside
of " normal agricultural " character.   It would be possible for the population to grow up to
6000.

CHEW MAGNA.—Although it lies on the Coal Measures, the destiny of this delightful village
is apparently to continue its normal growth into an agricultural town with the addition of
a sprinkling of folk having business in Bristol but desirous of enjoying the pleasures of a quiet
rural life in their leisure hours.   The present population is estimated at about 4000 and provision

is made for growth into a well-defined town up to 12,000, surrounded with a semi-agricultural Zone, and having the hillsides beyond this Zone protected in order to preserve the existing landscape beauties. The riverside areas south and east of the town are proposed to be preserved as permanent Open Spaces.

There is no railway and there are no new arterial road proposals affecting this rural retreat.

CHRISTON.—This hamlet lies on the sunny southern slope of an enclosed valley in the Mendip range, just above the edge of the low-lying land through which runs the Lox Yeo River. The present population is about 300, and the plan envisages development into a small residential town of about 8000 population with river and adjoining fields reserved as permanent Open Spaces.

There is a surrounding belt of semi-agricultural character; beyond this on the east and west, a Special Landscape zone; Banwell Hill (on the north) and Crook's Peak (on the south) are still further protected as Rural Reservations.

CONGRESBURY.—This village, present population about 2500, lies on the Bristol–Weston road at the junction with the link connecting that road with the Bridgwater road. It has a railway junction, which is, however, only a minor one, and it is situated on the edge of the low-lying alluvial plain controlled by the Somerset Sewers Commission. Normal growth into a country town within a space that could take a population of 25,000 is provided for, mostly upon the higher ground outside the Drainage Commissioners' area. To the north the wooded hill slopes are zoned for Special Landscape protection with Cadbury Hill and Camp reserved as permanent Open Space.

HUTTON, BANWELL, SANDFORD, AND CHURCHILL.—These villages are strung out upon the Weston–Bath road; which is to be widened and a bye-pass on the north of Banwell village is planned in the Scheme. These villages are expected to develop quietly as agricultural centres with some dormitory development related to Weston-super-Mare. The plan provides ample space for their development and prescribes intervening zones of agricultural character which will ensure the preservation of the identity of each community. To the south the hill slopes are protected for Landscape amenity; to the north lies the alluvial plain.

IRON ACTON.—This is planned to develop into a compact coalfield town of about 14,000 population, with a new bye-pass (forming part of the London to Aust route) passing through its centre. On the south is an Open Space reservation including part of the River Frome, and beyond this to the south-east is a new industrial area extending to Yate, Wapley Common and Coalpit Heath, which is well served with railways. South-west of the new town is an area off the economic coalfield which should be retained for agricultural use. On the west, north and east is agricultural land upon the coalfield, a district of no remarkable landscape value, and no proposals are made in respect of it, except that in the event of a revival of the coal industry resulting in an industrial invasion, steps should immediately be taken, by including the area in a Town Planning Scheme, to formulate a definite *policy of development* in order to guide the new activities upon right lines.

LOCKING.—The hamlet of Locking lies on the edge of the low-lying drainage area, with which, indeed, it is almost entirely surrounded. The present population is about 500 and provision is made for extension to the edge of the drainage area. This will accommodate a population of about 13,000; the character of the new development is expected to be mainly dormitory to Weston. A new road bye-passing the present hamlet is suggested as a backbone to the new development.

PAULTON, TIMSBURY, HIGH LITTLETON, HALLATROW.—These form with others a collection of related villages in the Cam Valley; the district lies on the coalfield and is already semi-industrialised; its future prosperity appears to depend on that of the Coal Industry. Uncontrolled development has probably gone too far for the original amenities to be recaptured, and the plan merely shows a general zone in which further development is most likely to occur.

The district is, however, full of possibilities for detailed planning, and it is very strongly urged that a local Town Planning Scheme should be initiated at the earliest possible date in order to make the most of what opportunities there may be remaining to formulate a policy of development for the undeveloped remnants.

PENSFORD.—This village, on the coalfield, is given room to develop (with the adjoining hamlet of Publow) into a town of about 16,000 inhabitants, encircled on the north and east by a semi-agricultural belt, and on the south by a " Special Landscape " zone. The course of the River Chew through the town is demarcated by a riverside Open Space reservation.

WELLOW.—A rural village in a landscape of normal character, but lying on the coalfield; it is one of many that are not planned in the Scheme to be stimulated, as it is thought that the village should be left to continue its placid rural existence. In the event, however, of any untoward development arising in the vicinity, it would be advisable to review the Plan and probably to initiate a small local scheme under the Town Planning Act.

A new road passes near the village, south of the railway.

WOOLVERS HILL.—This is a case of an almost virgin site chosen for new residential development. The site is on the flat land lying behind Weston, but is entirely above the 50-foot level and it rises at its centre to just over 100 feet; it lies near to, but not upon, a traffic route.

It is an example of the application of a constructive policy embodying the theory that it is wise to seek for, and allocate well ahead of time, a good site capable of development into a compact community, instead of perpetuating the sporadic and ribbon types of development condemned elsewhere in this Report. The site shown will accommodate a population of about 9500.

YATTON.—This straggling village (population about 2500) lies partly upon the Nailsea Coalfield, and is situated mainly upon a spur of rising ground jutting out into the low-lying area controlled by the Sewers Commission. Residential growth is to be encouraged in the direction of Frost Hill and Cadbury Hill, on the south-west of the village, these two districts being clear of the Coalfield.

The area provided (if fully built up) would make a town of about 15,000 population. To the east, north and west the village is surrounded with a low-lying area upon which industrial development will be encouraged, and through which runs the G.W.R. main line, and two branch lines having their termini at Yatton Station.

SECTION 8.   RURAL AREAS

§ i. *Introductory*

A description of the effect of the plan upon rural areas may be limited to three large typical tracts of country: the same ideas, *mutatis mutandis*, may be taken to refer to the rest of land that is not scheduled for Residential or Industrial use.

§ ii. *Normal Countryside*

The Normal Countryside north and south of Bristol under which the Coal Measures lie. Here the distinction from the Normal Agricultural (in which it will be remembered industrial development will also be permitted under restriction) is that as soon as coal working becomes practicable, co-operation of services should come into play to render every possible facility. The electric power map will show that it is only available at the moment over a very limited extent of the coalfield. There is one extremely valuable line from Midsomer Norton through Clutton and Pensford; but the Frampton Cotterell and Iron Acton area is not yet supplied. This does not imply any criticism of the electric supply, but the plan suggests the areas in which it is most likely to be called for.

§ iii. *Special Landscape Zone*

The Special Landscape area extending roughly from the Weston-super-Mare Road to the Wells Road and from Dundry to the south of Mendip. The plan envisages an entirely different state of affairs to the last described: if that forecasts and encourages change, this perpetuates existing conditions.

The area is traversed north and south by one main road only, the Bristol–Bridgwater: so far this route has not brought ribbon-building along it, and it is consequently one of the best traffic routes out of Bristol: *may it remain so.* The other radial out of Bristol, through Bishopsworth to Harptree, is fortunately daunted by the tremendous barrier of Dundry: there is a secondary approach from the Bridgwater Road through Winford. The attitude towards these roads would therefore be to make them suitable to local traffic, but to do nothing to encourage through traffic into the area. It is hoped that the new hospital near Winford will not be made the occasion for an unnecessary widening of the approach from the Bridgwater Road. There is, however, one road, at the foot of the northern slopes of Mendip, which is to be made into a main road: this need not encourage much development.

The only railway that touches the area is the branch line to Blagdon: this is likely to encourage growth at the rail head, which in the interests of water supply should be carefully controlled. Electric supply has also not opened up this area. The prognostic, therefore, is a continuation of its present state save for one disturbing factor along its eastern side, the underlying coalfield. In spite of the extreme rural beauty of this part, it was not thought to be possible to limit or prohibit coal-mining altogether. But it is to be carried on in a more isolated manner (without subsidiary industries) than in the Normal Agricultural zone. The Plan indicates clearly the attitude towards any mining operations that may become necessary. It is possible that trial bores may show that the comparatively narrow strip of the Coal Measures are not worth more serious exploitation than is done at the moment in one or two village mines which are too small to do any harm.

Fortunately, on the other hand, a large area of Mendip, from Shipham eastwards—the wildest part—is a water catchment area and so is or should be considered safe: this extends along the foot of the escarpment from Blagdon to West Harptree (part of the route of the widened road) and for some distance north of the Yeo Reservoir.

§ iv. *Low-lying Area*

The large area of Low-lying Land south of Mendip. It might at first glance appear that it is rather drastic to stop all building except for strict Agricultural use over this great extent, especially as it contains villages of attractive appearance as Mark (where actually there is a rise to the 50-foot contour). But again it is a question of the right interpretation of the Plan. The intention is to show that if there is a large future population to be housed, there are many more desirable places than upon the Marsh or Moor upon which to locate new villages or towns. Human common sense in remote ages was well aware of this and it will be observed that the population was concentrated on the Isle of Wedmore, round Brent Knoll and on the southern slopes of Mendip.* The Plan postulates a similar degree of common sense to-day but does not seek to interfere with individual requirements which for special reasons may need a residence on the marsh itself.

---

* The same concentration of villages is observable on the Polden Hills, the next long line of higher ground, south of the Isle of Wedmore.

PART THE FOURTH

THE REALISATION OF THE REGIONAL PLAN

PART THE FOURTH. THE REALISATION OF THE REGIONAL PLAN

CHAPTER I. STATUS OF THE REGIONAL PLAN

§ i. *Nature of a Regional Scheme*

THE Regional Report and Maps are in the nature of advisory documents, the result of the common deliberations of a group of Local Authorities, seeking, through a joint committee, to recommend the best form of development for the district as a whole. Unless a special Act of Parliament were to be passed implementing the recommendations of the Report, the production of schemes under the Town Planning Act is the normal channel through which the recommendations would be given a legal status.

But it must not be forgotten that the building of new towns or suburbs, the construction of new roads, the starting of new industries—all these construction works are not set in motion by the operation of the Town Planning Act: it is the way in which they are done that can be controlled by this means. In the Third Part, under the heading Persuasive Planning, some indication is given of the way in which the realisation of the Plan may be encouraged and even hastened, given of course the *primum mobile* of industrial and population growth.

Road construction and improvement are proceeding apace, irrespective of trade advance, owing to the change in methods of locomotion which suddenly found the country furnished with insufficient and obsolete roads: this deficiency is rapidly being made good under the Ministry of Transport's guidance and with financial help from the national exchequer. It is important, therefore, that Road Improvement should not be thought of as an isolated operation, apart from the community's activities in other directions. And this relation of Roads to Zoning (or the use to which different places are likely and desirable to be put) it is one of the major functions of the Regional Plan to determine, which thus prevents the danger of one aspect of planning being proceeded with, without due consideration for the many other factors which act and react upon each other.

There is also the value of the Regional Scheme in the education of public opinion: the clauses and statutory maps of a Town Planning Scheme are not, and are not intended to be, popular documents. In many cases they reveal only in an indirect way and as a result of close study what are its main objectives. It is hoped that this Report will have been found comprehensible to minds that may not have had legal or technical training, as it is intended to show, after a study of existing conditions, the general lines of future growth, and for the moment the artificial distinctions of administrative areas are left out of account in order that a view of the whole may be obtained. With this document in their hands, the general public can give a fuller and more enlightened support to their respective local authorities in their endeavours to realise its recommendations.

§ ii. *Alternative Methods of applying the Town Planning Act*

As has been said, the framework of the Regional Plan to become effective must be embodied in Town Planning Schemes prepared in accordance with the provisions of the Town Planning

Act. It is worth while examining the various areas to which schemes might be made to apply. The most elementary method would be for each of the seventeen authorities in the Region to set to work to prepare a Town Planning Scheme, each for its own area, including in each scheme the features of the Regional Plan which had been agreed to. The drawback of this simple method must at once be sufficiently obvious: a partnership having been set up in order to obtain a Regional Scheme suited to the common needs, the partners would proceed to lose the value of their association and to carry out the scheme in water-tight compartments. For the common good, certain burdens may have been placed upon a single authority—it now has to shoulder them unaided by its fellows. In other words, the partnership lasted while the scheme was advisory and on paper, but when the time came to give it a legal status and carry it out, it was then dissolved. In the other extreme—and for practical reasons not feasible in this area—a single Town Planning Scheme coterminous with the Region would be prepared by a joint committee, as provided for under the Act: the existing joint committee would thus become no longer an advisory body but an executive one to prepare and carry out a colossal Town Planning Scheme.

In other Regions a half-way method has been adopted: the area has been broken up into several groups of local authorities, large enough to shoulder joint responsibilities. This has partly occurred here, as shown on Diagram below.

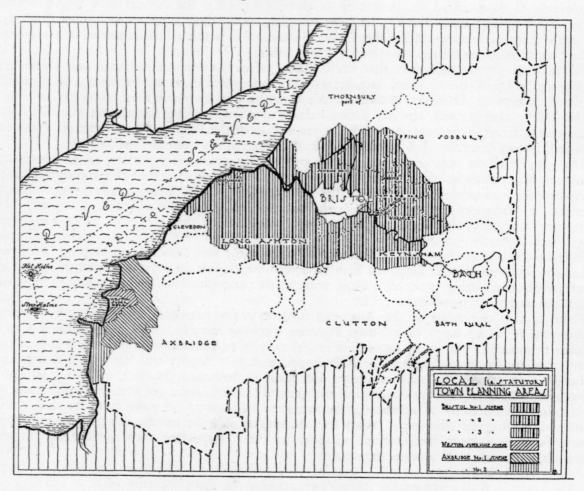

But as these groupings generally start from some nucleus of activity, there is a danger that some of the outlying areas may be left to shift for themselves.

It is also necessary to distinguish between the preparation of a Scheme and its administration in carrying out; the term in the Act for the body that *carries out* a scheme is "the Responsible Authority." The Act provides for this "Responsibility" for a scheme to be varied to suit any variety of special circumstances, e.g., "for certain purposes one local authority, and for certain purposes another local authority, or a joint body constituted specially for the purpose of the scheme." Thus it should be possible to pick out certain broad features of Regional Significance for which the group of authorities would be jointly responsible: e.g., main roads, regional (not local) open spaces, agricultural zones, etc. The other features of the carrying out of the scheme might be left to the individual authorities. By this means the local authority would deal directly with the truly local features of the scheme; there would be no delay in the cumbersome submission of details to a joint committee not concerned with local affairs. The individuality of the local authority for its own business would be maintained. But when the claim was regional, it would be given the support of regional responsibility. The scheme during realisation would have to be divided up into these local and regional components. The Minister of Health, in whose power is the ultimate determination of the Responsible Authority, might well be invited unofficially in advance to discuss the division of the Town Planning Schemes in order that the responsibility might fall upon the most suitable authorities.

§ iii. *Rural Schemes*

The "outlying areas" alluded to in the preceding paragraph might well be combined into two Rural Schemes, one for Gloucestershire and one for Somerset. In each case the respective County Council (under the powers recently conferred under the new Local Government Act) would be asked to participate; nor would there be any reason why any of the authorities in the Region (who might be preparing their own schemes) should not participate in these two Regional Schemes. The Responsible Authorities would be determined as above.

These two outlying schemes have been termed "Rural," but of course they would legally be Town Planning Schemes under the Act: for it must be clearly stated that without a statutory scheme the chief features (applied to rural as well as to urban and suburban conditions) of this scheme could not be enforced. But it must also be remembered that there is no limit to the simplicity of a Statutory Scheme or to the small number of constructive proposals which it contains. And as to the unwieldy size of these rural areas, some arrangement could probably be made for submitting the maps and draft schemes in sections.

§ iv. *Continuance of the Regional Committee*

If the area is thus divided up into a number of Town Planning Schemes and these again are subdivided according to their content (not their areas) into different groups of Responsible Authorities, it is clear that some form of co-ordination is necessary, by means of the full Regional Committee. Otherwise a divergence in practice would inevitably occur. A co-ordination of the clauses of schemes is a comparatively simple affair: indeed this could be done by the Ministry of Health when schemes were submitted. But a co-ordination of town planning practice is much more difficult. The interpretation of the permissive clauses in Zoning leaves a wide latitude for variation, and it has been pointed out that reasonableness of enforcement depends upon a *common policy* continuously applied.

Now it would be manifestly impracticable that every decision upon a permissive use should be referred to the Regional Committee—which would have to be in almost continuous session. It is difficult enough at times for the Responsible Authority (when it happens to be a joint one) to deal with these expeditiously. It is therefore suggested that the Regional Committee should meet once or twice a year in order to review the progress of the various schemes. By this means a common line of action could be adopted: it is not likely that any one Responsible Authority could depart to any serious extent from the spirit of the Regional Scheme in six months; and the action taken by all the Responsible Authorities would be the subject of mutual discussion and advice. The sharing of experience in administering the different areas of the Scheme should prove extremely helpful.

CHAPTER II.   AN ADVISORY COMMITTEE

IT is worth considering whether the Regional Committee, which consists principally of the Representatives of Local Authorities, might not be supplemented by an Advisory Committee such as exists in East Kent. The representatives of local authorities naturally and rightly turn to the Town Planning Act as the most direct way of implementing the Regional Scheme. But control of growth when it occurs is not enough : constructive action, Persuasive Planning, must not be neglected.

In East Kent, on the advice and under the guidance of the late Lord Milner, a Committee was set up (and still functions) on which, in addition to the Local Authorities, were represented the Land Owners, the Industrialists, Labour and other interests vitally concerned in the twin problem of exploiting the East Kent Coalfield and preserving the existing amenities of the district.

In this Region a similar committee would have great weight in furthering the development of the Region on right lines, and particularly in stimulating growth after the most economical and attractive manner. It is suggested that the following should be represented :—

> The Local Authorities.
> The Local Landowners.
> The Industrialists.
> The Electricity Companies.
> The Chambers of Commerce.
> The Merchant Venturers' Society.
> The Labour Organisations.
> The Transport Companies : Railways, Motor Bus, etc.
> The Rural Community Councils.
> The Bristol Kyrle Society.
> The Architectural Societies.

The local authorities in particular would feel the benefit of consultation and co-operation with these other bodies. Such a Committee, too, would have great weight if Parliamentary action were required : e.g., for such a necessary piece of work as the revision of the Geological Survey ; or if combined action were necessary to develop some local resources.

CHAPTER III.   THE LANDOWNERS, ANCIENT AND MODERN

§ i.   *The Effect in the Past on the Country*

IN any Regional Scheme the Landowners occupy a unique position and co-operation with them is essential.   It is confidently anticipated that the recommendations of this Report will be found to be in their interests.   Town and Regional Planning is merely an extension of the estate planning which has always been practised by the landowner in the past: the latter zoned his estate, though he was unacquainted with the term.   But he certainly divided his land up into areas according to the most appropriate uses: the Mansion House, Gardens and Home Park, the latter being to a large extent an open space available for the use of the local inhabitants; the chief residential area—the village—with perhaps one or two outlying hamlets or satellites, yet always compact; the social centre, church, hall, schools and shops forming the core of the village; the agricultural zone or farms, their buildings sometimes grouped into the villages at other times punctuating the farm lands; the woodlands and possibly waste or unenclosed lands.

It must also be remembered that side by side with this economic partition of the estate, the landowner had an eye to the landscape treatment of the countryside.   The typical appearance of large parts of rural England was finally set during the seventeenth and eighteenth centuries. Iberian, Celt, Roman, Saxon, Dane, and Norman had each contributed his quota: the Briton, whether Iberian or Celt, cleared the forest, made his ridgeways, founded settlements, and besides these utilitarian features, erected those mighty earth and stone works that first impressed man's hand upon the scene; the Roman, as may be seen in the admirable new map published by the Ordnance Department, planned out, on national lines, roads, villas, towns, camps, forts on a scale which has never since been equalled and of which this Region has its full share; the Saxon, neglecting town and villa, established the English village system, grouping the farms, cottages, manor house and church; the Dane restored the market town and borough. Working on this composite background the Norman and his descendants devised an architectural clothing and created the mighty series of cathedrals and castles that form the human climaxes of the countryside, entering into competition with and frequently dominating the natural scene; here, if there is no outstanding castle or cathedral, there is an unrivalled series of parish church towers.   All this time the shrinkage of the waste lands and forests and the reclamation of the alluvial flats continued changing the face of England, until towards the end of the sixteenth century it must have presented a bare if serviceable aspect outside the towns and villages; and the agricultural land under the open field system must have resembled, over large areas, a collection of allotment gardens.   There would be few hedges or trees outside the forests.

Now came in the change during the seventeenth and eighteenth centuries over the whole appearance of the countryside.   The formation of the great estates and the building of country houses surrounded by their parks gave a new richness to the scene: the allotments were absorbed into farms; the wastes separating the villages were reclaimed and enclosed.   Whether this was an advantage on purely social grounds or no, it increased the efficiency of farming and altered the general appearance of the countryside.   The owner of a large estate wished to draw attention to its extent by a boundary, wall or hedge: the larger and now permanent fields showed their divisions by stone walls or hedges, whichever was more appropriate, in place of the temporary dividing off of parts of the common fields with hurdles.   Isolated trees

153

in fields and hedgerows add to the park-like landscape, and under the systems of tenant farming they were not cut down. Coverts and belts of trees were added for sporting purposes.

This park-like effect of the country (which always so impresses Continental visitors) was evidently the result of a desire to irradiate the influence of the private garden and park over the surrounding country. The record of an early example in this Region has been preserved; in the seventeenth century French influence was in the ascendant, and an attempt was made to classify the landscape after the Continental model. An old engraving shows how the Duke of Beaufort thrust his radiating avenues in all directions round Badminton, obtaining permission from neighbouring landowners to traverse their property in order to focus his vista upon some church tower. Vestiges of several of these avenues can be traced to-day. Similar grandiose attempts were made elsewhere, but this formalising attempt was defeated by the invincible undulation of the greater part of English scenery : on the level marsh land no one could wish to create a great demesne.

But the desire " to improve the scenery of a country and to display its native beauties with advantage " (to use Repton, the eighteenth-century landscape gardener's phrase) persisted, and this energy was turned into the more feasible channel of Landscape Design. The new school accepted the natural informality of the country and aimed at emphasising it. Mr. Christopher Hussey, in his book *The Picturesque*, has drawn attention to the influence upon English country planning and planting which the great landscape painters, Claude and Poussin, exercised with their grand calm manner ; and the Dutchmen, Ruysdael and Hobbema, with their delight in the picturesque. It is by no means realised, if it can even be definitely known, how much of England was consciously laid out during this time : and a great deal, especially of planting, that was done unconsciously as to a definite scheme of design, dropped inevitably with the picture as did the individual buildings in a mediæval town.

§ ii. *Modern Conditions*

There are still portions of the country where these arcadian conditions described by Dr. Vaughan Cornish (see p. 69) are unchanged : but in many parts a double process has been at work. On the one hand estates have been broken up into smaller units ; on the other hand, development has become much more widely scattered (rather than more rapid) owing to the sudden freedom of movement in all directions given by the motor car and bus. It is not possible to stem either of these tendencies, the one based upon economics, the other on the human passion for locomotion as well as a genuine desire to make use of the country. But the old leisurely methods of control of the large estate will no longer suffice. The smaller ownerships must now be combined into large units for a control very similar to that exercised by the former large owner. He imposed restrictions upon his purchasers in order to preserve the amenities for everyone : he avoided the mixing up of incongruous elements, the one damaging the other—a factory next a church, a tin shed next a good house, etc. As in the past, so now, it is good business for all to develop rightly according to a plan.

§ iii. *Landowners and Zoning*

The effect of the zoning plan upon landowners is frankly to encourage growth in certain directions, to group it, in fact, rather than to allow it to straggle anywhere. In the past the demand for building land was so small that the building value outside the outskirts of the town was practically nil : now with more rapid and extended growth any land with convenient access might be considered to have a chance of being sold for building. It must therefore be shown what is the effect of grouping this housing and other growth on to a more limited amount of land and of limiting it upon a large extent of agricultural or unbuilt-on land. Firstly, let it be clearly understood that there is no suggestion of limiting the number of houses and the land requisite for them.

The very large margin of land scheduled as residential has already been shown : in addition to these defined residential areas, there is Zone D (Agricultural) on which groups of houses can be erected, provided they are properly laid out and can be economically drained, etc.   There is no limitation of houses on the score of space.   But there is limitation as regards density and position.   There was probably never much likelihood of the Marsh Land being extensively sold for building : but there are parts of the Landscape Reservation (upon which little more than houses for agricultural workers are to be allowed) where building might conceivably, but not very probably, have occurred if there were no Regional Plan.

The conclusion is, therefore, that while there is ample room with a very big margin on the right side of land available for building, there are areas in which it will be definitely limited. The same amount of building, in a word, will be somewhat concentrated on to a smaller amount of space (to the great economy of the ratepayers) instead of being spread over a wider extent. Now if, as already mentioned, the whole were in one or two huge ownerships, there would be no economic problem ; the owner would welcome the cheaper form of development as tending to keep down the rates and hasten sales ; the average building value from the sparser Zones being concentrated upon the denser Zone.   But as ownership is more split up, there would appear to be two ways in which an equitable arrangement could be arrived at :—

(i) By arranging in regard to the larger ownerships, that each owner should as far as possible have part of his property in Zones A and B and part in the more restricted areas.   This can probably be arranged to a certain extent, but the zones and reservations were not of course planned with this end in view.

(ii) By combining several ownerships into a convenient unit (say a parish or group of parishes) where the incidences of zoning are unequal, and one man is getting most of the building land, whereas another finds all or most of his land is more tightly restricted.   The Council for the Preservation of Rural England has put forward the suggestion that to meet this situation it should be possible to devise some system of pooling the Building Value Increment.   The arrangement would be a mutual and a friendly one, based upon a primary valuation, and it could be worked in consultation with the town planning authority.   The idea is frankly new : but a more drastic suggestion has been made in the *Morning Post* to turn the parish into a company and to allot shares according to the original value of the holdings of the members, all participating in the dividends.   The Pooling Scheme here described does not interfere with private ownership, but it distributes along reasonable lines an increment which might otherwise fall unfairly.*

There are a certain number of cases where the features of a scheme affect detrimentally an estate : for these definite hardships compensation is payable.   But it must be remembered that zoning restrictions which are approved by the Minister of Health as " reasonable " are exempt from claims for compensation.

§ iv.   *Rural Reservations and Private Open Spaces*

Those Reservations from which all building is eliminated are subject to compensation, if it can be shown that there *is* any building value.   The areas so shown are of limited extent and for the most part being bleak mountain tops or downland are required for water catchment.

Private open spaces are another matter : a certain number of these will probably become " Public " and be purchased for public use.   The owners of others who are in residence will probably welcome having them reserved under Town Planning Schemes as " private " open spaces.   This course in no way alienates the property from the owner and allows him and his heirs or future purchasers perpetual use of it ; but as it precludes building development, so it concurrently precludes the accretion of building values.   The owner therefore who is in residence, or his heirs, are safeguarded from the anomaly of taxation on a supposition of such value.   Wherever these parks are in the neighbourhood of urban growth, the gradual appreciation of the value of the private parks would in a generation or two force the owners to sell to pay for taxation on a value which they had never realised.

---

* See example of this Pooling Arrangement in Appendix C.

CHAPTER IV.   ARCHITECTURAL CONTROL

§ i.   *Design and Materials of Buildings*

FOR some time now it has been generally recognised that there is a present danger that perfect architectural freedom may degenerate into unbridled building licence.   Up to the beginning of the eighteenth century there existed a strong tradition in English Architecture which, almost amounting to instinctive design, produced buildings of great variety of shape, but always suited to their internal needs and external situation.   The Cotswold Hills are probably the greatest stronghold in England of this traditional continuity in domestic art. Local materials as well as traditional design had a great deal to do with the interrelated harmony of the buildings with each other and their suitability to the landscape : stone walling and stone slates, weathering as only local material can, become incorporated in the scene almost as works of nature.   Though the other parts of this region are perhaps not so rich in domestic architecture as the Cotswolds, the parish churches, considered as part of the Gloucester and Somerset group, are unrivalled in any part of Great Britain—especially in their most notable feature, the Tower, which sets the scale and standard of design for the village.

§ ii.   *Eighteenth Century Design*

The Renaissance did not penetrate country places until the end of the seventeenth and the beginning of the eighteenth century : it then introduced a new manner based upon rules of proportion to succeed to the older traditional methods.   It also introduced standardisation of features—windows, doors, hoods, cornices, etc.   These details were made from books of design which became common : the composition of the fronts were the result of certain rules of spacing and rhythm.   The result, while not so original as the earlier buildings, was eminently satisfying : the little Georgian house of the village or small town is appreciated to-day by all types of people.   Bath was at this time in the hands of a series of first-rate architects beginning with the Woods, father and son ; they no doubt helped to radiate an even higher and more scholarly type of design, which can be seen in many places throughout the Region.   But the homely Georgian, in which the greater part of Axbridge, for example, is built, is typical of the vernacular Renaissance architecture which appears so suitable to the English temperament. It is not exalted, it is not highly imaginative : but it is simple, satisfying and touched with the essential good taste of the period ; there is no vulgar ostentation or clamouring individuality and its effects are obtained with a great economy of means.

§ iii.   *The Nineteenth Century*

The nineteenth century broke up this later and orderly building, and except where trained architects have been employed, the building of small houses, shops and other buildings had no relation to environment either in design or material.   If rural beauty is to be preserved and suburban seemliness created, there must be some means of producing, economically, good modern building.

§ iv.   *The Bath Clause*

To the City of Bath belongs the credit of setting up under their 1925 Act a new form of Advisory Committee to which the local authority could refer any building which was considered to be unworthy of its position : the decision of the Advisory Committee is binding upon the builder and the City Council. Based upon this private Act, the Minister of Health has drafted a Model Clause for inclusion in Town Planning Schemes. All local authorities possessing town planning powers can therefore apply the means devised by the Bath Act if they wish and if the Minister of Health considers that they are in a position to make wise use of the powers. The City of Bristol has also incorporated the clause in a Private Act : by this means both Bath and Bristol can deal with their built-up areas as well as the areas included in their town planning schemes.

The Advisory Committee set up under these Acts or the Model Clause consists of :—

An Architect (chosen by the President of the R.I.B.A.).
A Surveyor (,, ,, ,, ,, ,, the Surveyors' Institute).
A Justice of the Peace (chosen by the Council).
None of them may be a member of the Council.

Moreover it is possible for several local authorities, such as those forming this Regional Scheme, to combine together to use the same Advisory Committee ; or there might be one for the Gloucestershire portion and one for the Somerset area.

But it is quite clear that the powers exercised under such an Advisory Committee are chiefly negative : the Committee has the right and duty to prevent the erection of buildings which will destroy the amenity of town, village or countryside. At most the Advisory Committee in stating the grounds of their objection can suggest how the design can be improved. Good design cannot be produced by such indirect means : and there is the disadvantage of the proposing builder being unaware what will be the fate of his efforts.

§ v. *Advisory Panels*

The Council for the Preservation of Rural England, accordingly, set itself to supplement this control under statutory power by advice and guidance of a voluntary nature. Observing that the Minister of Health in the circular letter accompanying the Housing (Rural Workers) Act, 1926, recommended the local authorities to co-operate with some voluntary advisory Panel in order that they might obtain advice as to the appropriateness or otherwise of contemplated works, the C.P.R.E. proceeded with the co-operation of the R.I.B.A. to set up Panels for this purpose. The voluntary panel, useful for an Act dealing with the repair of old cottages,* is equally available for new buildings and for the æsthetic aspects of lay-out and general town planning. The Minister of Health has fully realised this extended use of the Panel and in a White Paper† has advised local authorities to avail themselves of it. The Panel is also prepared to help intending builders in the early stages of the preparation of their plans and designs : they can thus ascertain whether what they propose to build is likely to prove acceptable to the Local Authority as to materials and design.

The membership of such Panels‡ is strengthened by the inclusion of representatives of the Landowners, Builders and the Surveyors to the Local Authorities. The Panel would of course work in close liaison with the Statutory Advisory Committee set up under the Model Clause. Indeed, if the Panel functioned well, there would rarely be need to apply the veto

---

* " If the work of reconditioning contemplated by the Act is carried out with reasonable skill and care very much may be done to preserve and perpetuate the styles of cottage architecture which have come down to us from former times ; while, on the contrary, if repairs and reconditioning are carried out without regard to the suitability of the materials and treatment or so as to involve the destruction of the proportion and beauty of the design, much damage might result." [Extract from circular letter from the Minister of Health accompanying the Housing (Rural Workers) Act, 1926.]

† White Paper No. 940, Nov. 29th 1928. Price 1d.

‡ The local Panel has been selected by the Wessex Society of Architects ; *Hon. Sec.:* H. E. Todd, Esq., A.R.I.B.A., 29 Orchard Street, Bristol.

of the Advisory Committee, but its power in the background would be invaluable. The scheme therefore contemplates improvement in the design of buildings by unofficial and voluntary advice (the Consultative Panel) and control of wilfully ugly buildings by means of official powers (Advisory Committee under Model Clause). If either course were adopted separately the result would be failure: it is useless to offer intending builders advice and guidance if they know they can neglect it with impunity: it is equally hopeless to expect improvement by merely exercising the negative power of rejecting designs when submitted to local authorities.

The important question arises whether every building which it is proposed to erect in the Region must either have received the imprimatur of the Consultative Panel or have been submitted to the Advisory Committee. The Model Clause leaves the discretion as to the latter course to the local authority. It is not, of course, desired to add to the complications of intending builders in the submission of their plans; but it is already necessary to obtain by-law approval and to conform with the town planning scheme. If the Consultative Panel is in close touch with the surveyors administering the town planning schemes, it should be possible quickly to establish certain standards and criteria by which the obviously bad buildings would almost automatically be submitted to the Advisory Committee for improvement; again, members of the Panel acting separately could rapidly go through the drawings submitted for approval, picking out those which the Council should send on to the Advisory Committee. This is not the place to devise the exact machinery, but given the desire to co-operate, there should be no difficulty. It is suggested, however, that in the Special Landscape Zone every new erection or altered old building should automatically be submitted to the Advisory Committee.

In order to facilitate the work of the Consultative Panels, the C.P.R.E. in consultation with the R.I.B.A. will probably issue standardised designs for small houses and bungalows, including window, door and other details: these will be accompanied by pamphlets giving directions as to the use of materials, etc. It must not be thought that this machinery for guidance and control is going to put up the cost of building: a careful study of bad design will usually show a number of expensive features which might with advantage be eliminated; others are ugly simply because they are badly proportioned—this refers particularly to windows; and because they are badly detailed—this refers particularly to doorheads. These features cost no more when the same amount of material is used architecturally and in good proportion.

A VILLAGE POST OFFICE (OLVESTON)

CHAPTER V.   RURAL PRESERVATION

§ i.   *Work to Hand*

THE work of watching over the countryside and villages is at present in the hands of a joint committee of the Bristol Kyrle Society and the Rural Community Councils of Gloucestershire and Somerset : this joint committee is working as an affiliated body of the Council for the Preservation of Rural England.*

It might be thought that, with all the apparatus of Schemes under the Town Planning Act, there would be no need for further organisations to safeguard the beauties of this Region ; but there are many directions in which vigilance and constructive work are still necessary.

In the first place there is the *rightful use of the country by the public*. This is work which Local Authorities can only attempt by the method of by-laws and fines, such as those directed against the litter nuisance. It is much better and more thorough to obtain the result by educative methods—by voluntary rather than by repressive means.

There are places which are open to the public by courtesy of the owners : these privileges are in constant danger of being withdrawn owing to misuse : by-laws do not penetrate here, but the vigilance of organisations such as Rambling Clubs, Footpath Associations, etc., can be of great value.

Advertisements can be controlled by the Local Authorities under the Regulation Acts and under their Town Planning Schemes ; but it is useful to have the vigilance of an outside body to stimulate action ; and there are the cases of those advertisements erected on the premises and referring to the business which is carried on there : this type of advertisement does not come within the scope of the present Acts, but pressure of public opinion can often effect what eludes the Law. The National Society, Scapa, with all its store of experience, is ever ready to help.

There is next the *organisation of public support to the Local Authorities* in their Rural Preservation schemes under the Town Planning Act. Without this outside countenance and co-operation there is danger of Schemes being still-born.

The preservation of ancient buildings is also a matter for an unofficial body : a survey of the old bridges and houses, large and small, of architectural interest should be undertaken. The Society for the Protection of Ancient Buildings is always prepared to give advice and help in getting suitable buildings placed upon the Schedule as Ancient Monuments. The Royal Society of Arts has a fund for the restoration of cottages of special beauty.

There is finally the fuller *Landscape and Village Survey* described in Chapter VII of the First Part. This is a large undertaking but it can be organised upon a local basis : each village (working upon a common system of recording and representation) can be responsible for its own area. The Schools, through their geographical departments, can work in touch with the University departments concerned. The Women's Institutes would seem to be the natural organisation to take up the Village Survey.

---

* *President :* The Earl of Crawford and Balcarres. *Secretary :* H. G. Griffin, 17, Great Marlborough Street, London.

§ ii. *Organisation of Effort*

It will be gathered from the above that there are many different organisations necessary for complete co-operation. The essential feature of the C.P.R.E. is this federation of bodies all working from different directions to the common end. It may be found necessary as the work grows to set up here a Branch which will epitomise on a smaller scale the varied interests of the Central Council.

In the meantime the Joint Committee of the Kyrle Society and the two Rural Community Councils is the headquarters body for organising Rural Preservation in the Region.

All the forces of goodwill must be mobilised if the existing countryside is to be preserved unimpaired, and if the new growth, instead of desecrating, is to add to it a new interest and beauty.

SOUTH SLOPE OF MENDIP FROM COMPTON BISHOP CHURCH

APPENDIX A

ANALYSIS OF TRAFFIC CENSUS, 1922, 1925, 1928

Route No.	Description of Road	Location of Census Point	Census Figures (per day)						Percentage Ratio			
			Numerically			By Weight			Numerically		By Weight	
			1922	1925	1928	1922	1925	1928	1922–5	1922–8	1922–5	1922–8
A4	Bath to London . .	Near Lambridge . .	—	3227	4433	—	4889	6323	—	137.3*	—	129.3*
A36	Avonmouth to South-ampton (via Bristol, Bath, Warminster) .	Tram Depot, Bris-lington . . .	5534	7801	—	9922	16624	—	141	—	167.4	—
,,	,,	6th milestone south, between Keynsham and Saltford . .	1659	2544	3320	2402	3878	5928	153.3	200	161.4	246.7
,,	,,	½ m. north of Limpley Stoke Viaduct .	547	993	1319	876	1899	2219	181.5	241.1	216.7	253.3
A37	Bristol to Shepton Mallet	Somerset Road (Knowle) . . .	3130	4003	—	6757	11149	—	128	—	165.0	—
,,	,,	1 m. south of Whit-church. . . .	799	1039	1592	1574	2061	2894	130	199.2	130.9	183.8
,,	,,	Temple Cloud . .	70;	910	1398	948	1440	1997	129.4	198.8	151.9	210.6
,,	,,	1 m. south of Ston Easton. . . .	403	526	873	514	1057	1493	130.5	216.6	205.6	290.4
A38	Derby to Plymouth (via Gloucester, Bris-tol, Bridgwater and Exeter)	North of Almonds-bury	—	—	3276	—	4025	5044	—	—	—	125*
,,	,,	Kellaway Avenue .	3722	5544	—	8629	13503	—	155	—	156.4	—
,,	,,	Winterstoke Road .	4180	4770	—	5820	10494	—	114	—	180.3	—
,,	,,	Lulsgate Bottom. .	876	1764	2729	1398	2573	4070	201.3	311.5	112.5	291.1
,,	,,	Lower Weare . .	1184	1732	2692	1467	2412	4171	146.3	227.3	164.4	284.3
,,	,,	Edithmead . .	1600	2349	3460	1787	3509	5557	147.4	216.2	196.3	311.0
A46	Stratford-on-Avon to Bath (via Cheltenham and Stroud) . . .	Grickstone . . .	—	—	1264	—	1414	2101	—	—	—	148*
	,,	Swainswick . .	599	868	1302	652	1226	1840	144.9	217.3	188	282.2
A362	Farrington Gurney to Warminster (via Rad-stock and Frome) .	1 m. west of Radstock	584	443	461	412	406	495	75.8	78.9	98.5	120.1
,,	,,	Mells Down . . .	315	283	379	230	386	601	90	120	167.8	261.3
A363	Bathford to Warmin-ster	Farleigh Wick . .	309	480	608	523	862	1019	155.3	196.7	164.8	194.8
A366	Hemington to Trow-bridge	Faulkland . . .	—	274	375	—	478	616	—	136*	—	128*

* No figures for 1922, ratio given between 1925 and 1928.

[Continued over

161

II

ANALYSIS OF TRAFFIC CENSUS—*continued.*

Route No.	Description of Road	Location of Census Point	Census Figures (per day)						Percentage Ratio			
			Numerically			By Weight			Numerically		By Weight	
			1922	1925	1928	1922	1925	1928	1922–5	1922–8	1922–5	1922–8
A367	Bath — Radstock — Oakhill	Nr. Dunkerton Bdge.	405	560	1092	492	817	1404	138.2	269.6	166	285.3
,,	,,	2 m. south of Radstock	518	633	742	487	703	981	122.2	143.2	144.3	201.4
A368	Bath — Corston — Banwell — Weston .	1 m. north of Marksbury	672	1267	1862	752	2134	3165	188.5	277.1	283.7	420.8
,,	,,	Near Sutton Court .	167	401	524	163	739	907	240.1	313.7	453.3	556.4
,,	,,	Blagdon	342	434	704	313	661	1022	127	205.8	211.1	326.5
,,	,,	1 m. west of Sandford	742	738	923	627	951	1140	99.4	124.4	151.6	181.8
A369	Marksbury — Hallatrow — Wells . . .	Between Crossways and High Littleton .	—	964	1443	—	1363	2249	—	149.6*	—	172.3*
,,	,,	Nedge Hill, Green Ore	402	853	1604	589	1437	2520	212.2	400	244	427.8
A370	Bristol — Weston — East Brent	Coronation Road (Bristol) . . .	4485	4524	—	8026	10545	—	101	—	131.3	—
,,	,,	Cambridge Batch .	1755	2880	5843	2197	4388	9047	164.1	333	199.6	411.8
,,	,,	Puxton . . .	1381	2247	4588	1975	3497	7481	162.7	332.2	177	378.7
,,	,,	Bleadon	1540	1694	2573	1599	2370	3517	110	167	148.2	220
A371	Weston — Cheddar— Wells and Shepton Mallet	½ m. east of Locking .	627	604	880	845	841	1203	96.3	140.3	100	142.3
,,	,,	½ m. north-west of Cheddar	875	1249	1879	1423	2174	2455	142.7	214.7	152.7	172.5
,,	,,	3 m. north-west of Wells	544	728	1226	828	1280	1854	133.8	225.4	154.6	223.9
A430	Bristol — Marshfield —Chippenham. . .	Whiteway Road, St. George	2575	2610	—	6440	8143	—	101	—	126.4	—
,,	,,	Tog Hill	—	—	501	—	1202	825	—	—	—	68.6*
A431	Bristol — Bitton — Bath	Marling Road, St. George	1672	1964	—	1472	6095	—	117	—	414	—
,,	,,	Longwell Green . .	—	—	1444	—	1910	2348	—	—	—	123
,,	,,	Near Cleeve Hill House	579	495	602	642	642	762	85.5	104	100	118.7
A432	Bristol — Chipping Sodbury	Eastville Park . .	5646	5141	—	12717	13741	—	91	—	108	—
,,	,,	Kendleshire . . .	—	—	1702	—	1714	2175	—	—	—	126.9
A4018	Bristol — Sea Mills —Avonmouth . .	Sea Mills Road . .	1536	1803	—	2625	4144	—	111	—	157.8	—

* No figures for 1922, ratio given between 1925 and 1928.

APPENDIX B

Trees for Roadside Planting.

Trees suggested in the Report for Afforestation in the different districts are generally suitable for roadside planting in those districts. In addition there are other varieties which are more especially suited for this purpose mainly on account of their ornamental value, e.g. :—

Sycamore (several varieties), Red Maple, Japanese Maple, Horse Chestnut, Sweet Chestnut, Tree of Heaven, Hornbeam, Purple Beech, Indian Bean, Flowering Ash, Honey Locust, Maidenhair Tree, Black Walnut, Tulip Tree, Magnolia, Plane, Fern-leaved Oak, Holly Oak, Cypress Oak, Acacia and Rose Acacia, Lime or Linden, Cornish Elm, Golden Drooping Elm.

Also the following, which may be conveniently classified as FLOWERING TREES.—Snowy Mesphilus, Cornelian Cherry, Hawthorn (red and white), Laburnum (*Wateris* and *Alpinum*), Bird Cherry, Double-flowering Cherry (*cerasus japonica alba ; — flore plena ; — rosa plena ; — Sieboldii ; — James Veitch ; — Wateriana*), Flowering Plum (*prunus pissardii ; — blireiana flore pleno ; — subhirtella*), Rowan, Whitebeam, Siberian Crab Apple (*pyrus malus baccata ; — floribunda ; — floribunda purpurea ; — neidwitz kiana*), Almond (*amygdalus communis ; — davidiana rubra*), Californian Chestnut (*pavia californica ; — rubra ; — indica*).

APPENDIX C

POOLING OF INCREMENT VALUE CONSEQUENT UPON RESERVATION OF LAND FOR AGRICULTURAL OR OPEN SPACE PURPOSES.

N.B.—This imaginary example is given for the purpose of illustrating a principle. The values assumed are, of course, entirely hypothetical.

Take 5,000 acres and assume that 4,400 are to be reserved and 600 to be developed. The 5,000 acres are owned as follows :—

										£
A owns 2,350 acres, average present value £28 per acre	..	..	..	..	=	65,800
B „ 1,500 „ „ „ „ £35 „	..	..	..	..	=	52,500
C „ 680 „ „ „ „ £40 „	..	..	..	..	=	27,200
D „ 370 „ „ „ „ £50 „	..	..	..	..	=	18,500
E „ 100 „ „ „ „ £60 „	..	..	..	..	=	6,000

5,000   170,000

Average value per acre, £34.   Average agricultural value per acre, £25.

£

Of A's land 2,200 acres are preserved from building, therefore £3 per acre must be recovered from building land   6,600

Of B's land 1,400 acres are preserved from building, therefore £10 per acre must be recovered from building land   14,000

Of C's land 620 acres are preserved from building, therefore £15 per acre must be recovered from building land   9,300

Of D's land 160 acres are preserved from building, therefore £25 per acre must be recovered from building land   4,000

Of E's land 20 acres are preserved from building, therefore £35 per acre must be recovered from building land   700

4,400 acres.   £34,600

Total present building value of the 4,400 acres to be preserved from building 34,600
To this must be added the present value of the land to be sold for building :

A	150 acres at	£28	.. ..	=	4,200
B	100 ,,	£35	.. ..	=	3,500
C	60 ,,	£40	.. ..	=	2,400
D	210 ,,	£50	.. ..	=	10,500
E	80 ,,	£60	.. ..	=	4,800

600 acres. £60,000

If this £60,000 is recovered from the land sold, the present total value of £170,000 will be maintained. £60,000 equals an average of £100 per acre for the 600 acres to be sold, and this would probably be a low average figure for building land *having the attraction of selection according to special suitability and permanently secured rural surroundings.*
In order to maintain the *status quo* the £60,000 must be allocated as follows :

A must receive	£6,600+£4,200	.. ..	=	10,800
B ,, ,,	£14,000+£3,500	.. ..	=	17,500
C ,, ,,	£9,300+£2,400	.. ..	=	11,700
D ,, ,,	£4,000+£10,500	.. ..	=	14,500
E ,, ,,	£700+£4,800	.. ..	=	5,500

£60,000

Therefore the proceeds of land sold for building at the price of £100 per acre, or more, should be divided in the following proportion :

A—108/600 ; B—175/600 ; C—117/600 ; D—145/600 ; E—55/600.

	Acres of agricultural land	Value (At £25 per acre)	Share of building value	
		£	£	£
A would then have	2,200	55,000	10,800	= 65,800
B ,, ,, ,, ...	1,400	35,000	17,500	= 52,500
C ,, ,, ,, ...	620	15,500	11,700	= 27,200
D ,, ,, ,, ...	160	4,000	14,500	= 18,500
E ,, ,, ,, ...	20	500	5,500	= 6,000
				170,000

This method of pooling the land to be sold would leave the undeveloped land to be retained in its present ownership—which is what is often desired.

APPENDIX D

(Extracted from Report of Petroleum Filling Stations Committee, Cmd. 3330, May, 1929. Price 4d.)

Section II of the Petroleum (Consolidation) Act, 1928, confers powers on County and Borough Councils to make byelaws :—

    (i) to regulate the appearance of petroleum filling stations in specified areas and in particular to specify requirements " as to the position, design, size, colour and screening of such stations or of any parts thereof," and

    (ii) to prohibit the establishment of petroleum filling stations and require their removal (on payment of compensation) from other specified areas.

These powers were granted " for the purpose of preserving for the enjoyment of the public the amenities of any rural scenery or of any place of beauty or historic interest or of any public park or pleasure promenade or of any street or place which is of interest by reason of its picturesque character."

The areas wherein the appearance of petroleum filling stations is regulated or their presence prohibited " shall be distinctly marked and shown upon plans to be signed by and deposited with the clerk of the Council making the byelaws."

It will thus be seen that the Act contemplates that, since the æsthetic character of individual places varies widely, every byelaw-making authority should, so far as possible, consider separately and on its own merits each part of their area which comes within the scope of the Act, and should then apply to that part byelaws appropriate to its particular requirements.

The Departmental Committee appointed by the Home Office have accordingly drafted a model set of byelaws which may be considered applicable to normal places, but point out that for special areas of beauty or historic interest more detailed or stringent byelaws may be desirable, e.g., the actual colour of pumps can be given or even the named varieties of trees or shrubs specified for making a screen. " Similarly, in the case of a picturesque village street, it would be open to the Council to make special byelaws requiring every petroleum filling station established within the area to which the byelaws applied to comply with such requirements, for example, *as that no part of any apparatus should be visible to the public from any point in the street*, that every roof and wall visible to the public from any point in the street should be respectively tiled and faced with the natural stone of the country, and that all screening used should consist of walls built of such stone."

The Committee make a special point of the fact that the Section of the Act does not actually give Local Authorities direct power of arbitrary control of every station that comes under the scope but allows them to adopt byelaws defining (as *infra*) the sort of station permissible and thus seeing that the stations conform to these byelaw requirements.

The Committee after hearing evidence from many sources has come to the following general conclusions as a guide to Local Authorities :—

    (1) that all advertisements should be prohibited except the sign, the name of the proprietor and of the premises, trade marks, proprietary names on or affixed to petrol pumps and oil containers, and the guarantee disc of quality ;

    (2) that uniform colouring should be employed throughout the station, except that a band of distinctive colouring not exceeding 9 in. in depth may be painted on petrol pumps and a similar band not exceeding 6 in. in depth may be painted on oil containers ; provided that in any case in which the band is the same colour as the remainder of the pump it may be bounded at the top and bottom by two thin lines of another colour not exceeding one quarter of an inch in depth ;

    (3) that unsightly material should not be used in the construction or roofing of the station ;

    (4) that flashing lamps should be prohibited ;

    (5) that the premises should be kept in a tidy and orderly condition ;

    (6) that as regards existing stations visible galvanised or corrugated iron should be painted but its use in any visible position on new stations or on extensions of existing stations should not be permitted ;

    (7) that plans and specifications of any proposed filling station and of any existing station proposed to be altered should be submitted to the local authority six weeks before erection or alteration is to be commenced ;

    (8) that we cannot recommend the prescription of either a general scheme of screening or a general colour, nor a requirement that all filling stations should be provided with a draw in, nor that any limitations should be placed on the size of filling stations.

With regard to the Sign mentioned in (1) the Committee have issued a supplementary report containing a design for the sign and a sample of lettering. The sign allows panels for the name of the Proprietor or Station, names of fuels, oils and other commodities retailed, and a panel for a further inscription.

APPENDIX

The following is the set of Model Byelaws which the Committee has drafted as a guide to Local Authorities :—

BYELAWS AS TO PETROLEUM FILLING STATIONS MADE BY THE   COUNCIL
    UNDER SECTION 11 OF THE PETROLEUM (CONSOLIDATION) ACT, 1928, HEREINAFTER REFERRED TO AS
"THE ACT."

PART I.

Byelaws applying with respect to petroleum filling stations within areas marked blue on deposited maps.

1. The byelaws contained in this Part of this Order apply to such parts of the area of the Council as are marked blue on the deposited maps.

2. No filling station, in any area to which this byelaw applies, shall be permitted by the occupier thereof to be visible unless the appearance thereof is such as not *to affect injuriously* the enjoyment by the public of any view of or from any rural scenery or any place of beauty or historic interest or any park or pleasure promenade or any street or place which is of interest by reason of its picturesque character.

3. Without prejudice to the generality of the last foregoing byelaw, the following provisions shall have effect with respect to every filling station in an area to which this byelaw applies, that is to say :—

    (1) except so far as is permitted by the First Schedule to these byelaws—

      (a) no visible advertisement, name or lettering used in or in connection with the filling station shall be exhibited within the area aforesaid :

      (b) all visible apparatus comprised in the filling station shall, if painted or otherwise coloured, be the same colour :

    (2) every visible wall forming part of the filling station shall be constructed of or faced with*—

      (i) bricks either of facing quality or salt glazed ; or

      (ii) clay tile or natural slate hanging ; or

      (iii) natural or artificial stone or terra cotta ; or

      (iv) timber framing and weather boarding ; or

      (v) half timber ; or

      (vi) rough cast ; or

      (vii) cement rendering ; or

      (viii) concrete blocks :

    (3) every visible roof forming part of the filling station shall be covered with natural slates, clay tiles, hardwood shingles, thatch, lead or copper :

    (4) any visible corrugated or galvanised iron which was used in or in connection with the filling station before these byelaws came into force shall be painted, and no other visible corrugated or galvanised iron shall be used in or in connection with the station :

    (5) no visible lamp giving intermittent illumination used in or in connection with the filling station shall be exhibited in the area aforesaid :

    (6) the filling station shall be kept in a tidy and orderly condition.

4. No person shall begin to establish, or alter the appearance of, any filling station within any area to which this byelaw applies unless at least six weeks before so doing he has given notice of his intention to the Clerk or Surveyor of the   Council, accompanied by such plans, specifications or other information as may be necessary for the purpose of showing the work intended to be done in connection with the establishment or alteration of the station and in particular showing—

    (a) the proposed position of the filling station in relation to any adjacent highway or premises ; and

    (b) any fence, wall or screen proposed to be used in or in connection with the filling station ; and

    (c) the materials of which all parts of the filling station are intended to be constructed ; and

    (d) the colours with which it is intended to paint or otherwise colour any part of the filling station.

5. The occupier of every filling station established at the time of the making of these byelaws shall for (two) years after that time be exempt from the operation of so much of these byelaws as requires any structural alteration of the filling station to be made.

PART II.

Byelaw prohibiting the establishment of petroleum filling stations within areas marked red on deposited maps.

6. No person shall establish in any part of the area of the   Council which is marked red on the deposited maps any visible filling station.

---

* Such materials would be selected as would be most suitable for the area concerned.

Part III.

Supplementary.

7.—(1) The Interpretation Act, 1889, applies for the purpose of the interpretation of these byelaws as it applies for the purpose of the interpretation of an Act of Parliament.

(2) In these byelaws, unless the context otherwise requires, the following expressions have the meanings hereby respectively assigned to them, that is to say :—

"Apparatus" does not include glass used in connection with any pump or with any lantern or other means of illumination :

"Deposited maps" means maps (in the Act referred to as "plans") numbered   which have been signed by and deposited with the Clerk of the   Council and are open for inspection in accordance with the provisions of subsection (2) of section eleven of the Act :

"Filling Station" means a petroleum filling station :

"Plans" includes sections and elevations :

"Standard Sign" means a sign made in accordance with the specification and sketch set out in the second Schedule to these byelaws :

"Visible," in relation to a filling station, means visible (otherwise than from aircraft) to the public from any place outside the filling station.

First Schedule.

Permitted deviations from requirements of byelaw Number 3.

1. The name of any filling station and of the occupier thereof may be displayed therein once, in a position not higher than the level of the lowest part of any roof, by means of letters not exceeding twelve inches in height.

2. For the purpose of indicating the brand of fuel or oil supplied from any pump or container—

(a) lettering and trade marks may be displayed

(i) on any part of the pump or container and on any glass forming part of a lantern attached thereto ; and

(ii) on any disc or other similar object attached to the pump or container and not exceeding twelve inches in any dimension ; and

(b) there may be displayed

(i) on the pump a horizontal band not more than nine inches wide ;

(ii) on the container a horizontal band not more than six inches wide ;

and no such band shall be painted in more than one colour, so however that upon any pump or container of such a colour as not to be readily distinguishable from the band the margins of any such band may be painted in one other colour to a width not exceeding one quarter of an inch.

3. There may be displayed in not more than three positions in or in connection with any filling station the standard sign.

Second Schedule.

Specifications and sketch of Standard Sign.

PRINTED BY JOHN WRIGHT AND SONS LTD., BRISTOL.